Search For Eden

by

Barbara Michel

This is a work of fiction. Locations are real places, but all characters have been created from the author's imagination. Names of characters or any resemblance to real persons, living or dead, is purely coincidental.

Copyright© 1996
BARBARA MICHEL

Son-Rise Publications
143 Greenfield Road
New Wilmington, PA 16142
1-800-358-0777
ISBN - 0-936369-90-6
Printed in the USA

Dedications

To my daughter, Loni Lynn, and my son-in-law, Jim; to my son, Christopher, and my daughter-in-law, Keli. God bless you, and may you always travel in the footsteps of Jesus.

Thanks to Gerald, my husband and friend, who aids me with my research, chauffeurs my travel ventures, and encourages me to be a prolific and determined writer.

Thanks to Florence Biros of Son-Rise Publications, my publisher and friend.

Thanks to Patricia Dunn for the beautiful painting used for the cover of this book.

My appreciation is extended to Donna Jackson for her quality typesetting and excellent layout.

Thanks to my Mennonite cousins, Eli and Lizzie Wenger and Ella Wenger, for their hospitality, their willingness to answer numerous questions, and for translating some of the Pennsylvania Dutch phrases.

Thanks to Amos Hoover, Muddy Creek Farm Library, Denver, Pa. (Lancaster County) for answering numerous questions and helping to translate English phrases into Pennsylvania Dutch for Search For Eden.

Table of Contents

Chapter 1	page 9
Chapter 2	page 21
Chapter 3	page 33
Chapter 4	page 47
Chapter 5	page 59
Chapter 6	page 71
Chapter 7	page 83
Chapter 8	page 91
Chapter 9	page 103
Chapter 10	page 113
Chapter 11	page 123
Chapter 12	page 133
Chapter 13	page 145
Chapter 14	page 157
Chapter 15	page 167
Chapter 16	page 177
Chapter 17	page 189
Chapter 18	page 199
Chapter 19	page 213
Chapter 20	page 225

Introduction to the Eden Series

Amish culture dates back to 1693 when the disagreement over shunning of excommunicated members drove the final wedge that separated the Anabaptists into the Mennonite and Amish societies. Their basic Biblical theology has remained the same. The Amish are thriving in this century, in spite of their rejection of modern ways. There were approximately 5,000 in North America in 1900, and today there are well over 100,000.

SEARCH FOR EDEN, the first novel in the Eden series, is set in Lancaster County, Pennsylvania. This is not the largest Amish settlement, but it is the oldest surviving community, the most densely populated, and is one of the most progressive. The details of Amish life vary in each settlement—even from district to district, but their basic values are widely shared. This series depicts the Amish in their contemporary culture. Amish cope with progress in a radically different way than modern societies, and have instilled insights that can enlighten those who are within the cultural mainstream.

The novels in the Eden series are an introduction to Amish culture and are not intended to be a comprehensive study in sociology. The Amish are portrayed as they believe, peaceful, moral, ethical, compassionate, and Biblically sound followers of Jesus Christ who have remained loyal to God and separate from what they consider worldliness.

The faith in God of these people and the strong family and church ties that bond them together are vividly displayed. Engrossing stories entwine kind and gentle characters and the episodes are stoked with authentic action and sprinkled with humor. Besides an appealing and lively read, these novels offer spiritual inspiration and encouragement.

SEARCH FOR EDEN, the first novel in the series, portrays that, due to human frailties, Christians sometimes falter and fail. One step in the wrong direction sometimes leads to another. God remains faithful. Full of love, grace and mercy, He offers forgiveness to the repentant and fills them with His Holy Spirit. This gives Christians strength, courage, and inspiration to live a more dedicated life. The following Scriptures are the basic thoughts that thread their way through SEARCH FOR EDEN.

". . . all have sinned and fall short of the glory of God, and are justified freely by his grace through the redemption that came by Christ Jesus."

Romans 3:23.

Even after salvation, Christians are tempted, and sometimes fail God. We need the grace of God that comes through Jesus Christ our Lord.

"Jesus answered, 'I am the way and the truth and the life'."

John 14:6

As Jesus is "the truth," we can not have peace with God while living in disobedience, yet this does not mean God will desert us. He continues to protect and bless while encouraging and giving opportunity to repent.

"If we confess our sins, he is faithful and just and will forgive our sins and cleanse us from all unrighteousness."

I John 1:9.

I thank God for my Christian heritage. He gave me my talents, called me to write inspirational novels, and continues to motivate me. Substantial prayer, as well as a great deal of research, goes into the writing of each novel. The kindness and openness of my Mennonite cousins, Eli and Lizzie Wenger, and Eli's sister Ella, contributed considerably to my desire to create the Eden series and inspire my continuing.

I pray you will find enchantment and spiritual enrichment on the following pages and enjoy reading the novels in the Eden series as much as I delight in writing them.

1

June. Lancaster County, Pennsylvania.

Rebecca Wenger stood at the counter in the back room of a flower shop, soothed by soft music and surrounded by dozens of colorful fragrant blossoms. A canary sang heartily from his cage by the window. Tranquility encompassed her. She bit her lower lip. *Does my peace have false roots?*

Swiping a withered leaf from her jeans, she struggled to ignore the twinge of guilt that pinched her insides. She selected a yellow rose that matched her ruffled blouse, caressed the velvety petals, then plunked it into a tall milk glass vase.

Could Margie have been wrong?

She pictured her *Englischer* cousin's long flowing dark hair and sparkling green eyes. Margie was lovable—at least Rebecca had thought so, before she'd taken her advice and removed her prayer cap to apply for a job in this flower shop.

At first, she'd felt unprotected and conspicuous, almost as though she were naked, but going without her cap gradually wore her down to acceptance. Margie had also talked her into dressing like an *Englischer*. She still felt self-conscious in jeans, but wore them to please her boss. She tossed her long tawny hair, enjoying the feeling of freedom she experienced as it swayed against her back; however, she hoped no Mennonites who knew her would see her dressed like this.

"That tells me this isn't right," she whispered, considering returning to her father's home and suffering her Old Order Amish grandmother's rebukes. She shook her head. She was eighteen. Wasn't this job a step toward fulfilling her calling to enter nurse's training? After all, her Mennonite Church approved of nursing. "If only *Mammi* Mary weren't so . . ."

She plucked a pink carnation for another arrangement from a container and sniffed it. Her mind scrolled back two months to the day she'd gone shopping with Margie and made her decision to leave home in search of her Eden.

The gravel had crunched on Wengers' driveway, a vehicle jerked to a stop, and a horn blasted. Rebecca had quickly finished rolling up her hair, pinned it firmly, and donned her prayer cap. Shoving her dull-green bedroom drapes aside, she'd glanced out the window and gasped. The car her *Englischer* cousin drove was so brilliant a red it made her blink and squint.

Rebecca's father sanctioned her friendship with Margie, but *Mammi* Mary, who lived with them, was skeptical. Hoping the older woman would not glimpse the red car, get upset, and try to thwart her leaving, she hurried outside to join her cousin.

Margie leaped from the car and tossed her long dark hair, a smile brightening her heart-shaped face. "Isn't Daddy's new car gorgeous?"

"*Ja.*" Rebecca glanced toward the garage. Her father's car was black, including the bumpers, and had no trim. All Mennonite cars in her district were the same. The contrast between the two vehicles astounded her.

Margie side-stepped anxiously. "Let's go!"

Rebecca tried not to covet as she compared her own subdued deep-blue print dress to the scarlet roses embroidered on the bodice and hem of her cousin's white sun dress.

"Hop in!" Margie swirled her full skirt and slid behind the wheel in one fluid movement. She waited for Rebecca to get in the passenger side. Glancing at Mary, who stood at the front door, she rolled her green eyes. "If I were you, I'd get out from under that old woman's thumb."

"*Mammi* means well, Margie, but I've thought about leaving." Guilt swept through her, although she struggled to ignore it.

"Have you talked her into letting you enter nurse's training with me this fall?"

"No." She ran her fingers over the smooth tan leather upholstery. "Dad supports my decision, but he doesn't want to upset *Mammi* Mary."

Margie backed the car out of the driveway. "No one could stop me. You should have more pluck."

Rebecca blinked. "More what?"

"Courage. Why don't you get a job and save money to go into training on your own?"

Although leaving home was a temptation, Rebecca smiled at her misguided flippant cousin and thought about *Mammi* Mary. The woman was so strict because she'd been raised Old Order Amish. Grandfather Wenger had been a carpenter. He'd felt he needed a pick-up to carry supplies, but the Bishop had forbidden it. When he went against the *Ordnung* and bought a vehicle, the Bishop gave him the choice of giving it up or suffering *Meidung* (shunning). He'd kept the truck.

Margie rolled her green eyes toward Rebecca. "You could do with a little of your grandfather Simon's stubbornness!"

Picturing the old man, now deceased, Rebecca sighed. When the shunning started, he'd been unable to stand it. He'd left the Amish community and begged Mary to go with him. "*Mammi* accompanied Grandfather Simon to a Mennonite church, but her heart and mind remained Old Order Amish."

"That's no reason for her to press you into her mold."

Margie could be right, Rebecca thought, the urge to leave home tiptoeing around the fringe of her longing, again.

Grinning, Margie glanced at her. "There's pink lipstick and a mirror in my purse."

Unable to resist, Rebecca retrieved the mirror and peered at her reflection.

Margie laughed. "Your golden-brown eyes sparkle, almost all of the time." She sighed. "I wish I had your oval face and delicate features."

I am pretty. Rebecca bit her lower lip. A sermon about vanity would be forthcoming, should *Mammi* perceive so vain a thought. She shoved the mirror back into her cousin's purse as though imagining *Mammi's* reaction had been a rebuke.

On New Holland Pike, Margie pressed on the accelerator and the vehicle leaped forward. "Why was your grandfather's truck such a big deal? Some Amish have cars."

"The Beachys do, but my grandparents were Old Order."

"Didn't some of your *Englischer* mother's culture rub off on you?"

"Mama joined the Mennonite Church when she married my father. To my knowledge, she never broke any Mennonite rules."

Margie looked exasperated. "I know. When she died, my heart ached for you."

"Even after five years, I miss her so," Rebecca said, picturing her mother's sweet face. "Since *Mammi* Mary moved in with us, I've been pressured to comply with her ideas."

Margie pursed her lips. "There has to be some way for you to get your freedom."

Rebecca sighed. "Someday, I'm going to find my Eden."

"Eden?" Margie laughed. "That isn't far from Route Twenty-three."

"I don't mean the town. I mean like Eden in the Bible. My Eden will be peaceful and free. I don't want to be unfaithful to God, Margie. I just want to get away from *Mammi's* ancient rules and become a nurse."

"You feel God wants you to be a nurse. It's up to you to find a way." Stopping her vehicle to make a turn, Margie pointed to an approaching Amish buggy. "Get a look at the handsome creature who's driving. Speaking of Eden, there's a man I wouldn't mind spending time with behind some bush."

"Margie!" She glanced at her cousin, but the young Amishman drew her attention. She'd seen him at Zimmerman's store in Intercourse and once at Central Market. Each time he'd been occupied with a business transaction and hadn't seemed to notice her.

Margie grinned. "His name's Aaron. My boyfriend and I met

him one Saturday night in Lancaster. He secretly has a car that he keeps at a filling station."

Stopping his horse at the light, Aaron removed his straw hat to swing it at a bee. His dark wavy hair shimmered in the sun. He stared at Margie's bright-red car, his dark eyes sparkling.

Margie pressed the button to lower her window. "Hi, Aaron!" she called boisterously, waving her arm out the window as she pulled away.

He looked surprised, then smiled and waved. "Hi, *wie gehts* (How are you)?"

Abashed, Rebecca averted her face, but curiosity made her look out the rear window. Aaron continued to peer at the car until his buggy turned the corner, cutting off his view.

"That's what I call a real hunk!" Margie sighed. "It's too bad he's Amish."

Tightening her lips, Rebecca eyed her cousin. "Did you need to yell like some harlot?"

Margie laughed. "I was just being friendly. He told us he was twenty-four. He's clean-shaven, so he's available--if you're interested."

Rebecca shook her head. "I wouldn't want to get involved with an Old Order Amishman."

"Right! That would only be exchanging your strict way of life for one that was more so." She laughed. "It might be fun, though—temporarily."

Rebecca's eyes widened. "Margie!"

She laughed. "Don't worry. My boyfriend would kill me." She turned right onto Route 30. "I'm heading for Park City Mall, unless you have some other idea."

"Fine. I want to stop at Phar-mor."

Margie's eyes sparkled. "I'm going to Watt and Shand's, and there's an outfit in Boscov's that I just have to have."

Rebecca studied her cousin's sandals. "You always wear such pretty shoes."

"You could afford clothes if you got a job."

"Like what?"

"There's a florist in Lancaster who's looking for someone to answer the phone and deliver flower arrangements. I considered the job, but..." She shrugged. "I'd rather have fun this summer."

"I want to do what's right, Margie, but someday I'll get enough nerve to begin my search for Eden."

"You'll never find it under your *Mammi's* thumb."

"I suppose not."

"I'll get you a copy of Vance Troy's newspaper ad. Just considering a job with him can't hurt."

A flower shop. A vision of being encircled by vivid aromatic blooms made Rebecca's heart race. As Margie turned right onto Harrisburg Pike, Rebecca asked, "Would you help me find an apartment?"

"You bet!" Her green eyes glistened, and she laughed. "I'd have to give you lessons on how to act like an *Englischer*."

"I don't have to be anything but myself!"

Margie wrinkled her nose. "It would be more fun if you tried out the kind of freedom I'm used to."

Determination gradually increased Rebecca's courage. Once she demonstrated that she could make it on her own, maybe *Mammi* would approve of nurse's training. "I think I'll take the job," she said slowly, "if Mr. Troy will hire me."

"Great!" Margie flipped her hand. "Eden, here she comes!"

The door behind Rebecca slammed. She jumped and whirled, her mind snapping back to the present. The overhead lights shimmered on Vance Troy's sandy hair as he entered the room. He juggled a box of roses, a container of daisies, and a basket of white chrysanthemums. He was five-foot-ten with a medium frame and clean-cut features. There wasn't a wrinkle in his tan slacks, but he wore his matching shirt unbuttoned at the neck, giving him a casual appearance. A generous smile made creases at the corners of his brownish-green eyes. "You have a knack with flowers, Rebecca."

She sniffed a yellow rose. "Blossoms remind me of vitality and life."

Setting the mums on the counter, he pointed to several large basket arrangements and laughed. "I assume you're not referring to those."

"The flowers are gorgeous, but I don't relish delivering to funeral parlors."

"Joe's delivering them in the van." Reaching out, he grasped her hand. "I set the three center pieces, a kitchen planter, and the other vases of flowers in the rack in the station wagon."

"Thank you." She smiled, but withdrew her hand.

"How soon will you be ready to make the deliveries?"

"This is the last bouquet. One more sprig of baby's breath will complete it."

"Good." He bent closer to inspect her handiwork and nodded his approval. "We have a lot to do this afternoon, so I'd like you to get back as soon as possible." He handed her some invoices and envelopes. "The addresses are all here."

"I'll try to rush the deliveries, Mr. Troy."

"Don't get a speeding ticket." Chuckling, he opened the outside door for her.

"Oh!" Joe Dinger's tall frame shadowed the opening, his hand outstretched as though he'd been reaching for the knob. "Hi, Becky." He looked at Vance. "I'm ready to deliver the funeral baskets."

Vance grinned. "Don't mix them up with the wedding decorations."

Joe laughed. He looked a couple of years older than Rebecca. His brown eyes assessed her as he combed one hand through his short dark hair. A smile softened his handsome features. "If you like, we can deliver the orders together."

"She's going in the opposite direction, Joe," Vance said, then returned his gaze to Rebecca. "Are you free to have dinner with me tonight?"

"Thank you, Mr Troy, but I want to get a birthday present ready to mail to my grandmother." Smiling, she grabbed the paper bag containing the Old Order Amish outfit she'd made for *Mammi*. It was complete with a medium-blue dress, an apron, a prayer cap and a black bonnet. She'd even purchased a pair of shoes and black stockings for the old lady.

"Don't forget this." Joe swung her bright-red purse, then looped the handles over her arm.

Vance held the door for her. "We'll have dinner together some other time then, Rebecca." He hurried to the white station wagon she used for making deliveries, opened the door behind the driver's seat, and propped the vase in the rack.

Sliding behind the wheel, Rebecca flung her bag and purse onto the passenger's seat. Vance was attractive, kind, and generous, but he wasn't a Christian. Even though she pretended to be an *Englischer*, she vowed she wouldn't get emotionally involved with a man if he weren't Mennonite. Vance retreated as she started the engine, but turned to smile and wave before entering his shop.

Tourists who were anxious to see the nearby Amish communities poured into the city. She'd been driving such a short time that heavy traffic made her nervous. As she pulled from the parking space, her eyes flicked over a gray Taurus that cruised down Queen Street. She glanced at the blond man in the passenger's seat, but it was the driver who caught and held her attention.

Aaron! She studied the Old Order Amishman Margie had called to as they passed his buggy. She'd seen him twice since, but didn't think he'd noticed her.

After delivering all of the orders except two vases, she checked the address for one of them and turned in that direction.

Pulling into a familiar driveway, she set the brake, shifted to park, and let the engine idle. Taking one of the vases, she headed for the patio. This was one of Mr. Troy's regular customers, so she tried hard to please him. She rang the doorbell, then stepped back.

Greg Mattis opened the door quickly, almost as though he'd been waiting for her. He was in his early twenties, but his brown hair was thinning on top. Excess weight stretched his orange T-shirt, and fat bulged over his belt. "Good afternoon," he said, reaching for the flowers.

As Rebecca stepped forward to proffer the bouquet, she tripped on an uneven tile and lost her grip on the vase. She shrieked as it crashed on the patio and hurled shards of glass in all directions.

Water splashed, and the flowers tumbled into a colorful array around her feet. The puddle of water widened and oozed under her yellow tennis shoes. She peered curiously at the vase. Apparently it had a false bottom that had contained a packet of something. "What's that?"

Seizing the packet before the water reached it, Mattis shoved it into his pocket. "It's freshener for the flowers."

"But . . . we put freshener in the water."

He shrugged. "There's extra for when I change the water."

"Oh." She stared at the shattered glass, wondering why Vance hadn't told her about the additional packet. "I'm sorry about the flowers, Mr. Mattis." Bending, she began to gather the scattered blooms. "I'll go back for another arrangement, and you can keep these as an apology."

"Forget it. It was an accident. I'll clean that up."

She straightened, handed him a pink carnation with a broken stem, and grinned sheepishly.

"Thanks." Accepting the flower, he chuckled, but something strange glittered in his eyes.

Rebecca turned and hurried back to the wagon. As she got into the vehicle, a slip of paper in her pocket crinkled, reminding her she hadn't had Mr. Mattis sign that he'd received the delivery. Vance insisted on it, so she supposed, even though the vase had been broken and the flowers damaged, a signature might be necessary.

I'll make a note on the receipt concerning the breakage, she thought. Hating to return to his house, she made her way back across the lawn, took one step onto the patio, then froze. Greg Mattis's husky voice drifted to her through a screen. Evidently he was talking to someone by phone.

"Yeah, but when she busted the vase, she saw the packet of stuff." His voice sounded harsh and threatening.

Her hand moved to her throat. *Why's he making such a big deal over a package of flower freshener?*

"If it was up to me," Mattis continued, "I wouldn't take any chances. She's smart, and she probably caught on. She could ruin not only me, but your entire operation!"

Operation? A chill trickled down Rebecca's back.

"Yeah, well, if I were you, I'd silence her to make sure."

Silence me? Whirling, she rapidly retreated, praying the man hadn't seen her. Her hands were sweaty as she gripped the steering wheel, and beads of cold sweat dotted her forehead. What had she bungled into? The wagon hopped as she backed onto Queen Street, nearly colliding with an oncoming car. Jerking to a stop, she roared the engine and shot out of the driver's path and onto a side street.

"I'm probably being silly," she said, yet apprehension gnawed at her. What if that packet wasn't flower freshener? What else could it be? Could Vance Troy or Joe Dinger be doing something illegal? Both men had been friendly and considerate. She frowned. What about Doug or Gene, the greenhouse workers? Could one of them be pulling something behind Vance's back? What about his other business contacts? Whom should she talk to? Whom could she trust?

Why'd I let Margie talk me into leaving home? She blinked tears away to clear her vision. "God help me!" She tried to picture her grandmother's reproving face, but all she could remember were the love and concern in the old woman's eyes.

Not knowing what to do, she figured she might as well deliver the last vase of flowers.

A black Daytona waited at the intersection. *Gene*, she thought, eyeing one of the greenhouse workers. Had he been the one notified of the broken vase? Glancing her way, he smiled. Instead of it soothing her quandary, it increased her anxiety. What was behind his dark-blue eyes? He shoved a truant lock of chestnut hair from his forehead. His round face, which before had looked boyish, now seemed to appear suspicious.

Rebecca stepped on the accelerator, thankful Gene was caught at the red light. The wind whipped through her open window, tossing her long hair, but it no longer seemed like a symbol of freedom. Her last delivery was in Strasburg. She wished she could just forget it and go home. She turned onto East King Street and followed Route 462. As she branched right onto Strasburg Pike, her tormented mind replayed the phone conversation.

A glance over the back of the seat made her shiver. Did the remaining vase have a false bottom? Did they all? Deciding to check, she pulled off the road and stopped to retrieve the vase. Her fingers trembled as she studied the bottom. The seam had been expertly camouflaged, but she could detect a faint line. One twist unscrewed the bottom and a packet of powder dropped onto her lap. Tossing the bottom ring of the vase onto the seat, she reached for the packet. Her hand hovered over it as she pondered the possibility of leaving her fingerprints or smearing someone else's.

When the vase was reassembled and back in the rack, she grappled through the invoices for an envelope. Not touching the packet, she worked it into the envelope. "Now what?" she asked, her voice squeaking. This stuff was probably nothing except a chemical for plants. Mattis could have been talking about someone else. She frowned. But what if the powder were some sort of drug? She remembered reading an article that described the increasing drug problem in Lancaster and cringed.

On the reverse side of a flower shop's invoice, she wrote, "check false bottoms on milk glass vases for possible narcotics." Wiping off any fingerprints, she slid the message in with the packet and sealed the envelope. After addressing it to the police station, she drove to the post office in Strasburg. As the envelope dropped into the mailbox, she wondered if she should have taken the packet to the police station. She shook her head. Vance had said he had friends on the force!

While stopped at a traffic light on Main Street, she spotted Gene's Daytona heading into town on route 896. Was he following her? Knowing he would be at the intersection before she could move, her stomach cramped, and her heart throbbed.

2

Gene looked at Rebecca as he turned right onto Main Street. His chestnut hair was tousled by the wind. A police car sped to the intersection, then also turned right onto Main. Was it worry that shimmered in the greenhouse helper's dark-blue eyes?

Rebecca gripped the steering wheel, wondering if she should deliver the last vase of flowers—now minus the packet. When she turned right onto South Decatur Street, she glanced at the phone booth on the corner. *Whom can I call for advice?*

Spotting Vance's red sports car crossing a side street, her heart beat quickened. She would flag him down for help. But, what if Vance had been the one Mattis had called?

She gasped. *Could he be after me?*

She decided to skip the last delivery. A black car raced down another side street. Gene? Was he planning to stop her at the next intersection?

Could she turn down an alley, avoid both men, and head for home? She hadn't been driving long and under the circumstances, she became flustered. She meant to brake, but her foot slipped and she jammed the accelerator. The car shot forward and her moist hands slipped on the wheel, causing the vehicle to swerve. At the sickening scrape of metal, her throat constricted. "No! Oh, no!"

Pulling the station wagon into a parking space directly in front of the parked green sedan she'd sideswiped, she fought tears. Her eyes flicked over a red brick building. *The First Presbyterian Church. Margie's Presbyterian.* She assumed any church would be a sanctuary. Grabbing her red purse and the paper bag containing the Amish outfit she'd made for *Mammi* Mary, she left the vehicle and scurried to the building. She peered over her shoulder to make sure no one was watching. Then, she tried the door, found it unlocked, slipped inside, and breathed a prayer of thanks.

Hugging her bag, she leaned against a wall and massaged her throbbing temples. With the station wagon parked nearby, Gene would know she was in the area. The damage to the parked car was slight, but by fleeing, would she be guilty of a hit-and-run accident? If she contacted the police, and Gene really was after her, he would probably show up before the authorities.

I need time to figure out what to do! Staring at her bag, a plan formed in her mind. She heard someone running a vacuum cleaner, but no one was in sight. She whispered a prayer that no one would see her.

Finding the ladies' room, she entered quickly. Passing the mirror, she glanced at her reflection. Gold flecks turned her eyes to amber, making them flash like caution lights. Because of them, her father had nicknamed her Amber, although he rarely used the endearment—except in private.

Opening her bag, she withdrew the plain, medium-blue Amish dress she'd made for her grandmother Mary and shook it, grateful there were no noticeable wrinkles. With trembling fingers, she took off her blouse and jeans; then, donning the dress, she pinned it. Shoving her yellow tennis shoes into the empty paper bag, she pulled on the black stockings and shoes and thanked God she'd bought them for the old woman. They were slightly large, so she stuffed toilet tissue in the toes and pulled the laces tight.

She combed her fingers through her long tawny hair, glad that she hadn't given in to her wild whim to cut it short. Pulling the mass back, she twisted it and held it in place while she put on the prayer cap and black bonnet. The disguise seemed perfect! She prayed she could pull off this sham long enough to figure out what to do.

Picturing the tiny transistor radio in her purse, she thought about listening to the news. When the police received the packet, they would inform reporters.

Not if the stuff is a narcotic, she thought, figuring the police would keep silent until they could make an arrest. Would it be advisable to hide until then?

She tossed her jeans and bright-yellow blouse into the bag with her yellow tennis shoes. Her scarlet purse looked conspicuous, so she rammed it into the bag as well. The items were symbols of rebellion, although Margie had given her the purse and radio.

I'll call Margie, she thought, knowing her impetuous cousin would be elated over this intrigue. *She'll come for me.*

She peered out the restroom door. Seeing no one, she tiptoed swiftly to the front door and opened it a crack. Hearing someone's approach, she felt forced from the building. Opening the door farther, she slipped outside. Her heart leaped when she noticed Gene sitting in his parked car across the street, staring at the scraped sedan. He would recognize the station wagon and know she'd done the damage.

She turned her head so that her face was hidden by her bonnet, but the brim also obstructed her view. It took every ounce of willpower she could muster to keep from running. To avoid passing Gene, she was forced to walk toward Main Street. Not wishing to arouse suspicion, she bowed her head to appear shy, but couldn't resist glancing back.

Gene peered curiously at the church door, apparently waiting for her to materialize. How long would her disguise fool him? Was following her his own idea or had Vance sent out an alarm? Who had been on the other end of Greg Mattis's phone call?

At the corner, she whirled right, crossed Decatur Street, and ducked into a phone booth. Grappling in her purse for a quarter, she dropped it into the slot, and dialed Margie's number. After ten rings with no answer, she replaced the receiver and sighed deeply.

What next? She pictured her father's broad shoulders, tanned face, and gentle blue eyes. A longing to return home gripped her. She vowed never to get angry with *Mammi*, no matter how overbearing she seemed. The old woman had been doing only what she thought was right.

Rebecca retrieved her quarter from the coin return. With trembling fingers, she dropped it into the slot and dialed her home number. Tears of relief blurred her vision as her father's phone rang. A sudden thought seized her. *If I go home, I could easily be traced.*

Who was responsible for those odd packets? How could she go home until she found out? If she were in some sort of danger, would going home jeopardize her father or *Mammi*? How could she go to the police, now that she'd mailed the only possible evidence? Wouldn't it be wise to wait a few days?

"Hello," David Wenger's voice boomed.

Staring across Main Street at the red brick face of the Bank of Lancaster, Rebecca opened her mouth to ask her father to come for her, but the words stuck in her throat.

"Hello," David repeated. "Who is this, please?"

Rebecca gripped the receiver until she could feel her fingertips throbbing. Concerned over the possibility of drawing her family into danger, she hung up.

Clutching her bag, she intended to leave the phone booth, but spotted the flower shop van and froze. Joe Dinger was headed south on Route 896. Was he hunting her, too?

Glancing over her shoulder at the pizza shop, she wondered if she could vanish inside; however, as though paralyzed, she stayed in the booth, praying Joe hadn't recognized her. When the van was out of sight, she left the booth, kept her head bowed, and walked rapidly away.

At Shenk Street, she turned right. Having no planned destination, she turned first one way, then another, until she'd lost her sense of direction.

A horse snorted. Pausing, Rebecca stared at the animal, then at the empty gray Amish buggy. It looked like an oasis. Would it afford a sanctuary until she could figure out what to do? Glancing around and seeing no one, she slid open the door and got into the back seat, intending to climb down and disappear before the owners came back.

The horse stomped, blew, and shook his head.

"Take it easy," Rebecca whispered. "You'll draw attention."

Licking her dry lips, she wiped the perspiration from her forehead, and hugged the paper bag containing her clothes. She shivered as she thought about the car accident. There hadn't been much damage, still . . . She realized she was biting her lip when she felt the pain.

Footsteps approached, and someone stopped beside the carriage. Keeping her face averted, Rebecca braced herself, expecting someone to seize her arm and yank her to the street.

"*Wass gait do aa* (What's going on here)?" a woman asked in Pennsylvania Dutch, the German dialect spoken by Amish and Mennonite.

Rebecca slowly faced a middle-aged Amish woman who had soft-gray eyes and a pleasant expression. She wore a light-blue, long sleeved dress and a navy bonnet.

The woman's graying brown eyebrows lifted slightly. "Bisht Du alles recht, mei liewe Maedel (Are you all right, dear girl)?"

Rebecca wondered what to say. "*Ich brauch hilf* (I need help)," she stammered, thankful her grandmother had insisted she practice speaking in Pennsylvania Dutch. Her mother had learned some, but had spoken mostly English. Her throat tightened, and she tried to moisten her dry lips. When the woman smiled, a ray of hope filtered through the debris in Rebecca's mind.

"*Bisht Du am warte uff ebber* (Are you waiting for someone)?"

Panic threatened Rebecca, for she knew the woman would question her being alone. "My brother ran into trouble," she said, although she had no brother. Lying was new to her, and her words stung her lips. "He said to ask the owners of this carriage for help, until he could return for me."

The woman's smile broadened as she climbed into the front seat of the carriage. "I guess *der gut Man* (God) had us visiting here for a purpose. *"Wo bisht Du von* (Where are you from)?"

Rebecca's mind whirled. There were so many Amish in Lancaster County, that she could name one of several communities. But what if she named the one this woman was part of? "I'm . . . from Mercer County," she mumbled.

The woman's eyes widened. "You traveled all that way with your brother?"

Rebecca thought about her cousin Margie. "We came in a car with an *Englischer*." She swallowed and looked away.

"They left you and your brother to fend for yourselves?"

"*Mir hen es so welle* (We wanted it that way)." There was understanding in the woman's eyes. Rebecca felt shame, but cornered, she justified her fabrication. "My brother wants to live in Lancaster County."

The woman looked mystified. "But, because of the lack of available land, our people are moving away. My cousin just left for Ohio, and recently some from our district have moved to Kentucky."

"*Ja*, but my brother was corresponding with someone who wished to move to Mercer County. They were supposed to meet to discuss an exchange."

"Then you'll be staying in the area?"

"If my brother gets a farm."

"*Ach*." The woman's brow furrowed in thought. "There are so few farms available in this county, and prices are high. Where is the property where your brother wishes to locate?"

"I . . . don't know." Rebecca's stomach twisted as her anxiety grew. "He's private about his business affairs. The man my brother was to meet had some trouble." She considered the wonderful hospitality of the Amish people. "My brother went to help him, so he told me to ask the family who owned this carriage if they would take me in for a few days."

"We'd be glad to, dear. I'm Esther Beiler. What's your name?"

Even though Rebecca was saddled by guilt over her dishonesty, she felt it necessary to hide her identity. "Call me Martha."

A man climbed into the carriage. "*Wer hen mir do* (Who have we here)?"

"Someone *der gut Man* has sent to visit us for a while, Isaac. Her name's Martha." Esther glanced at Rebecca. "What's your last name, dear?"

". . . Kauffman." Her deceit gnawed at her insides, and the canyon it created was swiftly filling with shame. She'd always been honest, even in the face of *Mammi's* reprimands. Had she let Margie's wild tales about narcotics rings and what they do to informers warp her discernment and steal her courage?

Isaac's blue eyes twinkled between the brim of his straw hat and his bushy brown beard. "You're welcome to stay with us as long as you like, Martha." Smiling, he picked up the reins.

When Isaac turned the carriage northward, Rebecca's heart faltered. She'd hoped the family lived south of Strasburg, thus farther from her home. Her father's farm was only a few miles north of New Holland. "Where is your farm, Esther?" she asked, trying to keep a tremor out of her voice.

"Near Bird-in-Hand."

Alarm seared through Rebecca. The Beilers probably did their shopping at Zimmerman's in Intercourse. There were people there who knew her. She would have to make excuses to stay away in order to protect the Beilers as well as herself.

Closing her eyes, she listened to the clop-clop of the horse's hooves. The Amish community was so close to modern lifestyles, yet they didn't become a part of it. The societies were worlds apart. She would be safe with the Amish, for no one would look for her there.

A black Daytona passed the carriage, and she smothered a gasp. It was Gene! Did he know she was in the carriage? If he reported her whereabouts, would someone be after her?

When the vehicle vanished in the distance, Rebecca slumped against the seat, praying the man had lost track of her. What about in the days to come? Would Gene search for her? Would Vance or Joe? What about the police? Was the scrape on the green sedan bad enough for them to try to locate her? Even if those strange packets of powder had been flower freshener, Vance would be angry because she'd marred the bumper of his station wagon.

"God help me," she prayed silently, then chewed her lower lip. How could she expect God to come to her aid? She'd turned her back on her teaching, been disobedient, and now was lying to the Beilers. Feeling dirty, she tried to shake the guilt that continued to grow, but it was futile. *How high a price will I pay for disregarding my beliefs?*

Sick at heart, she stifled a groan. Why had she listened to Margie? Her cousin's promises had been propaganda, and she'd permitted herself to be brainwashed as though she were a child instead of being eighteen. Margie claimed to be a Christian, but Rebecca realized the girl's teaching had left much wanting.

Sighing, she wished she could undo the past month. After tasting the world and finding it bitter, she yearned to return home. Even *Mammi's* strictness would be welcome, now.

I can't go home until the police investigate the flower shop. She felt, no matter what it cost her, she must protect her family.

As the carriage neared Intercourse, she cringed. If only *Mammi* had discovered her intention and destroyed her plan to apply for the job with Vance Troy. If only Margie hadn't given her the want ad in which he had advertised for help.

When Isaac turned the carriage onto another road, Rebecca figured they weren't far from their destination. Picturing the Amishman named Aaron, she wondered if he would recognize her and prayed their paths wouldn't cross. A vision of him settled in her mind and refused to go away. Where did he live? Did he know the Beilers? What if he remembered seeing her somewhere? Misery shrouded her.

Life's ironic, she mused. Her aim had been to find a Garden of Eden; but instead of discovering a blissful future, this was like fleeing with uncertainty into the past!

She studied the back of Esther's head, then looked at Isaac's profile. *I'll never let any harm come to these quiet and gentle people*, she vowed.

Rebecca was deep in thought as the buggy continued down Old Leecock Road and turned onto Harvest Drive. How long could she remain hidden?

Picturing Vance Troy's smiling face and easy manner, she wondered how, or if, he could be involved in selling drugs. Considering Joe Dinger's wholesomeness, sorrow enveloped her. She liked Joe. Gene and Doug had been pleasant, too. If she had enemies, how could she discover who they were? The police would soon have the anonymous tip she'd sent them as well as the sample packet that could be evidence. They would handle the situation. Once they understood, would they blame her for leaving the accident scene? She sighed. This would all be over in a few days. *All I have to do is relax and wait.*

Although she loved Lancaster County, the view of level fields and gently rolling land did little to comfort her. Leaving her father's farm had been foolish. How many times would she regret it? But, could she have done differently? She knew God wanted her to be a nurse. Why didn't He tell *Mammi*?

"This valley is the garden spot of America," Esther said over her shoulder.

Rebecca opened her mouth to say she knew, but recalled telling the woman she was from Mercer County. Supposing it was better to remain silent than to speak out and blunder, she said nothing.

As they passed a field of tobacco, she looked at the straight rows and well-tilled soil, remembering how much work tobacco demanded. The muscles in her back tightened as she thought about the hours she'd spent hoeing in her father's fields. This year, he would have to cultivate the plants alone. Another kind of guilt gripped her as *Mammi* Mary's words drifted through her mind. *Don't complain about hoeing, Rebecca dear. Der gut Man commands us to be stewards of the earth.*

Isaac glanced over the back of his seat. "Does your family grow tobacco on their Mercer County farm, Martha?"

Shocked from her revery, she swallowed. "No." She grappled in the recesses of her mind for facts about Mercer County that insisted on evading her. "We have . . . cows." She looked out the window, praying he would stop questioning her.

Isaac turned the buggy down a lane. They passed under the spreading branches of a huge oak tree, then rounded a curve. Straightening, Rebecca tried to take in the entire Beiler farm quickly. The basic house was red brick with a large porch. A small frame addition, probably a summer kitchen, joined the right side of the house. A four-room frame unit, the *Dawdy Haus*, was connected to the main house at the back left corner. The structure wasn't stylish, but it was homey. Tended flower beds brightened the fenced-in yard where two young boys romped with a medium-sized black dog. Was her coming here putting those innocent children in danger? Her stomach lurched. She felt as though she were astride the crest of a tempestuous wave, forced to go where it took her.

"*Kom ann* (come on), Martha," Esther said, climbing from the buggy.

Rebecca smiled, but her insides churned. The boys raced toward Esther as she approached the gate. Then, noticing Rebecca, they stopped. Two pair of light-blue eyes studied her from under straw hats. The smaller set of brows was blond, the older boy's were light-brown. The dog barked.

"It's all right, Jedidiah," Isaac said around a laugh. "Martha's a friend."

Reaching a hand toward each of her boys, Esther smiled. "Martha's going to stay with us for awhile." She glanced at Rebecca. "The little one's John. He's three. Reuben's five."

"Hello, boys," Rebecca said, "*wie gehts* (How are you?)"

The eldest smiled shyly. The few freckles across his nose seemed to brighten. Light-brown hair poked from under his straw hat. "I have to help Papa with the horse," he said, heading for the carriage.

The older man grinned at his son. When the boy was settled on the seat, Isaac slapped the reins against the horse's rump, and the carriage rumbled toward the barn. Yipping, Jedidiah scrambled after it.

Crossing the porch, Esther opened the kitchen door. "*Kom ann* and meet the girls, Martha."

Stepping through the opening, Rebecca glanced at the long oak table with a dozen chairs that sat in the center of the room. Spotless white-and-beige vinyl covered the floor. A twelve-year-old girl in a light-blue dress arranged moon pies on a cookie sheet. Looking up, she grinned, dimpling her cheeks. Her velvety-brown eyes sparkled as they met Rebecca's.

A young woman about Rebecca's age bent to remove a laden cookie sheet from the oven. Her dress, though somewhat faded, was a pretty shade of pink.

"Girls, this is Martha," Esther said. "She's going to stay with us for a few days." She turned back to Rebecca. "Ruth's my youngest girl." She motioned toward the older girl. "Sarah's my middle daughter."

Placing the hot tray on the stove, Sarah turned and poked a tiny truant lock of blond hair back under her cap. Her smile was warm, and her bright blue eyes illuminated her pretty oval face. "Hi, Martha, *wie gehts*?" Sarah's tall, slender body moved gracefully as she gripped a pancake turner to shovel the moon pies from the tray to paper towels on the counter.

Esther removed her bonnet, so Rebecca did likewise. Clinging to her paper bag, she pictured her jeans, yellow blouse, bright-yellow tennis shoes, and the red purse that Margie had given her. What was she going to do with her ridiculous items? For a moment, she wished she'd left them in a trash can, but thinking about the tiny radio in her purse, she was thankful she still had it. It was her only link to the outside.

Deeply engrossed in thought, she gripped the bag and stared at the floor. What if one of the Beilers glanced in her bag?

"Bisht Du OKay (are you okay) Martha?" Sarah asked.

"Oh." Rebecca controlled a shiver as she looked into the girl's cheerful face. "I'm . . . tired."

Pulling out a chair, Sarah smiled. "Sit and relax."

Ruth approached with a glass of lemonade. "This will help refresh you."

" Gross Dank (Great thanks)."

Ruth returned to the counter and continued forming the moon pies.

Smiling, Sarah approached Rebecca. "I'll take care of your bag, Martha."

What did the girl have in mind? Gripping the parcel, Rebecca fought to hide her anxiety.

3

"I'll keep my bag with me, *Gross Dank*." Rebecca cleared her throat to camouflage the tremor in her voice.

Sarah held her sweet smile. "I'll take it upstairs to my room, Martha. You'll be sleeping in Elizabeth's bed."

"Elizabeth?"

"Our older sister. She now has a place of her own."

Rebecca relinquished her grip. Clinging to her bag would arouse suspicion. Would Sarah respect her privacy and not look in the bag? As Sarah vanished up the stairway, Rebecca's mind whirled, searching for possible excuses for the jeans and ruffled blouse. Just thinking about the forbidden clothes made her sick.

Sarah skipped back down the stairs. "I put your bag on your bed, Martha. After supper, I'll make room in one of my drawers for your things."

"*Viel Dank* (Many thanks)." Rebecca had nearly answered in English. Since Amish mostly speak Pennsylvania Dutch in their homes, except when they are in the presence of *Englischers*, she'd better remain alert. She sipped her lemonade, the tartness reviving her. So far, this family hadn't questioned her beyond her ability to improvise, but how many more lies would she tell? She frowned as guilt cloaked her. Where would this deceit end? If that strange packet was flower freshener, this charade was ludicrous and the accident stupid!

Ruth smiled. "Doing something might make you feel better, Martha. You can help me with the pies, if you like."

Standing, Rebecca walked mechanically to the counter, picked up a crescent-shaped pie and placed it on the cookie sheet. Her cousin Margie had never had to do kitchen chores, and Rebecca had envied her. She recalled her harbored resentment toward *Mammi* because the old woman had demanded she learn to do all the household tasks well. Now, the training would come in handy. For the second time that afternoon, she silently thanked *Mammi* Mary. Her grasp of the German dialect seemed adequate—as long as no one spoke too fast.

"You girls start supper," Esther said. "I'll be back, shortly." Opening the door, she went out.

Ruth watched her go, then broke off a piece of warm moon pie. "Want to sample one, Martha?" She shoved a bite of golden crust into her mouth. "I mixed this batch."

Accepting the portion of pastry the girl offered, Rebecca bit off a crunchy bite, savored the taste, then swallowed. *Es war wonderbar gut* (it was exceptionally good). She glanced at the dozens of moon-shaped, single-serving pies. "*Wass* (What) are you going to do with so many?"

Ruth stared at her, unblinking.

To cover her blunder, Rebecca smiled. "It's your turn for meeting this Sunday, *gel* (isn't that right)?"

"*Ja.*"

As Rebecca arranged more pies on a tray, she sighed. Her mistake could have been costly. Passing the tray of treats to Sarah and witnessing the girl's friendly smile, she vowed not to tell more lies. The web she'd already spun could become a dreadful embarrassment. She blinked back tears as shame fountained within her. God was forgiving, but how could she seek forgiveness and consolation from Him if she continued to evade honesty?

Opening the oven door, she checked the last tray of pies. At home she had an electric stove. Since Old Order Amish didn't believe in being connected to the outside world by gas pipes, electric lines, or phone lines, the Beilers had a propane stove. She was thankful that this family didn't use a wood stove, for in this area, some still did. Beilers' refrigerator was also run by propane. Some

Amish used a gasoline motor to generate electricity for refrigeration, utilizing the same engine to run the washing machine on wash day.

Rebecca ran her fingers over the smooth birch cabinets and cupboards.

Ruth watched her. "Sarah's friend is a cabinetmaker. He put in our cupboards last year." She giggled. "Sarah's sweet on him."

"Ruth," her sister said. "You behave. I have no sweetheart."

The younger girl's velvety-brown eyes sparkled with mischief. "You say that but you--" She cut off her statement as Esther entered the kitchen.

Sarah removed a bag of carrots from the refrigerator, took them to the sink, and began to scrape them. Rebecca admired the girl's gentle nature and quiet ways. Sarah was attractive, but her inner beauty would have shone, regardless.

Getting a knife, Rebecca began to chop the scraped carrots into the pot Sarah had set on the counter. Peace waved through the Beiler home like strains from a soothing symphony, but Rebecca found it difficult to enjoy. How long would it be before she would regain control of her chaotic emotions? When would it be safe for her to go home?

Biting her lower lip, she looked out the kitchen window and wished she could forget Vance Troy and his flower shop. She found it difficult to believe that he could be involved in anything unethical. She remembered the time a little old man had entered the shop with only enough money to purchase a rose for his wife's eightieth birthday. The man's eyes had become misty as he gazed longingly at a pink-throated orchid. Then, sighing, he ordered a red rose. Vance rang up the purchase and took the rose into a back room, but wrapped up an orchid instead.

Joe Dinger usually went to pick up the new vases, she thought. Had he purchased the false-bottomed containers so he could have an illegal business on the side? Her teeth clamped harder on her lip. She didn't want to believe that of Joe. Any time they had been together, he'd been a gentleman—yet . . .

She sighed, relieved that she hadn't given the Beilers her true name. Was keeping her identity a secret living a lie?

"Is something wrong, Martha?" Sarah asked.

Rebecca ignored her, until she felt the girl's fingers on her arm. She tried to smile as she remembered that she had told them her name was Martha. "*Es speit mich* (I'm sorry) that I didn't answer you. I was thinking about something."

Ruth giggled. "Don't let Papa catch you. He calls that daydreaming and says that idle hands will be used by the devil."

"He's right," Rebecca said.

Ruth grinned until her round cheeks became rosy spheres, and the corners of her eyes crinkled. "We have to keep busy when Papa's in the house."

"*Ja, vell.*" Esther gave her youngest daughter a pat. "There's enough to do that we don't have to hunt for it or wait for it to find us. I'll fetch potatoes for supper." Taking a basin, she vanished down the cellar stairs.

Sarah took the last tray of pies from the oven. Glancing at Rebecca, she smiled. "Tonight, one of our neighbors will be eating with us. You'll like him. He's tall and strong."

Ruth's eyes sparkled as dimples appeared in her round cheeks. "See? Sarah's sweet on him, *gel*?"

"No I'm not."

"*Ja*, you are."

"He's a friend, Ruth."

The younger girl giggled. "Is that why you're blushing?"

"Silly girl." Sarah turned away to finish scraping the carrots.

Rebecca figured her denial wasn't true. One thing Amish young people were permitted to cover up was their courtship. Even though everyone seemed to know, a couple usually denied their relationship until their wedding was announced. It was an old custom that was played like a game.

The kitchen door swung inward. Gasping, Rebecca whirled, but it was only little John.

The three-year-old came in, peered curiously at Rebecca, then eyed the moon pies. Grinning like a cherub, he looked at Sarah. "Can I have one?"

"It's close to supper time, John."

Motioning to her little brother, Ruth broke one of the pies in half. With sparkling blue eyes, he went to her. She proffered the treat and whispered in his ear.

He giggled. "*Ja! Denke au.*" Biting into the pastry, he headed for the door. "*Es is gut* (it is good)."

Sarah propped a hand on her slender hip. "Ruth, you're spoiling him."

"*Ja*, but he's the baby, *gel*?"

"Mama better not catch you slipping him treats before meals." She shook her head, but her smile dissolved her attempt to be austere. "You've been snitching, too." She pointed to her sister's thick waist. "One of these days, you're going to have to consider your figure. Maybe no boy will want you, if you're too plump."

"I'm a good cook and that's what counts, *gel*?"

"You hope."

The cellar door opened and Esther came into the kitchen with a large pan of potatoes. At the sink, she ran water on them.

"Does your neighbor eat with you often, Sarah?" Rebecca asked, thinking she detected a shimmer in the girl's blue eyes.

"Lately he has been."

Ruth reached in a drawer for a knife. "That's because he's sweet on you, too."

"That isn't true."

"*Ja* it is."

"Girls," Esther said quietly. "That's enough idle talk." One thin eyebrow lifted as she peered at Ruth. "Did you feed the hens?"

"Not yet, Mama."

"You may do it, now, dear, and gather the eggs."

Heading for the door, Ruth veered enough to wrinkle her nose at Sarah and give her a playful poke.

"I'll help peel the potatoes." Rebecca retrieved the knife Ruth had put on the counter. As she picked up a potato, she glanced out the window at John and the black dog. They seemed tireless, making Rebecca's fatigue more apparent.

An image of her father's worried face seemed to form before

her. How could she contact him? Where was the nearest phone? If only she'd paid attention when they rode in. Picturing her tiny radio, she wondered how long it would be before she could slip away to listen to a news broadcast. Would there be a report concerning the hit-and-run accident? She managed to appear calm, although her nerves were shrieking.

Sarah plopped a peeled potato into the waiting pot of water. "Aaron has to go home right after supper."

The sound of the man's name ricocheted through Rebecca's brain and electrified her nerves, causing her to drop the partially peeled potato. Her throat tightened as she tried unsuccessfully to swallow. Esther glanced at her. Smiling to camouflage her dismay, Rebecca resumed her task.

An image of the Aaron she'd seen on occasion crept into her tormented mind, creating more chaos. The man had been so taken by Margie's red car that he hadn't even noticed her. Or had he? If he were the same man, would he recognize her and ruin her temporary haven? Would he expose her for the liar she'd become?

Struggling to maintain an outward calm, she took a deep breath, reminding herself that the Amish used names over and over. There were probably two dozen Aarons.

Forcing her thoughts away from numerous possibilities that all frightened her, she thought about *Mammi* Mary. A scene from the past played before her in a haunting panorama.

Mary had patted the sofa beside her. "*Kom* and sit with me."

Rebecca had obeyed — as always. Resentment had bubbled within her as she faced the austere old woman. Mary's thin gray brows seemed to shadow her faded blue eyes, and her lips drew taut. Rebecca had wondered what new law she was conjuring up. One of these days, she intended to flee captivity and *Mammi's* uncompromising rules.

Mary pressed an embroidery hoop that held a pillowcase into Rebecca's lap. "Keep your hands busy, dear."

Rebecca stared at the gray outline of a basket of flowers on the fabric. Sighing, she took the needle, threaded it with green floss, and began to stitch around a leaf.

David Wenger came in to sit in his favorite chair. Life would be easier, if *he* were the one making the rules. He was still a good-looking man and had a full head of dark hair, although it was beginning to turn silver at his temples. His shoulders drooped from hard work. His job at New Holland Equipment would have been enough, but he had to keep the farm going. Rubbing his large calloused hands together he gazed at Rebecca. "Oh, Amber," he said, murmuring the name he used privately. "You're so much like your mother."

Smiling, she studied him, never doubting his love. She glanced at *Mammi*, wishing the old woman would take the staves out of her corset and limber up her old-fashioned ideas. "Have you and *Mammi* further discussed my entering nurse's training, Papa?"

Mary straightened her back. "We haven't reached an agreement, Rebecca."

"I'm eighteen. It's time I begin my training."

Mary's features stiffened, portraying her reluctance. "You should find a nice young man and get married."

Someday, I'll leave and get a job, Rebecca had thought. *And I won't tell Mammi where I am.*

"That'll take care of the potatoes," Esther said, bringing Rebecca out of her reverie. Putting the lid on the kettle, she carried it to the stove.

Rebecca figured that *Mammi's* determination to keep her from nursing and to pressure her into marriage had set her up to accept Margie's solution. Had the look in the old woman's eyes been only sternness? Had her taut lips always meant disapproval? Now, Rebecca could discern the love and concern that had shimmered in Mary's eyes as well. As the pangs of disloyalty seared through her, she fought a grimace. If she'd tried harder, would she have understood *Mammi* better?

It serves me right, she supposed. She was hurting only herself. No. She'd brought sorrow to her family and was now deceiving these lovely people. *Am I as horrid as I seem?* She straightened her shoulders. *I'll confess my folly—soon.*

A fast-approaching buggy drew her to a window. The horse

pulling the conveyance was jet-black—except for a splash of white on his forehead. The buggy stopped at the front gate with a jerk as the young man driving yanked on the reins. The high-spirited beast stomped and snorted. A woman in her mid-twenties sat on the seat cuddling an infant. Her lips drew taut as she looked at the driver. She said something, seemingly dismayed. The young man laughed.

"Elizabeth's here," Ruth said, bursting into the room to set a basket of eggs on the bench by the door. "I get to hold baby Priscilla first."

Esther sighed. "I wish Eli wouldn't drive so recklessly, especially when Elizabeth and the baby are with him."

Ruth giggled. "Eli can't help driving like that, Mama."

Sarah glanced out the window. "*Ja*. He likes Aaron's new buggy. Besides, Ransom was a race horse, and he's hard to hold back."

Mischief twinkled in Ruth's dark eyes. "Aaron got a new buggy and a high-stepping horse to go courtin', *gel*?"

"Ruth." Sarah spoke softly, but the warning in her glance quieted her younger sister.

Rebecca watched the couple. Eli jumped from the carriage, favoring his right arm which was in a sling. Hurrying to the other side of the buggy, he helped Elizabeth climb down with the baby. Going to the back, he retrieved a cardboard box. Blond hair curled from under his straw hat, and his blue eyes sparkled. Hesitating in the yard, he spoke to John and the dog.

Elizabeth came through the gate and started up the path. A slight breeze blew her long, light-green skirt. Ruth raced across the porch and down the steps, stopping in front of her sister to take the baby.

Esther glanced through the open doorway at her slender eldest daughter. "Eli has helped Elizabeth so much since her husband was killed."

"Oh!" Rebecca turned to face Esther. "*Wass* happened to him?"

"He fell from the top of the silo last year during harvest." Sadness shadowed Esther's face. "Moses was a good man, and our dear Elizabeth is alone at twenty-five."

"How old is the baby?"

"Four months."

Coming into the kitchen like a ray of sunshine, Elizabeth hugged her mother and Sarah.

Taking Rebecca's arm, Sarah tugged her forward. "This is Martha Kauffman."

Elizabeth smiled. "Hi, *wie gehts* (how are you)?" After shaking hands, she removed her deep-blue bonnet and hung it on a hook. Her small, straight nose and pretty oval face was like Sarah's. The hair that showed in front of her prayer covering was the same chestnut color as Ruth's, and gold flecks sparkled in her soft-brown eyes.

Gusting into the house, Eli set the box on a counter, removed the cake it contained, then turned to leave.

"Eli," Sarah said, "must you be so impolite?"

His blond brows rose as he glanced quizzically at her. "You should treat your suffering brother with more respect. You know I broke my arm, just so Aaron would have an excuse to spend more time here."

Now that Rebecca realized Eli was Esther's son, she could see a resemblance to little John. Eli's cheekbones were higher and his face not as round as the little boy's, but his expression of innocence made her smile.

Sarah lowered her lashes demurely. "Eli, we have company."

He laughed. "Since when is our big sister company?"

"I'm referring to Martha Kauffman."

"Who?"

Sarah laughed softly as she turned to look at Rebecca. "Martha, I'd like you to meet my wild older brother."

"Oh." Eli stared at Rebecca, and color crept across his shaven cheeks. "Hello, *wie gehts*?" He grinned. "I'm not usually so crazy. It's... because of the inconvenience caused by my broken arm." He backed toward the door, but tripped over Jedidiah who had followed them in. Yipping, the dog dove under a bench as Eli's straw hat toppled to the floor. Regaining his balance, Eli swooped to seize his hat, spun, and fled.

Elizabeth laughed. "That serves him right for giving me such a wild ride."

Esther frowned. "Was he terribly careless, dear?"

"No, Mama. It's just part of his *Rumspringa*."

"*Ja*," Esther said, sighing. "But we must permit young people to have their freedom, so they'll be more willing to live a strict life after they join the church, *gel* (right)?" Glancing at Rebecca, she frowned. "Isaac's concerned, because at twenty, Eli should be a member of the church."

Elizabeth touched Esther's arm comfortingly. "He'll settle down soon, Mama."

Rebecca glanced out the window. Eli had stopped to talk to his baby brother. Then, climbing into the buggy, he slapped Ransom's rump with the reins. The animal raced toward the barn. Rebecca smiled. "Eli drives well with one arm."

"He's full of life," Elizabeth said. "He'll tackle almost anything, even with his right arm in a sling."

Esther sighed. "We must pray about his wickedness."

"Oh, Mama," Sarah said, "the car he has in town, the one we aren't supposed to know about, will probably tame him, *gel*?"

"*Ja*. If it doesn't ruin him first." The older woman looked pensive. "I'm also concerned about the illegal drugs that I hear are increasing in Lancaster."

Rebecca's heart lurched as a vision of the questionable packets invaded her mind.

"Rachel Zimmerman's worried," Elizabeth said. "She told me her eldest son said it was easy to find a contact if a person wanted to buy cocaine. She asked him how he knew, but he avoided answering her."

Rebecca swallowed hard. Could the packets in Vance's flower vases have been cocaine? Not wanting anyone to perceive her distress, she lowered her eyes and pretended to be reading a copy of *The Budget*, a newspaper printed in Sugar Creek, Holmes County, Ohio that kept the Amish communities in contact with each other.

Esther's frown deepened. "I pray your brother doesn't try drugs."

Sarah hugged her. "You can trust Eli."

"Temptation to be like others is great for young men." Esther waved a hand. "You girls haven't given me any worry."

Elizabeth held her sweet smile. "Girls are different, Mama, *gel* (right)?"

"*Ja*," Ruth said, but the twinkle in her dark eyes made Rebecca wonder what the girl might someday get into.

Laughing, Reuben scampered into the kitchen. "Where'd you go, bad dog?"

Esther shooed him and the dog outside. "You boys play in the yard until supper."

"You can help set the table, Martha," Elizabeth said.

Her warm smile relaxed Rebecca. She was thankful the woman didn't require an explanation concerning her presence. Retrieving a pile of plates, Rebecca placed them on the table.

Elizabeth passed her a tray of glasses. "Aaron will be eating with us. He's a King, first son of Noah."

"Aaron will be taking over the family farm, soon," Sarah murmured with admiration. "With all his own work, he came to help with the chores that Eli finds difficult doing left-handed."

Rebecca smiled. "You really do care for him, don't you?"

Turning away, Sarah lifted four-month-old Priscilla from Ruth's arms. "I admire him for the way he accepts responsibility. He takes care of his family and helps us, too."

"Aaron's been managing their farm for over a year," Elizabeth said. "Is it because Noah hasn't been well?"

"*Ja*. But he's been feeling better of late."

Esther set the water kettle on the stove. "It's an answer to our prayers."

"Are there other boys in the family?" Rebecca asked.

"Three others," Elizabeth said. "Aaron's the eldest. The second son took his bride and moved to Kentucky where the two older sisters had been living with their families. The youngest boy is sixteen."

A wistful expression captured Sarah's features. "Joseph's twenty. He left, and I haven't seen him for nearly a year."

"They've finished the *Dawdy Haus*," Elizabeth said. "Noah and Anna have already moved into it, *gel*?"

"*Ja*." Ruth glanced at Sarah. "Aaron rattles around in the big house all by himself."

Sarah held the baby in one arm and propped a fist on her hip. "His younger brother and sister are there."

"Sometimes." Ruth grinned. "Maybe he'll choose a wife and get married this November."

"Maybe." Turning away, Sarah cooed at the baby.

Ruth grinned. "You hope, *gel*?"

"Stop your silliness." Sarah frowned. "The men are coming. Get the basins and take them outside." Was the pink glow on Sarah's face betraying her feelings for the man called Aaron?

Esther glanced around the kitchen. "One of you girls go to the *Dawdy Haus* for *Mammi* Hazel."

Elizabeth smiled. "I'll fetch her."

Rebecca fought to still her anxiety over meeting Aaron King as she filled the water glasses. She scanned the table. There was a huge platter of sliced ham, a bowl of mashed potatoes, one of sweet potatoes, and a dish of buttered carrots. There were also containers of applesauce, cottage cheese, pickled beets, and celery. A stack of sliced homemade bread and a platter of recently churned butter sat at each end of the table. A cake and a bowl of pudding waited on the counter. The Amish set a bountiful table, and this was an example of the way they liked to eat.

As the men came to the house, their laughter made Rebecca's heart thud. Once she confirmed that Aaron was a stranger, she would be confident that her identity would remain a secret.

Hoping to appear demure, she stood at the far side of the room. Isaac smiled as he entered, and the curious but warm appraisal in Eli's expression put her somewhat at ease.

"Martha, this is Aaron King." Isaac motioned toward the man who stepped through the doorway into the kitchen.

Rebecca felt the color drain from her face. He *was* the man she'd seen driving a car in Lancaster. "Hello... *wie gehts*, Aaron?" She spoke quietly, praying he didn't recognize her.

Removing his straw hat, he hung it on a peg by the door and turned to assess her. "Hello... Martha."

Struggling to camouflage her anxiety, she blinked. Was it curiosity that shimmered in Aaron's dark eyes—or suspicion?

4

The ladies bustled around the kitchen, completing the last minute details for supper. Elizabeth put Priscilla in the downstairs crib and helped little John into his seat. Grinning, Eli watched Rebecca.

Isaac took his place at the table. "Martha will be staying with us for a few days."

"*Ja?*" Aaron's right brow quirked.

An elderly woman tottered into the kitchen from the *Dawdy Haus*. Her dark-blue dress reached nearly to her ankles, and tiny wisps of white hair showed at the front of her prayer cap. The top of her head barely reached Elizabeth's shoulder. Pausing, she leaned on a cane and glanced around the room.

Sarah stopped near the old lady. "*Mammi*, I'd like you to meet Martha Kauffman."

"Hello, Mrs. Beiler," Rebecca said. "*Wie gehts?*"

"Doing *vell*." Hazel's thin lips stretched into a smile as her perceptive brown eyes surveyed Rebecca. "*Un Wie gehts?*" she asked in a crackling voice.

"Visiting here is *wonderbar* (great)!"

Sarah pulled out a chair for Hazel and waited for her to be seated. Smiling, she tenderly patted the old woman's shoulder.

Avoiding Aaron's eyes, Rebecca took her seat, inwardly grimacing at the thought of spending the entire meal across the table from him. Heads bowed for silent grace. Moments later, Isaac said amen, picked up the platter of ham, served himself, then passed the platter.

As Aaron forked a slice of ham, his interrogating eyes caught Rebecca's. "How long do you plan to stay with the Beilers?"

"I'm not sure." She hoped he would not question her further. Living this lie was bad enough, without having to repeat it.

Grinning, Eli plopped a mound of mashed potatoes onto his plate. "You can stay as long as you like."

Sarah laughed softly. "Don't forget about your broken arm."

"I do fine single-handed — in some ways."

"You'd better be careful," Ruth said accepting the bowl of carrots. "You might get your left arm broken, too, *gel*?"

He grinned, and his blue eyes went to Rebecca's face. Blond hair swirled around his ears.

Sarah seemed to be guarding her glances at Aaron, apparently not wanting him to catch her looking. He glanced her way often, but his expression was unreadable. He frequently looked Rebecca's way as well, making the lump in her throat grow larger.

Looking up, she caught him studying her face and nearly choked. The tasty bite of mashed potato seemed to turn to plaster in her mouth. Determined to stare him down, she held her focus steady. Finally, he lowered his eyes to spread butter on his bread, but the excessive inquisitiveness in his expression had stolen her appetite.

The sun streamed through a naked window and caressed his dark wavy hair. His broad shoulders and muscular arms shaded his plate. Under other circumstances, she would have been attracted to this handsome man. Glancing up, he caught her scrutinizing him. The flush of blood that heated her cheeks made her angry. She lowered her eyes and focused on his suspender. Amishmen in that district wear only a single strap. She again met his gaze. He seemed to be interpreting her discomfort. There was something brewing behind his dark-brown eyes. How much did he know? The warmth in Eli's smile and the kindling interest in his glances made the lack of trust in Aaron's more apparent.

Pretending to be distracted was difficult, for the walls in Amish homes are bare, except Beilers had a number of calendars hanging near the stove. Would avoiding Aaron's gaze make her seem shy or would he think her strange?

She glanced at the purple smocked pillow that lay crunched in a rocker in the corner, then at Jedidiah who sat under the wooden bench by the door. At night, the men put their barn shoes under it. Rebecca studied the hats on the pegs above the bench, trying to guess which one belonged to Aaron.

Yawning, the dog crept across the kitchen to stretch out behind Reuben's chair. The canine seemed to be keeping one eye open. Reuben's hand moved slowly to his side, and a slice of carrot bounced on the floor near Jedidiah's nose. Chomping it, the dog looked up expectantly. Rebecca smiled. If anyone else had witnessed the act, they hadn't let on. Then, the littlest boy dropped a bite of ham.

"John," Elizabeth corrected softly.

"*Ja?*" He blinked, his eyes two blue spheres of innocence. A grin spread across his baby face, and his cheeks dimpled.

"You be a *gut* boy."

"*Ja.*" He lowered his long blond lashes, but his grin remained.

Aaron continued to study Martha's face, feeling as though he'd seen her. *Where?* As he ate, he struggled to recall an image that flitted through the recesses of his mind. An *Englischer?* He tried to picture Martha without her head covering and her long tawny hair whipping in the breeze. Then an evasive memory of a Mennonite girl toyed with his senses. Had the girl's father called her Amber? He cleared his throat. "*Wo bisht Du von* (Where are you from), Martha?"

She hesitated, seemingly uncomfortable. "Mercer County."

He thought of relatives of a family who had moved there from near Bird-in-Hand. "Do you know any Millers?"

"There are none in our church."

"I assume you didn't travel alone." Her apparent uneasiness encouraged suspicion to tip-toe around the perimeter of his mind. "Did your father accompany you?"

She lowered her thick tawny lashes, drawing his attention to their golden tips. "My . . . brother."

"*Wass's* name?"

". . . Matthew."

Her voice had softened until he had difficulty hearing her. "*Wass's* your last name?"

". . . Kauffman." She looked as though she were about to jump and run. *Fer wass* (Why)?

"Does your brother know you're here with the Beilers?" When she glanced up, her eyes flooded him with a soft golden-brown hue that nearly made him gasp.

"He's aware that I'm with a kind, gentle family I can trust."

"How will he know where to come for you?"

She squirmed. "I . . . have a phone number."

"You'll be leaving then?"

Lowering her eyes, she forked a slice of carrot and circled it through a puddle of butter on her plate. "Sometime."

"Back to Mercer County?" He figured it was impolite to interrogate this lovely girl, but he couldn't seem to help himself.

"*Ich . . . wehs net* (I . . . don't know)."

He frowned. "That's strange."

"Not . . . really." She swallowed, looking as though she wished she could disappear. "It depends on how successful he is settling his business."

"He's starting a business?"

Color crept across her smooth white cheeks, and she refrained from meeting his gaze. "He's . . . bargaining for a land exchange." Her voice had lowered even farther.

Aaron felt rude pressuring her and had decided to wait until they were alone to satisfy his curiosity; however, her last statement had opened a topic that germinated more questions. "Where's your brother planning to locate?"

Rebecca fought not to cringe under Aaron's scrutiny, but her tongue felt scalded from her lies. Blaming him, she drew her lips taut. "My brother doesn't discuss his business transactions with me, Mr. King." She struggled not to wriggle.

"Aaron," Isaac said, "Martha is our guest, and we don't want to make her uncomfortable by asking her too many questions. *Gel* (right)?"

Aaron frowned. "*Ja, vell —*"

Rebecca was so grateful, she could have kissed Isaac's bearded face. She wanted to remain obscure for a few more days. Did Aaron know Vance Troy or Joe Dinger? What about Gene or Doug? What if he discovered she'd worked in Vance's florist shop? Would he connect her to the hit-and-run incident? If something illegal was going on, would he blame her for being part of that, too?

For the remainder of the meal, Aaron ignored her. He would have to refrain from asking questions in front of the Beilers. *He won't catch me alone*, she vowed.

Standing, Isaac pushed in his chair. "Reuben, you come to the barn with me to help with the chores."

The five-year-old nodded.

Eli got up, flashed a smile at Rebecca, grabbed his straw hat, and went outside.

Aaron followed the men to the door, took his hat from a peg, then turned to Esther. "*Gross Dank* for supper. *Es war wonderbar gut* (it was very very good)." When his eyes found Sarah, they lingered. Then, gripping the doorknob, he looked at Rebecca.

She smiled. "*Gute Nacht* (Good night), Mr. King."

"*Gute Nacht*. It was nice meeting you . . . Martha."

The way he'd paused before he said her name made her heart lurch, and the sagacious shimmer in his dark eyes seemed to hold more than curiosity. Trying to appear shy, she lowered her lashes and began to collect the plates.

Mammi Hazel made her way to the sink, hung the crook of her cane over the counter, and prepared the dishwater. In Amish families, everyone who was able did their part.

As Rebecca helped with the clean-up, she convinced herself that Aaron King must be a reasonable man. After all, Sarah was sweet and intelligent. The girl wouldn't get involved with a man who was unworthy of her affection, would she?

She sighed, thankful the men were gone. Her muscles ached from the tension Aaron's presence had caused. Priscilla began to whimper. Rebecca glanced toward the crib. "May I rock her?"

Elizabeth smiled. "*Ja.*"

The infant quieted as Rebecca lifted her. Rocking and humming, her mind went back to Aaron. What if he talked to Isaac and Eli about her? Her breath caught. Had he seen her wearing that horrid brilliant-orange sundress Margie had encouraged her to purchase? What if he'd noticed her dressed in jeans? Her heart raced as another horror struck her. Had he noticed her with her father the day at Central Market when she'd first observed him? Might he have seen her driving Vance's station wagon?

Chewing her lower lip, she thought about the last time she'd seen Aaron driving a car. She had to smother a gasp as she realized Eli had been the passenger. Had he seen her, too? Was the shimmer in his blue eyes friendliness or curiosity? She grimaced. Had Aaron left for the King farm or were the men comparing notes?

An image of Joe Dinger pressed to the forefront of her mind. She pictured his amicable face, dark hair, and sparkling brown eyes. Pondering his kindness and thoughtfulness, she wondered if he would help her. Could she locate him without coming in contact with any other employees of Troy's? She frowned. Could Joe help her without getting into trouble himself? Dare she take that chance? Was Joe innocent or could he be the one who hid the packets in the vases?

I can't trust anyone!

Several Amish young men had cars that they hid in town. Some were beginning to bring them home, although they couldn't park them on Amish property. How many of them could have seen her? Did any of them know about her job with Vance?

Oh, God, she prayed, brushing her lips across the baby's blond ringlets. *Please help me.* Running away from home and telling lies made her feel alienated from Him. *Under the circumstances, how can I find my way back into God's grace?* Hot tears burned the back of her eyes, and she blinked rapidly to keep them from spilling down her cheeks.

"Aaron's a good man, Sarah," Elizabeth said.

Sarah dried a plate methodically and put it away. "He hasn't joined the church, yet."

Elizabeth reached for the dirty potato pan. "How old is he?"

"Twenty-four." Sarah frowned. "His younger brother left because of the pressure to join the church. I hope Aaron isn't pressed too far as well."

Waving a dish towel, Ruth giggled. "He probably would leave, if it weren't for Sarah."

"*Wass* (What)?" Elizabeth glanced at Ruth, then at Sarah and smiled. "It's unusual for a man his age not to be married. *Gel?*"

Sarah sighed. "It's unusual for one that age not to have joined the church, too."

"He's like Eli," Ruth said, grinning. "He probably has a car in town, too."

Listening made Rebecca feel worse. Picturing herself without her prayer cap and her long hair whipping in the wind, she grimaced. Why had she permitted Margie to convince her to buy flashy clothing? Remembering that she was wearing brilliant-red lace underwear, she felt sick. She was Amish on the outside, but it didn't even reach her skin. *Margie's solution to my problem seems frivolous and shallow, now.* Shame crept over Rebecca like sludge as remorse captured her heart. She felt unclean in a way that soap and water could not cleanse.

How could she avoid being identified, accused, and condemned? If she fled, possibly she could escape the Beilers, but there was no eluding God's all-knowing eyes.

Priscilla began to cry, bringing Elizabeth to the rocker. "She's hungry. It's past her feeding time."

Getting up, Rebecca proffered the baby. Her arms felt empty, and the storm in her heart raged on. She went to the window to see if the men were still at the barn. Rays from the setting sun shimmered on the top of Aaron's buggy. The man hadn't left.

"I'm finished, Ruth," Hazel said, drying her hands and gripping her cane. "*Kom ann* to the *Dawdy Haus* with me. I want to show you a new stitch tonight."

Ruth made a face. Remembering her own reluctance to Mary's insistence, Rebecca understood. Erasing the displeasure from her expression, Ruth accompanied the older woman from the kitchen.

Footsteps on the porch made Rebecca jump. Turning, she stared at the door, feeling like a chicken under the descending claws of a hawk.

Isaac swung the door open, stepped into the kitchen, and smiled at Rebecca. Relieved, she smiled back.

"Is Aaron gone?" Sarah asked, peering out the door behind her father.

"He's helping Eli mend a harness before he leaves. He's anxious to be on his way, though, for his mother isn't well."

"Oh!" Elizabeth frowned. "Is Anna off her feet?"

"*Ja*. Aaron thinks she has the flu." He eyed his eldest daughter. "Eli said he'd take you home after he finishes in the barn." Sitting on the bench, he pulled off his heavy work shoes.

Rebecca wondered if it was a mistake to avoid Aaron. Should she make herself available, just to find out what he knew? The thought made her shiver.

Padding across the room in his stocking feet, Isaac sat in his chair and picked up a copy of *Die Botschaft*, an Amish-Mennonite newspaper published in Lancaster. When the last of the dishes were put away, each of the women chose one of several chairs, sat, and picked up their sewing.

"You must come to visit me, Martha," Elizabeth said, handing her the sleeping baby. "Eli will be glad to bring you."

"*Herzlich Dank*. I'd love to visit you sometime."

Elizabeth gathered up Priscilla's things. "It'll be dark soon. I wish Eli would hurry."

The sun had set by the time he came in. "You ready?" he asked Elizabeth.

"*Ja*." She wrapped her cape around her shoulders and tied her bonnet. With Priscilla in her arms, she went out.

Pausing at the door, Eli glanced at Rebecca. "Would you like to ride along?"

"*Gross Dank*, Eli, but not this evening. I'm tired."

"Some other time, then," he mumbled, his face turning pink as he rushed from the room.

Rebecca turned to look at the mending in Esther's lap. Hating the task, she suppressed a shudder. "Is there any mending I can do?"

Esther smiled. "We can manage, Martha."

Rebecca prayed the woman hadn't perceived her aversion. An uneasiness crept over her. "I . . . think I'll get . . . some fresh air."

Sarah glanced wistfully out the window, then returned her attention to the sock she was darning.

Rebecca paused on the porch. The sky had darkened, although there was still a glimmer of crimson at the horizon. Nothing moved, but she could hear Eli's buggy as he headed for the main road. She looked for Aaron's carriage. It was gone. A cricket chirped, and a night bird called. Strolling across the lawn, she sighed. Would Aaron be back tomorrow? She hoped not, for she needed time to think and plan.

Now that the man who could possibly expose her was gone, she ambled to the barn. Pausing at the fodder room door, she peered into the darkened interior. Lantern light glimmered at the back. A cow lowed. A horse whinnied, and she could hear the team munching oats.

Stepping inside the barn, she moved to the first stall, inhaling the sweet scent of fresh hay. "What's your name?" she asked a draft horse. He blew and stomped. Reaching out, she petted his broad forehead. A mouse squeaked behind her. As she turned, a few bits of chaff sifted through a crack in the floor above and drifted listlessly to the straw. Chills traveled down her spine. Were eyes scrutinizing her? Apprehension, as well as the coolness of evening, drew her back outside. A whippoorwill called from an apple tree in the barnyard, and a cat squalled near the carriage shed.

A scuffling noise in the barn startled her, and she whirled, to face the door. Jedidiah appeared in the opening, yipped, then raced to greet her. Laughing, she bent to stroke the dog's head. "Do you want to go for a walk with me, Jed?"

Wagging his tail, he followed her as she wandered around the corner of the barn. With the trusty canine by her side, her anxiety dissolved. She rested her hand on a rough wooden fence post, then lifted her skirt, climbed over the top board, and crossed the pasture, the moon lighting her way.

At the other side of the meadow, she ducked under a wire fence and crossed the hay field. A small stream babbled through the farm. The Beilers had built a dam, so they could use a water pump. Stopping, she watched the wheel that was turned by water that spilled over the crest of the dam. The steady thump, thump lulled her. She peered at the crank attached to the wheel. As it was forced around, the cable was drawn forward, then released. She followed the cable with her eyes until it vanished into darkness. It was connected to a pump over a well several hundred feet away. It was a simple, but ingenious, way of drawing water and storing it in a reservoir. From there it flowed into the house by gravity.

One-by-one, stars began to twinkle. Peering at them, Rebecca wandered upstream to where the water was shallow. Flat stones formed a broken bridge across the stream. She hopped from one rock to another, then jumped to the field on the other side. Jed splashed through the water to join her.

A nearby row of berry bushes grew higher than her head. An oak tree spread its huge branches, their shadow creating a black void. The darkness seemed to beckon, so she moved to the tree and leaned against it. The sturdiness of the oak reminded her of her father. How far away he seemed. "Oh Papa," she whispered, sensing his grief over her leaving home the way she had.

A twig snapped beside her, and she glanced at the berry bushes. A rustling sound made her heart leap. A rabbit scrambled from under the brush and raced across the hay field. Barking, the dog gave chase.

"Jedidiah!" Rebecca called. "Jed! Come back!"

The black canine was soon swallowed up in the night. When all became still, Rebecca figured she was safe. Who would guess she was out here alone? As peace slowly engulfed her, she began to hum. The notes came automatically, but she soon realized she was humming one of the hymns her mother had taught her. Being an *Englischer*, she had known hymns that *Mammi* Mary didn't heartily approve of. Rebecca smiled as she sang the English words of comfort that filtered through the debris in her restless mind. "Blessed assurance, Jesus is mine, Oh what a foretaste of glory divine..."

Stepping away from the tree, she moved to where she could gaze at the canopy of stars above her. She continued to sing, swaying with the tempo. Was it right to sway? *Mammi* Mary forbade it.

Finishing one hymn, she began another, the words mingling with the breeze and flowing across the tobacco field in a soft, sweet lilt. "Rock of ages, cleft for me. Let me hide myself in Thee." Her phrases drifted away and seemed to be carried aloft by invisible wings.

The thought of hiding brought Rebecca out of her dreamy state. *How long will God protect me?* Her eyes traveled to the horizon where the hills formed dark mounds, and words from Scripture drifted into her mind. "I will lift up mine eyes unto the hills, from whence cometh my help. My help cometh from the Lord, which made heaven and earth."

Rebecca felt unworthy. A desire to be truthful filled her, and she vowed not to tell any more lies. She figured she should confess her disobedience before she could expect God's forgiveness. *When this flower vase mystery is cleared up, I'll go home*, she thought, planning to admit her mistake to her father, then ask *Mammi*, as well as God, for forgiveness. She shivered, wishing she could force the reoccurring image of the scraped green car from her mind.

Three steps took her to the edge of the tobacco field. She tapped a clod of soft dirt with her toe, and the scent of moist earth drifted to her. She admired the plants. *Sturdy little sentinels*, she mused, bending to touch a velvety-soft leaf, disregarding the chance of getting tobacco stain on her fingers. Barring bad weather, there would be a good crop. The Beilers depended on tobacco as their cash crop, as did many Amish families in Lancaster County. Remaining here would mean helping with the hoeing. She straightened, for the thought of it made her back muscles tighten.

"You ungrateful wretch," she whispered, comparing her reluctance to the generosity of the Beilers.

Wondering if she should return to the house, she peered back at the small stream. The water shimmered in the moonlight as it wound its way across the meadow. Behind the dam, the water pooled, looking like a huge silver tray that mirrored the sky. She watched the silhouette of a deer as the animal meandered across the field to get a drink.

A twig snapped near the berry bushes behind her, and she turned to stare into the darkness, expecting another rabbit.

"Amber?"

She gasped. Someone had discovered the name her father called her in private. How? Frozen, she stared at the deep shadow by the bushes, straining to see the man. It would be useless to try to outrun him. Why had she ventured so far from the house? She shivered. Regaining some of her senses, she knew she had to deny her identity. "I'm . . . Martha."

"Is that what your father calls you?"

He sounded like Joe Dinger. Was it possible? How had Joe found her? Was he there to help—or to silence her? The man took a step forward. Rebecca's heart faltered, her blood felt hot, and her bones seemed to turn to liquid. Holding her breath, she clutched her face with icy fingers.

5

Rebecca stared into the deep shadows at the partly concealed figure. Her heart drummed, and her mind reeled. The man strode from the darkness. Shoving his hat back, he permitted moonlight to bathe his face.

"Aaron!"

"Who'd you expect?"

"I thought . . . I was alone." She struggled to regain her composure. "*Wass* are you doing here?"

"I followed you."

"*Fer wass*?" she gasped, nearly blundering by using the English word, "Why."

"Do you think it's wise for a young lady to wander about alone after dark?"

Determined not to be interrogated, she tilted her chin.

He propped his fists on his hips. "I wanted to speak with you in private."

Forcing a smile, she acted nonchalant. "Did you hide your buggy so I'd figure you'd left?"

"Eli borrowed it to take Elizabeth home while I finished mending a harness. I was waiting at the barn for him to return."

In order not to squirm under his scrutiny, she looked away.

Grasping her arm, he turned her to face him. His dark eyes narrowed as he bent toward her. "*Wer bisht Du* (Who are you)?"

"Martha Kauffman." The lie stung her lips, but squaring her shoulders, she eyed him.

Releasing her, he stepped away. "Your reason for being here seems sketchy."

"Should my being here be a concern of yours?" She kept her tone sweet, striving not to anger him or create more suspicion.

"Have you told the Beilers the truth, Martha?"

"You speak of truth, yet you deceived me."

He took a step backward, and his lips parted. "How?"

"By letting me think you were no longer here."

He sighed. "*Wass* are you doing with the Beilers?"

"Isaac explained that. *Gel* (Isn't that so)?"

"*Ja*, but I feel there's more to your visit than you're telling us, Amber."

She suppressed a groan. Aaron must have heard her father using that name that day at Central Market. Had he seen her face clearly? It was becoming more difficult to appear calm. "Why do you call me Amber?"

"You looked so frightened when I used the name."

"You startled me. I would've jumped if you'd called me Jed!"

His brows drew closer together. "You remind me of a girl I've seen around Lancaster."

She smiled vibrantly to camouflage her dread. "You could've seen one of my distant relatives. My father says we have kin in Lancaster County."

"*Ja*? Why aren't you staying with them?"

What she thought to be wise answers were sinking her deeper into an unknown abyss. She shrugged. "We haven't corresponded, so I'm not sure where they are."

"I'll help you locate them."

She swallowed. "I'm satisfied with the Beilers."

The crease between his eyes deepened. "I'm going into town tomorrow. If I can't find the girl I've seen, I'll be back to question you."

"You have no right to question me, just because you saw someone who looks a little like me." Grinning, she tried to manufacture confidence.

Aaron sighed. "The girl intrigues me."

"*Ja?* You should be interested in someone Amish instead of searching for trouble with some city girl, *gel?*"

His rich laugh lessened the tension. "As long as you're telling the truth, there's nothing to worry about. *Gel?*"

"Dishonesty appalls me, Aaron."

"It does me, too." He shook his head. "Why do I get the impression that you're hiding something?"

"Maybe you're bored and imagining trouble."

"*Ja?*" He folded his arms. "I read fear in your eyes when I met you, and it didn't diminish during supper. *Wass's* frightening you?"

"I'm . . . not used to being away from my family. I feel like a stranger."

"Any Amish girl should feel at home with the Beilers, *gel?*"

"*Ja*, but . . ." Stunned by his kindness, she turned away. Her mouth felt scorched from the lies she'd told him. How could she have failed God so soon after she'd promised Him to be honest? Blinking to control the sudden excess moisture in her eyes, she battled to restrain a sob; yet tears ran down her cheeks.

"Martha?"

"Leave me be." Her voice caught.

He moved to where he could see her face. "Oh, Martha." Reaching out, he touched her arm. "*Es speit mich* for pressuring you. I haven't been neighborly." With fingertips, he lifted her chin to study her face. "I never got a close look at the girl that reminds me of you. Once, I heard her father call her Amber." He smiled. "Your eyes are a soft golden-brown color, so may I call you Amber?"

"No." The syllable resounded sharper than she'd meant it to. When he recoiled, she modified her reaction. "I want us to be proper, but you can call me Amber if no one's near."

"All right . . . Amber." His voice was almost a caress.

"The Beilers will wonder where I am." She turned toward the house.

"Wait. I saw the same girl in Zimmerman's store, once. I was under the impression she was Mennonite." He frowned. "But when I noticed her in Lancaster, she was wearing jeans, and her hair was flying free." Suddenly, he grinned. "She reminded me of Ransom.

My horse used to be a racer, and he's still full of fire."

Rebecca cringed, but the comparison made her laugh. Blinking, she asked, "Shouldn't you be more reserved? Why do you stare at strange young women?"

"I didn't stare!" His eyes lowered to the ground, and he kicked at a stone. "You say you're from Mercer County?"

"Stop it Aaron." Gritting her teeth, she vowed not to tell him more lies. "If you insist on chasing your phantom lady, don't drag me into it."

"Phantom?" He chuckled. "You're different from other Amish girls. One minute you're wary, the next you seem confident. You amuse me."

"I have no intention of humoring you, Aaron King."

He shrugged. "Isaac said your brother's trying to make arrangements to occupy a farm in this county. Will you be living with him?"

"No. I mean . . . *Ich wehs net* (I don't know)." Noticing the suspicion that began to creep back into his eyes, she sighed. "I'll probably stay — temporarily, for he'll need someone to keep house." She bit her tongue on yet another falsehood.

"You're full of secrets, Amber."

"I have no secrets." Swallowing hard, she wrestled not to choke on her words. Anguish seared her soul.

Aaron's intrigue grew. If all were as this young woman had said, why did she appear leery? He watched her reaction. "If you're telling the truth, nothing should worry you. *Gel* (isn't that true)?"

She glanced at him, then quickly away. "We'd better start for the house. *Gel*?"

"*Ja*. Eli expects me to be in the barn." He grinned. "If he finds us out here alone, he might tell folks we're courting." Even in the dim light, he detected the color that stained her cheeks, and his grin broadened. She turned away, apparently to hide her blush. He clasped her hand. "*Kom ann*." Her arm stiffened as though she were going to jerk her fingers free. Instead, she accompanied him. Wondering if she were accustomed to night strolls, he tightened his grip on her hand. "Promise me you won't stray this far from the house again after dark."

"Jed was with me."

Aaron laughed. "You can't trust that dog—especially if there's a rabbit within a mile, gel?"

"I found that out." She gave him a wary side-glance.

Interpreting her apprehension, he wondered what she could be concealing. At the edge of the stream, he stopped. The first rock was thirty inches out.

Martha frowned. "Leaping from the rock to land was easy, but the span seems farther from shore."

"Wait." Aaron headed downstream to search along the edge of the water for a flat rock. Procuring one, he lugged it back and splashed it in the stream about fifteen inches from the edge. It shimmered in the moonlight. "Try that."

She jumped. Her foot landed precariously and slipped. Shrieking, she clutched the air, then gasped as she sat with a splash in three inches of cool water.

Aaron leaped forward and lifted her to land, then broke into laughter.

Clenching her fingers into fists, she drew her lips taut. "You should've told me that rock was slimy! How will I explain my dripping skirt to the Beilers?"

"*Ja, vell . . .*" He wrestled to control his mirth, but a persistent grin tugged at his lips.

She flounced her skirt. "You probably did this on purpose, Aaron King, just to make me look foolish."

"You're doing that very well on your own. *Gel?*"

She propped a hand on her slender hip. "You seem to bring out the worst in me."

Jedidiah romped across the meadow, splashed into the stream, and lapped water. Sloshing to the opposite bank, he turned to wait. He panted, and his eyes sparkled from the chase. Apparently assuming they weren't coming, he waded back across the stream. Stopping in front of Martha, he shook the excess water from his coat.

"Jed! You're soaking my apron. You're no more of a gentleman than Aaron."

Bending, Aaron patted the dog's head. "It's all right, boy. All wet hens act like that. *Gel?*"

She acted indignant, but her sweetness shone through. Turning away, she gingerly placed her foot on the first stone, then skipped from stone to stone across the stream.

Aaron followed. Before they reached the barn, he heard a buggy. "Get to the house, Martha, before Eli sees you."

"*Fer wass?* Are you afraid to take the blame for ruining my dress?"

"Not your dress." He grinned. "I could be blamed for ruining your reputation."

Rebecca's eyes widened. "No wonder you're not married. No decent girl would have you." Remembering that Sarah cared for this man, she was embarrassed. To protect Sarah, he wouldn't want to be caught alone at night with another girl. Whirling, she fled, but his soft laughter followed her to the porch.

She turned to see Aaron and the dog vanish into the barn. Worry plagued her. He intended to go to town to search for Amber and would undoubtedly ask questions. Envisioning his determined expression, she bit her lower lip.

Shaking her wet skirt, she wondered what she was going to do for dry clothing. Would Esther question her bringing so little with her? When she told them she had nothing to wear, they would probably wonder what she had in her bag.

When Ransom's nose came around the last bend in the lane, Rebecca moved into a shadow close to the house, not wanting Eli to spot her. Leaning against the bricks that were still warm from the afternoon sun, she thought about what she was going to tell the Beilers. Her skirt was a mess, and mud clung to her shoes.

Unmoving, she waited until Aaron's buggy rumbled back out the lane. She chewed on a fingernail, praying he wouldn't uncover the truth. If he did, would she run? Leaning her head against the smooth bricks, she closed her eyes and fought despair.

Aaron drove out Beilers' lane, his mind on Martha. He was anxious to go into Lancaster to search for the girl with long, tawny hair. Had he seen her clearly enough to identify her? Had he put undue pressure on Martha?

"What will I do if I find the girl in town?" he muttered, frowning. *What will I do if I don't?*

His thoughts resembled a kayak in whitewater. What if Martha were in trouble? What would happen if he exposed her? It would be more Christian to try to help her.

"Help her what?" He sighed deeply. Why couldn't he just accept the girl as the Beilers had? Was there really something mysterious about her or was his imagination working overtime?

"I'll put her out of my mind," he said, but as he rode, he pictured Martha's lovely face, and the look in her soft golden-brown eyes haunted him.

"Martha?"

Rebecca jumped, and her eyes widened. "Eli!"

Taking a step backward, he peered at her. "*Es speit mich* (I'm sorry) that I startled you."

"I thought I was alone." Within an hour, she'd been surprised twice when being alert could be essential.

"You seem troubled. Is something wrong?"

"I'm . . . uneasy over being away from home." Her statement was true, but misleading. Was that any better than a direct lie?

"If there's anything I can do to make you feel more welcome, just let me know." Sitting on the rail, he leaned against a porch post.

"Your family is so kind." Watching his face, she tried to calculate how far she could trust him. The family wasn't supposed to know about his car. Could she get him to tell her about the vehicle? "Do you go into town often?"

"On Saturday nights."

"*Wass* do you do?"

He shrugged. "Different things, I guess."

Rebecca took a step forward and bent slightly toward him. "Where I come from, some of the Amish boys secretly have cars. Do any of your friends own vehicles?"

His grin broadened. "*Ja*."

Blinking innocently, she smiled. "Do you think you'll ever be tempted to buy one?"

He laughed. "Would I give in to a temptation like that?"

"Maybe."

His eyes sparkled in the dim light. "If I had a car, would you go for a drive with me?"

Her heart beat faster as she envisioned him taking her to Margie's, but lowering her eyes, she acted demure. "I'd think about it."

He held his grin. "Then, I'll think about it, too." His gaze lowered to her shoes. "Mud?"

"I went for a walk and slipped into the stream."

"Your dress looks wet."

Picturing what she must have looked like in the water, she laughed.

"Why don't you change clothes and go for a walk with me. I promise to keep you dry."

"*Herzlich Dank* (hearty thanks), but I've had enough for one night." She stepped off the porch to wipe her shoes on the grass, then slipped into the house. She felt Eli's gaze warm on her back.

Sarah looked up from her mending and smiled, but her lips parted when she noticed Rebecca's wet skirt.

"I was appreciating your stream, and . . ."

Ruth laughed. "You'll dry."

"Maybe you should change your dress, dear," Esther said.

"It's nearly bedtime. I'll be fine until then."

Sarah stood. "It's time for Reuben and John to go to bed." She handed Rebecca the sock she was mending. The perpendicular threads were evenly in place, and a needle dangled from the end of a darning thread.

Accepting the sock, Rebecca was grateful there were no more inquiries concerning her soaking. Sitting on a kitchen chair, she wished she'd stayed outside with Eli. Mending was bad enough, but she abhorred darning socks. Ashamed over the thought, she held the needle horizontally and began weaving it over and under the threads.

Scooping up little John, Sarah headed for the stairway. "*Kom ann*, Reuben," she called over her shoulder.

Esther arranged her sewing items in her basket. "That'll take care of the mending. I'll finish that sock, Martha, and you can go upstairs to Sarah's room."

Trying not to appear anxious, Rebecca stood slowly. "*Gute nacht* (Good night), then," she said quietly.

Standing in the middle of Sarah's room, Rebecca stared at the paper bag containing her clothes. Her fingers itched to get her radio and listen to a news report. *I must wait until Sarah's asleep.*

"I cleared a place in my drawer for your things, Martha."

Gasping, Rebecca whirled, wondering if she'd spoken aloud.

"*Es speit mich* that I startled you." Sarah pulled out her bottom drawer. "Would you like to empty your bag?"

"No." The word came out too quickly, and curiosity blossomed on Sarah's face. Those garments belong to my *Englischer* cousin, so I'll leave them in the bag."

Sarah's brow knit. "Where are your clothes?"

"I . . . don't have any with me."

Sarah's hand hovered in the air as though she'd intended to touch her face, then forgot. "You came from Mercer County without a suitcase?"

"My brother was late for his meeting, and he forgot to give it to me." The lie made it simple to look dismayed. She blinked back tears. "I don't know what I'm going to do."

"*Ach*, don't fuss." Sarah smiled. "I have dresses that will probably fit you, and I have an extra apron." Holding her smile, she studied Rebecca's wet skirt.

Rebecca sighed. "I feel so foolish."

Sarah laughed softly. Taking two plain white nightgowns from her drawer, she offered one of them to Rebecca.

As Rebecca unfolded the garment, she noticed that it was almost new. Glancing at the frayed one Sarah had kept for herself, her admiration for the girl grew. "Let me wear the old one, Sarah."

"I'm used to wearing it. It feels like a friend."

Unpinning her apron, Rebecca laid it aside, then hesitated, perplexed. *I'll be doomed if Sarah gets a glimpse of my scarlet lace undies.*

Sarah studied her, then smiled, apparently taking her reluctance to undress as modesty. "I must kiss Reuben and John good night. I'll be back in about ten minutes." Leaving the room, she closed the door.

Rebecca rapidly stripped, hid the incriminating lacy items behind the bed to dry and slipped into the nightgown. Reaching into her bag, she opened her purse and grappled for her radio.

With her ear to the speaker, she tuned in a station, but before any news came on, Sarah's footsteps neared the bedroom door. In a sweeping movement, Rebecca turned off the radio, shoved it under her pillow and straightened.

"I see you're ready for bed, Martha."

"*Ja*, and I'm exhausted." She hung her wet dress on one of the clothing pegs that lined the inside wall. Yawning, she stretched out on the bed and covered herself with the quilt. "Has it been only one day since this morning?"

Sarah's soft laughter filled the room with cheerfulness. "Some days seem longer than others."

"This was one of them." Closing her eyes, Rebecca fought sleep. Before morning, she had to hear a news broadcast.

Turning out the oil lamp, Sarah undressed in the shadows, and climbed into bed. "*Gute Nacht*, Martha," she said around a yawn. "Four-thirty a. m. comes fast."

"*Gute Nacht*, Sarah. *Schlof gut* (sleep good)." Slipping her hand under the pillow, she found her radio and ran her fingers over the smooth plastic. Just touching it gave her comfort.

Minutes later, hearing Sarah's even breathing, Rebecca figured the girl was asleep. Her nimble fingers turned the radio on. The click seemed to echo in the room. Her heart lurched. She waited, but Sarah didn't stir. Slowly, she turned up the volume. With her ear against the speaker, she searched the stations for news.

Battling sleep, she continued to seek for a broadcast, but assumed she would probably have to wait for an on-the-hour report.

A soft melody encouraged her to close her eyes. An image of

Aaron King formed before her. He smiled, and a warm feeling spread through her. His expression slowly changed, first becoming curious, then accusing. Blinking, she chased the image, refusing to let the man haunt her thoughts.

Soft music lulled her, and she drifted in and out of consciousness. When the news began, it was only muffled words somewhere in the distance. The man's voice droned on as he reported the national news, then he began the local coverage.

Suddenly Rebecca was wide awake. Had the man said something about a hit-and-run accident in Strasburg this afternoon? Had he mentioned her name? Is that what had wakened her?

When the weather report began, Rebecca snapped off the radio and shoved it under her pillow.

Nothing about the strange packets, she thought. What had she expected? It was too early. The police wouldn't receive the packet and her message until tomorrow. Even then, they would probably investigate before they released the news. Was she safe here? Not knowing was making her almost paranoid.

I can't stand any more of this deceit, she thought. Her lower lip trembled, moisture collected in her eyes; then tears rolled down the side of her face and lost themselves in her hair. Turning onto her stomach, she stifled her sobs in her pillow.

The night wore on, but sleep evaded her. Since leaving home, she'd called her father twice a week. He would have been waiting by the phone all evening. Again, he would have conveyed *Mammi's* message for her to return home.

"*Mammi* was right," Rebecca whispered, although she felt at eighteen she should not have been pressured to comply with Mary's Old Order demands—*especially concerning my call by God to be a nurse*. Did that make a difference now? She was letting God down, too.

A dog barked in the distance. Rebecca thought about the rabbit Jed had chased earlier that evening. She felt like a hunted animal, too. Was she—or was hiding from someone in Vance's shop crazy?

I must contact Dad to let him know I'm all right. If she asked

Sarah about the closest available phone, would she get suspicious?

As pre-dawn stole into the room, Rebecca fell asleep. The alarm sounded, jarring her frazzled nerves.

Sarah got up and dressed, approached Rebecca's bed and looked at her weary face. "I'm going to start breakfast, but you don't have to get up, yet. The men do the barn work before they eat."

"*Viel Dank.*" She closed her eyes as Sarah left the room. She longed to believe that yesterday's events had been a bad dream, but reality assaulted her senses, making more sleep impossible. Gritting her teeth, she flipped the quilt aside, got up, and groped behind the bed for her undergarments. The red lace bra and bikini panties seemed even more damning in the first bright rays of dawn. Her dress had dried, unwrinkled. Thankful, she slipped it on and drew a long breath. She wondered what the day would bring as she worked in the straight pins to close the back of the garment.

Forcing a smile, she started down the stairs, then stopped with a jolt and gripped the banister. *If Aaron King uncovered my secret last night, will he be here this morning to accost me?*

6

The aroma of sizzling bacon and brewing coffee wafted up the stairs to meet Rebecca. She skipped down the last few steps and crossed the kitchen. A small piece of cinnamon roll had broken off and lay on the counter. Popping the sticky morsel into her mouth, she savored its spicy sweetness.

Esther turned from the stove. "Good morning, Martha. Did you sleep well?"

"The bed was comfortable, *Gross dank*," Rebecca said in order to avoid mentioning her nightmares. "I'll set the table." Accepting the pile of plates from Ruth, she returned the girl's compelling smile.

Reuben came downstairs, rubbing the sleep from his eyes. He groped his way to the bench, yanked on his barn shoes, plopped a straw hat on his head, and went outside. The screen door banged.

Ruth grinned. "He's learning what it's like to be a man."

Rebecca watched the boy plod toward the barn. "He's only five."

"He doesn't do much, Martha, except run errands and help with a little barn work."

Sarah poured milk into a large pitcher and clunked it onto the table. "His training began just before he turned five. Father's never strict with him, but he doesn't have to be."

Snapping off a piece of crisp bacon, Ruth munched it. "Wait until he's old enough to drive a car." She giggled. "Eli will probably be anxious to show him how."

Esther turned to look at her youngest daughter. "Long before

Reuben is driving age, Eli will be a member of the church."

"*Ja*? You hope, Mama." Ruth's grin continued to mold her rounded cheeks. "He might keep his car and join the Mennonite church. *Gel*?"

"That's enough about your older brother, Ruth," Esther reminded quietly. "Eli will probably settle down soon."

"*Ja*, but now he goes into town every Saturday night." Ruth's dark eyes sparkled. "He promised to take me when I get older."

Esther handed her a large knife. "Slice the bread and stop your silly chatter."

"*Ja*, Mama." The knife swooshed through the fresh bread.

Noting the sparkle in the girl's dark eyes, Rebecca prayed she could convince Ruth to avoid searching for a Garden of Eden in the wrong places.

When the men came from the barn, anxiety rampaged through Rebecca. Releasing her grip on the back of a chair, she fought to appear relaxed. Glancing out the window, she sighed. Aaron was not with the men.

Mammi Hazel appeared in the entrance from the *Dawdy Haus*. Smiling, Rebecca hurried to help her pull out her chair. Sarah seemed to dote on the old lady. Had I shown half as much deference to *Mammi* Mary, I wouldn't be in the mess I'm in, but it was love for Mary that gripped her heart, not self-pity.

During silent grace, Rebecca thanked God for more than food. Silverware clinked on plates as platters of eggs dwindled, the bacon vanished, the mountains of bread shrank and the fried mush seemed to dissolve from the tray.

As Eli ate, he stole glances at Rebecca. Curiosity shimmered in his blue eyes, but so did admiration. "I have some free time this afternoon, Martha, so if there's somewhere you'd like to go, I'd be glad to hitch the buggy and drive you."

Envisioning her father, she smiled. "I'd like to use a phone."

"I hope your brother doesn't come for you for awhile," Eli said, swallowing his last bite of bread.

When the meal was finished, Sarah brought the Bible to her father. She looked at Rebecca with a bright smile. "Devotions start the day right."

Isaac began to read. "He that overcometh shall inherit all things; and I will be his God, and he shall be my son. But the fearful, and unbelieving, and the abominable . . . and all liars, shall have their part in the lake which burneth with fire and brimstone . . ."

The chosen Scripture ravaged Rebecca's mind and heart, and her thoughts wandered from Isaac's reading. She felt alienated from God, thus the verses made her nauseous. *I long to be honest, God. Whom can I trust?*

Isaac reached for *Die Ernsthafte* Christenpflicht (A Serious Christian's Duty), and began to pray.

At her home, Rebecca had *A Devoted Christian's Prayer Book*, an English translation. She closed her eyes, but couldn't shut out the negative echoes in her heart. Fright clawed at her as she tried to envision the possible drug dealer Greg Mattis had been warning, then remorse over hiding the truth from the Beilers bubbled into her throat. She fought tears by planting seeds of anger, but only torment grew. One day of deceit seemed years long. If only she could erase the last couple of days and go home.

The backwash from a tidal wave of apprehension swept her into an ocean of uncertainty. *If only I knew what was going on in the flower shop.* Keeping her expression from betraying her was a struggle, for even now, God was protecting her. If she continued to withhold the truth, how long would this refuge last? *From now on, I'll be honest*, she vowed. *That doesn't mean I have to confess my identity to the Beilers immediately, does it?*

Encompassed by silence, she realized that Isaac had ended his prayer. Slowly, she lifted her head, finding the family peering at her, respectful of her devotion. It made her sense of fraudulence more acute. Smiling, Esther patted Rebecca's shoulder, then got up to clear the table. The men went outside, and Rebecca moved to the sink to draw water to wash the dishes.

The morning passed, free of Aaron King. After lunch, Eli stood by the door, fumbling with his hat. Finally, he said, "Martha, if you want to go to a phone, I'll take you."

Dubious, Rebecca glanced at Esther.

The woman hung up the dish towel. "It would probably be a good idea to tell your brother where you are, dear."

Rebecca pondered. Should she call Margie first—or contact her father to tell him she was all right?

Apparently interpreting her silence as acceptance, Eli grinned. "I'll hitch the buggy."

"*Gross Dank.*" She raced upstairs for her change purse, so anxious she nearly forgot to put on her black Amish bonnet. Tying the strings, she went outside. The summer sun held promise. Even though it was too warm, she breathed deeply. When Eli stopped the buggy at the gate, she climbed in. Then, pondering the location of the phone, she bit her lower lip. What if there were people? "Where's . . . the phone, Eli?"

"Don't be frightened of me, Martha," he said, misinterpreting her apprehension. "It's only a mile down the road."

She forced a smile. "Your corn's doing well," she said, hoping to divert his thoughts.

"*Ja.* We were concerned about not getting enough rain, but the Lord's been gracious, *gel*? Last year our corn was exceptional." He drew a long breath, then frowned. "Harvest time would have been great, if it hadn't been for the silo accident. Moses was sure-footed and not afraid of height."

"*Wass* happened?"

"No one knows. He was smiling one second and falling the next."

"*Es speit mich* that Elizabeth was left alone. She's adjusting to his death. *Gel* (Is that not so)?"

"*Ja.*" He and my sister loved each other so much," he said quietly. Elizabeth was in shock until after the funeral. When Priscilla was born, Elizabeth became extremely overprotective."

"She doesn't seem to be, now."

"*Ja*, but it took her several months to adjust to losing Moses. She still visits his grave twice a week." He pointed across a tobacco field. "There's the phone shack."

The buggy wheels had barely stopped turning when Rebecca stepped down and raced toward the small building, praying Eli would stay far enough away not to hear her conversations.

Intending to call Margie, she counted her change and stacked the coins in her palm. Her hands trembled as she dropped a quarter into the slot. As though her fingers had a mind of their own, they sought her home number.

"Hello," David Wenger said.

"It's me, Papa." Her words were tremulous.

"Rebecca! Where are you?"

"I'm staying with a fine Amish family."

"Amber, honey, who are you with?"

Her fingers tightened on the receiver. "I called to let you know I'm all right."

"You say the words, but I hear doubt in your voice."

"I'm fine, Papa." The thought of what she'd been through the past two days beat her with giant phantom wings.

David sighed wearily. "The police were here, honey. Vance Troy is accusing you of damaging two vehicles, then fleeing."

Her stomach cramped. "I might have stumbled onto something illegal, Papa. I want to remain where I am until the police have time to investigate something questionable I sent them."

"Oh, Amber." He sounded worried. "Two men keep calling, asking where to find you."

Picturing Greg Mattis or a cohort of his, she smothered a gasp. "You told them?"

"I wouldn't have, even if I'd known where you were."

"Who's asking?"

"One says his name is Joe Dinger. The other one says he's a friend, but refuses to give his name. Come home, Amber. We'll go to the police and get this mess straightened out."

"I can't, yet."

"Are you in danger?"

"No." She hoped it was true.

"I pray for you every day, honey."

Her throat constricted. "I love you, Papa."

"I love you, too." His voice sounded strained.

"Tell *Mammi* I love her."

"I will." Another sigh escaped from deep within him. "Are you sure you can't come home, Amber?"

She shut her eyes tight. "I will—as soon as I can."

A fast-approaching buggy made her glance out the window. She gasped as she recognized Aaron King.

"Are you all right?" David's alarm was apparent.

"*Ja*. The gentleman coming is a friend of the family I'm staying with. I have to go."

"Wait. If you come home, I —"

"Good-bye, Papa — for now. I love you." As she hung up, the tears she'd struggled to restrain spilled down her cheeks. Leaving the shack, she kept her face averted. Feeling a hand on her shoulder, she stiffened, not wanting Eli to question her.

Insistent, the hand turned her to face him.

"Aaron," she whispered, peering at his stern face.

Seeing her tears, his expression softened. "*Wass* is wrong?"

"I . . . want to go home.." She gasped for air that didn't satisfy her lungs.

"You're welcome to stay with the Beilers as long as necessary."

"I don't have any money. I don't have clothes!" Weak from remorse and frustration, she leaned against him, pressing her face against his light-blue cotton shirt.

His arms gently encompassed her. "You don't need money, and Sarah will find you something to wear." His embrace tightened slightly. "You'll be all right, Martha."

"Aaron! *Wass* do you think you're doing?" Eli's tone was brusque.

Releasing Rebecca, Aaron stepped away. "*Es speit mich* that I've offended you."

Eli scowled. "*Vell*, you don't need to get so — familiar. *Gel*?"

"I didn't mean . . ." He sighed. "I was on my way to your place to help you get the benches ready for meeting tomorrow."

"Oh. *Herzlich Dank*." Eli touched the cast on his right arm and looked a little sheepish.

"I need to speak with Sarah. I'll meet you at the house." Spinning on his heel, Aaron strode swiftly to his buggy, leaped to the seat, slapped Ransom with the reins, and drove off in a cloud of dust.

Rebecca stared after the retreating buggy. The way Aaron had stalked to her and gripped her shoulder, he must know something. Would he talk with Sarah about it first? *What did he uncover in Lancaster?*

"You're pale." Stepping forward, Eli touched her arm.

"I'm . . . homesick." She moved to his buggy and climbed in.

Settling in the driver's seat, he smiled. "Maybe a ride will help. Shall we take the long way home?"

"I'd rather not. I promised Sarah I'd help her with the preparations for tomorrow."

"*Ja.*" Turning the horse, he headed home.

She held her smile and wiped the moisture from her forehead, then pondering what Aaron might have uncovered, a cold chill settled over her.

"Have you taken a liking to Aaron, Martha?"

"*Wass?*"

He met her gaze. "Do you care for Aaron?"

"I hope he's a friend. He and Sarah have . . . an understanding, don't they?"

"*Vell*, it sort of looks that way."

"It stands to reason that he'd care for her, for she's sweet and lovely."

Eli laughed.

Worrying about what Aaron would tell Sarah, Rebecca lapsed into silence. She'd won the girl's friendship. Would Aaron disclose information that would destroy it?

"Whoa," Eli said, stopping his buggy at Beilers' gate.

"*Gross Dank.*" She slowly stepped to the lane. Aaron's buggy was parked near the front walk. With a throbbing heart, she stood staring at the porch. Eli drove his buggy toward the barn. Instead of going into the house, she stopped to pet Ransom.

The kitchen screen door opened, and Ruth poked her head out. "Martha, Aaron wants to talk to you."

The apprehension that had churned within her turned into

rapids and whirlpools of torment and confusion. "This is it, Ransom," she whispered.

Trying to appear nonchalant, she strolled to the porch, stopped to pet Jed, then slowly entered the kitchen. She smiled at Aaron, praying to camouflage her anxiety.

"Aaron has a problem, Martha," Sarah said. "I'd help him, but I promised to go to Amos Zimmerman's to sit with their sick little girl while they're selling baked goods at their stand."

Puzzled, Rebecca looked at her, then at Aaron. "*Wass* can I do to help?"

"My mother has the flu, my father has to go to the stockyard this afternoon, and I can't be home." He frowned. "My younger sister needs watching, so I'd appreciate it if you could *kom* over for a couple of hours."

"Oh." Relief filtered through the debris in her restless mind, and her smile became genuine. She hoped her face hadn't been pale enough to arouse his curiosity. "I'd be glad to *kom*."

"I'll give Eli a hand with the benches, then I'll drive you to my place."

Rebecca expected to read jealousy in Sarah's expression, but the girl's smile was genuine, depicting a trust that Rebecca vowed never to violate. When she turned, Aaron had already left for the barn.

Sarah kissed Rebecca's cheek. "*Herzlich Dank* for filling in for me, Martha."

Rebecca hugged her. "You're like the sister I longed for but never had."

"I pray we'll always be close, Martha." Going to the window, she watched until Aaron entered the barn.

"He sometimes seems irritable," Rebecca said, intending to find out if he'd told Sarah anything concerning her.

"It's because he has so much responsibility, and the Bishop's pressuring him to join the church." A frown creased her lovely brow.

Picturing the automobile she'd seen him driving, Rebecca understood his diffidence. Intending to explain the vehicle to Sarah, Rebecca turned to her. An unexpected desire to keep his secret flooded her. Surprised, she turned away and fluffed the pillow on a nearby rocker. Then, realizing it would have been a mistake to admit to seeing Aaron's vehicle, she sighed. How could she have explained that to Sarah?

Slowly, she brought her chaotic emotions under control, but when she heard Aaron's voice outside, her heart pounded erratically. Donning her bonnet, she hurried to his buggy, avoiding his searching gaze. She wanted to say something witty, as he joined her on the seat, but her brain felt scrambled and sense eluded her.

When they were nearly out of sight of the house, Aaron cleared his throat. "You seem uncomfortable with me, Martha. *Fer wass*?"

". . . I'm . . . shy," she mumbled, staring at her folded hands.

He laughed, then sobered. "I went into town last night."

She intended to face him boldly, but managed only a cautious glance. "Did you have a good time?"

"I made inquiries concerning the man who called his daughter Amber."

She figured questions would make her seem innocent. "Did you find him? Was his daughter with him? Does she look like me?"

"Do you know a man named David Wenger?"

Fighting panic, Rebecca swallowed. "Is he from Lancaster County?"

"*Ja*, Martha."

Unable to deny knowing her beloved father, she took refuge in silence.

Aaron cleared his throat. "David Wenger lives north of New Holland. I found out he goes to the market at Bird-in-Hand every week. I'm going there on Wednesday to wait for him."

Ice crystals seemed to form in her blood, but she smiled. "Maybe you'll meet his daughter, too."

"I hope so, Martha." His right brow lifted slightly. "Will you accompany me?"

Her heart lurched. "I can't on Wednesday."

"*Fer wass*?"

"I . . . promised Sarah I'd help with the mending."

Suspicion glinted in his brown eyes. "Someday soon, then?"

Turning her face upward, she studied the slate sky. "It looks like rain. *Gel?*"

"*Ja.*" Sighing, he withdrew into contemplation.

Was his silence worse than his inquiries? It seemed as though he knew something. Was he giving her a chance to confess her identity? *It's too soon, Lord.*

As they rode, she pondered. Her inability to hide her anxiety from Aaron made him more apprehensive. She decided to cultivate his friendship. If he liked her, he would be more likely to stop bombarding her with questions.

Ransom turned into Kings' lane. Apprehensive over meeting Aaron's family, Rebecca's heart faltered and questions assailed her mind. What if his father had noticed her that day at Zimmerman's store? Would he expose her? She frowned. Had her father done business with Noah King?

Kings' house was an eight-room white frame dwelling. An old apple tree spread its leafy arms near the large porch. A four-room addition had been added to the back of the house for Aaron's parents. The flower beds needed care, signifying that Mrs. King had probably not felt well for some time. A yellow cat, stretched out on the top porch step, lazily opened one eye as Ransom pranced up to the gate.

"I'll introduce you to Mother and my younger sister, before I leave," Aaron said.

Rebecca accompanied him to the porch, then paused to pet the sleepy cat.

"His name's Restless." Aaron chuckled. "He doesn't live up to it anymore."

Rebecca stepped into the roomy kitchen. A double window above the sink let in sunlight that brightened the room. Leafy plants tumbled from pots on the sill. Rebecca admired the wood of the numerous cabinets and cupboards. "Sarah said you built the cabinets at Beilers'." Running her hand over the smooth counter, she looked at Aaron. "Did you build these?"

"*Ja.*" His attempt to appear humble, as Amishmen believe one should, failed, and pride of accomplishment glinted on his face.

"You do exceptional work." She turned to examine a door. "You even formed an artistic pattern with the wood grains. Have you considered going into business?"

"*Ja*, but . . ."

"Aaron, is that you?" a woman called from the downstairs bedroom.

"*Ja*." He faced Rebecca. "Since Mother wasn't feeling well, I had her come to my bedroom from the *Dawdy Haus*, so she would be close if she needed anything."

"*Kom ann* in, Sarah," the woman called.

Aaron motioned for Rebecca to accompany him. He paused by the woman's bedside. "Mother, I'd like you to meet Martha Kauffman."

"Oh?" The woman looked puzzled.

On legs that suddenly seemed boneless, Rebecca moved closer to extend her hand. "Hello, *wie gehts*, Mrs. King."

The woman smiled weakly as she took Rebecca's proffered hand. "Call me Anna." Her eyes were brown, like Aaron's, but pain had dimmed their sparkle. Her gray hair was thin on top from years of fastening her prayer covering with straight pins, and her face was creased from illness. There was anguish that seemed to be more emotional than physical in her expression—as though something gripped her heart, tormenting her soul.

"Sarah couldn't come," Aaron said. "Martha is visiting the Beilers and graciously offered to come in her place."

"*Viel Dank*, Martha." The woman looked at her son. Noah took Nancy to the barn with him, so Jesse could help with the chores. Make sure Nancy understands that she's to stay with Martha."

"*Ja*." He smiled. "You rest. She'll be fine." Guiding Rebecca from the room, he closed the door. "Mother will call, if she needs you." Moving to a window, he peered toward the barn. "They're coming."

Rebecca looked out. A boy in his mid-teens, swinging a pail and whistling, approached the house. His straw hat sat at a jaunty angle, revealing a tumble of auburn locks. An older man followed him. A straw hat shadowed his hair, but his beard was gray. His steps were labored, and his shoulders were bent from hard work. A girl of about ten walked by his side.

"Who's the girl, and where's the little one that I'm to take care of?"

Aaron jerked his head to face her. His lips parted as worry crept into his expression. "Didn't Sarah explain?"

"Explain what?"

"About Nancy. She's . . . she's . . ."

7

"She's what?" Rebecca asked.

Aaron looked perplexed. "The girl with my father is Nancy."

"Oh... but..." Rebecca contemplated the strange expression in the girl's eyes as well as the odd fashion she swung her arms.

"Nancy's twelve," Aaron mumbled. "She's... retarded." He sighed. "We don't talk much about my sister's condition, so I shouldn't have assumed Sarah had told you." He surveyed Rebecca. "Do you still want to stay with her?"

"*Ja.*" Smiling to reassure him, she met his unwavering gaze. "Sarah said you had other siblings."

"I have two older, married sisters and a brother a year younger than myself who moved to Kentucky with their families." He looked dismayed. "I also have a brother, twenty, but he's... gone."

She remembered Sarah mentioning another brother who had left home. Had something happened to him? Compassion waved over her, and she gently touched Aaron's arm. "You mean he's dead?"

"He is as far as the community is concerned, but we still pray for him." He drew an anguished breath. "Joseph chose another way of life."

She thought about her grandfather Simon. "Did your brother suffer *Meidung*?"

"He hadn't joined the church. If he had, he would've been shunned."

Her fingers tightened on his arm as she witnessed his sorrow.

"Did he join a Mennonite church?"

Aaron shook his head, then met her gaze. "Would that have been so bad?"

"*Ja.* I mean, I guess so as far as most Amish are concerned."

"*Ja, vell,* I have my... convictions concerning that, but..." He sighed deeply. "Joseph runs with a wild crowd. He was involved with... an Amish girl, but broke his promise, seeming to prefer the company of... questionable friends." Wiping a hand across his furrowed brow as though to erase his distress, he watched his father approach the house. "Dad's aged considerably since Joseph left. That's why I have to be careful not to... cause him more grief."

"How could you do that?"

"I..." He shrugged.

"Does your brother come to visit?"

"Not often. Each time he comes, it's worse. He's slipping farther and farther away—which torments Mother."

Understanding the anguish on Anna's face, and realizing Aaron suffered, too, she tenderly touched his forearm. "I'll pray for Joseph."

A warm smile teased his lips. He covered her hand with his, their gazes locked, and he gently squeezed her fingers. Footsteps resounded on the porch. He released her hand and stepped aside as the door swung inward.

"Aaron! Aaron!" Nancy rushed to him.

"Hi, Nancy," he said quietly. Gently touching her shoulder, he calmed her. "I brought you a new friend. Her name's Martha."

A scowl distorted her features. "I want Sarah."

"She couldn't come today."

Nancy's lower lip protruded. "I won't play with anyone else." She glared at Rebecca. "You don't look like Sarah. I don't like you."

He gently tucked a stray lock of hair back under Nancy's prayer cap. "You can make a new friend."

"No!" Whirling, she ran to a wooden rocker, flung herself into it, and rocked feverishly.

Aaron looked distressed. "I didn't think she'd react so strongly, although strangers sometimes confuse and upset her." Reaching toward the peg on the wall closest to the door, he retrieved his straw hat. "I'll take you back to Beilers'."

"I don't give up so easily, Aaron." Rebecca looked at the moping child. She was small for her age; her face was narrow and her complexion wan.

"Go home!" Nancy's large brown eyes resembled a puppy's.

Rebecca's heart went out to the girl. Interpreting Aaron's dismay, she smiled reassuringly. "I'll manage."

Noah followed his youngest son into the kitchen. The sixteen-year-old jerked off his hat, displaying tousled auburn hair. Freckles danced on the bridge of his nose, and his green eyes surveyed Rebecca. His grin broadened as he looked at his older brother. "Someone new?"

Aaron smiled at Rebecca. "I'd like you to meet my father and Jesse." He looked at his father. "This is Martha Kauffman, a friend of Sarah's. She came to watch Nancy, but—"

Noah smiled. "*Viel Dank* for *koming* Martha." He looked beseechingly at his daughter. "Nancy, come and shake hands with Martha."

"I wanna play with Sarah!" Grasping the multi-colored afghan that covered the back of the rocker, she pulled it over her face.

Sighing, the older man looked appealingly at Aaron. "Jesse and I are going to the stockyard."

A car horn blasted, and Jesse raced outside. After glancing at Nancy, Noah plopped his straw hat on his gray head and hurried to the car that would take them to town. Ransom pawed the earth, blew, and whinnied. Looking at the horse, Aaron sighed.

Rebecca took a step toward him. "You'd better be on your way, before Ransom decides to go without you. *Gel*?"

An ambivalent smile curved his mouth. "*Herzlich Dank*, Amber."

She followed him to the porch and waited until he was in the buggy. In answer to her wave, he smiled, but it didn't camouflage his perplexed expression. He merely tapped Ransom's flank with the reins, and the horse was off at a run.

Moving to the edge of the porch, Rebecca pressed her head

against a support post and watched the retreating buggy. Her father would probably be at Zimmerman's store this afternoon. Did Aaron plan to confront him? Forcing her worry to the back of her mind, she went inside, pondering over how to console Nancy. Would the girl understand a story? She noticed a rag doll in a tiny crib in the corner. Like all Amish dolls, it was dressed Amish and had no facial features. Crossing the room, she picked it up, cradled it in her arms, and approached Nancy. "Your baby's crying. Do you want to rock her or do you want me to?"

One brown eye peered at Rebecca from behind a fold of the afghan.

"She's a nice baby, Nancy. *Wass's* her name?"

"Sarah." Seizing the doll, she yanked it from Rebecca's grasp. "She doesn't like you."

"That makes me feel bad." Reaching out, Rebecca put the obstinate lock of hair back under the girl's cap.

Nancy jerked away. "I like Sarah."

Rebecca smiled. "So do I. Sarah's my friend, too."

Blinking, Nancy stared at her. "Does Sarah like you?"

"*Ja.*"

After peering at the floor for a moment, the girl smiled. "If Sarah likes you, then I will, too." Jumping up, she ran to a wooden box under a window, flipped open the lid, and took out a book of Bible stories. "Can you read, Martha?"

"*Ja.* Come and sit with me in the parlor, and I'll read you a story." Rebecca entered the adjoining room and sat on the quilt-draped bench. The room was furnished with other odd pieces, a brown armchair, a navy one, and a wooden rocker. Two stands held lamps, one oil, the other battery-powered.

Proffering the book, Nancy clapped her hands like a delighted three-year-old. Then, slumping to the bench and curling her feet under her, she peered at the book with large eyes.

The child's attention span was short, so before the story was finished, she jumped up and went back to the toy box. Rebecca kept her busy playing numerous games, interspersed with excerpts from Bible stories. When the clock on the top of the cupboard chimed five, Rebecca wondered about the evening meal. Taking Nancy by the hand, she went to Mrs. King's bedside. "*Wass* can I prepare for supper, Anna?"

The woman pressed her hand against her forehead. "I must get up."

"You should rest. Just tell me what to fix." Rebecca couldn't help permitting her eyes to roam Aaron's room. The walls were cream-colored and the dark-green window shades were at half-mast. Braided rugs lay on the polished wood floor beside the bed and in front of the oak dresser. An open Bible lay on the stand by a window. Had Anna been reading it--or Aaron?

Lost in thought, Rebecca didn't notice when Nancy's hand slipped from hers. She peered curiously at a sweater and two wrinkled shirts that hung limply over the ladder-back chair by the stand. A man's dirty sock lay crumpled by the dresser leg. Rebecca fought a grin.

Anna sighed. "There are potatoes and carrots in the cellar, Martha. I was going to make a meat loaf out of the ground beef in the refrigerator, but it's getting late."

Rebecca touched Anna's forehead. "You're running a fever. I'll make the meat loaf."

"I must have supper on the table at six o'clock."

"There'll be time, Anna, if I form the meat loaf into balls and cook them in a skillet on top of the stove."

"You're an angel." A weary smile curved her thin lips. "*Dank der gut Man* (thank God) Aaron found you."

To keep a perplexed expression from her face, Rebecca smiled. She figured if the woman became aware of her deceit, she'd change her mind. Turning, she saw that Nancy was gone. Hurrying from the room, she quietly closed the door. Anxiety flooded her, for the girl wasn't in the kitchen. Giddy laughter drew her to the porch.

Nancy was tying her doll's bonnet under the cat's chin. Restless looked disturbed. Squalling, he jerked free, leaped from the porch and raced toward the barn, the black bonnet hiding his face, and the long ties flipping in the breeze.

Rebecca laughed. "Let's go to the cellar for the vegetables,

Nancy. You can help me with supper."

Rebecca had the girl set the table, but soon discovered the chore was beyond her ability. It kept her busy, though, leaving Rebecca free to mix seasonings into the meat.

When supper was nearly ready, Rebecca took Nancy to the bench to finish sewing an apron for the child's doll. Glancing up, she saw Aaron surveying her from the doorway. She hadn't heard him come in. A warm blush crept across her face, so she turned away, busying herself with the last few stitches on the doll's garment. Knotting the thread, she broke it and handed the completed apron to Nancy.

"You've done all right. *Gel*?" Aaron said.

"*Ja*."

Jumping up, Nancy ran to her brother. "I like Martha. She's my friend!"

Smiling, Aaron hugged his younger sister. He glanced at the table, the stove, then at the closed bedroom door. "Is Mother still in bed?"

Rebecca joined him in the kitchen. "She wanted to help with supper, but I encouraged her to rest. She has a fever, Aaron. Do you think she should see a doctor?"

His brow creased. "Father and I want her to, but she insists she'll be all right."

"Are Noah and Jesse home?"

"*Ja*. They have to turn a new steer into the pasture, but they'll be in, shortly. His grin broadened. "Supper smells good."

"I helped Martha get supper." Nancy bounced in front of him. "We made an apron for dolly. See?" Handing him the tiny garment, she waited for his approval.

In his large hand, the small piece of white material looked lost. When his eyes found Rebecca's, respect and admiration shimmered in their depths. An unexpected feeling kindled within her, caressing her like rays of sunshine. She wanted to turn away, but she was mesmerized by his gaze.

"Aaron!" Nancy cried, breaking the spell. She grabbed his arm. "That's my dolly's apron."

"It's . . . real nice." He proffered the garment.

Snatching it, she went to the corner with her doll.

The men came in, so Rebecca served the meal. She avoided Aaron's eyes, for the questions that seemed to creep into them disturbed her. After taking a tray into the bedroom for Anna, she took a place at the table. She got through the meal without mishap, but was dismayed when Aaron insisted on helping with clean-up. His nearness and smile were disarming, especially after Noah took Jesse and Nancy to the barn.

As Aaron handed her the dish towel, her fingers touched his. A strange warmth traveled up her arm, across her shoulders, and settled in her heart. She jerked away. The sensation was wonderful, but it frightened her.

"When you're ready to leave, Amber, I'll take you home," he said quietly.

"I'll say *gute nacht* (good night) to Anna." Hanging up the towel, she went to the bedroom.

Anna was asleep, but the woman's fever hadn't broken. Rebecca's concern increased. In the kitchen, she donned the navy shawl Sarah had loaned her and tied her bonnet. Not meeting Aaron's eyes, she crossed the darkened porch. Together, they headed for the buggy. Stars blinked between clouds, and the moon cast a silvery glow over the farm.

Something moved on the shadowed buggy seat, and two beady little eyes glowed from a large head. Rebecca gasped. Grasping her arm, Aaron jerked her backward. She lost her footing and stumbled into his arms. Regaining her balance, she looked up into his concerned face. The moonlight bronzed his complexion and shimmered in his dark eyes, making her catch her breath.

"Stay back," he said, stepping between her and the buggy.

"*Wass's* that thing, Aaron?"

"I don't know. Go back in the house."

As he approached the buggy, it seemed to come alive with scratching and rustling noise. Alarm glued Rebecca to the spot. The thing wasn't large, but it seemed weird. The creature came forward acting as though it were going to spring.

"Aaron!"

8

"Be careful!" Rebecca gripped Aaron's sleeve.

"Stay back." Tension crept into his voice. The creature poked its head out the door, and moonlight beamed on its face. Aaron burst into laughter.

"Restless!" Rebecca stared in amazement. The cat still wore the doll's black bonnet. The garment had shadowed his face, making his head seem large and threatening.

"*Wass* are you doing wearing a lady's bonnet?" Aaron wagged a finger at the animal. "Have you no shame?" Chuckling, he untied the knot under the cat's chin.

"Nancy put the bonnet on him this afternoon. He ran before I could remove it. He looks cute. *Gel?*"

"*Ja, vell*, a straw hat would be more appropriate for a gentleman." He looked at her with laughter in his eyes. "It's safe, now that I've rescued you from the ferocious beast."

"*Wonderbar* (great)! You're a hero." Laughing softly, she got into his buggy. He could be wonderful--when he refrained from interrogating her.

For the first mile, they rode in silence. Rebecca's thoughts wandered. Had she met Aaron under other circumstances, maybe ... But, no. He was Amish. Even if that didn't matter, there couldn't be anything but friendship between them—because of Sarah.

The June evening was pleasantly cool, and the musical clop-clop of Ransom's hooves soothed her. Moonlight filtered through the trees, creating lacy patterns on the road ahead. Aaron pensively stared at his horse's ears. Was he thinking about Sarah? Was he deeply in love with her? *Is he worried that she will be upset because he spent time alone with me?*

Her hand rested on the seat between them. When Aaron's fingers covered hers, she peered quizzically at him, but he looked ahead, avoiding her eyes. Logic warned her to withdraw her hand, but her heart pleaded with her not to. The pressure of his warm fingers made her blood rush.

There was no traffic, and they were still out of sight of the house. Aaron swung his horse into Beilers' lane, but stopped in the shadow of the huge oak tree. For a few moments, he was silent, then he sighed. "I want to talk to you, Amber."

Apprehensive, she waited.

Instead of accosting her, he reached out and drew her into his arms. Surprised, she looked up. Their eyes met inches apart. Then, his head lowered, and his mouth covered hers.

She knew she should pull away, if not for Sarah's sake, for her own. But, as Aaron's lips teased hers in a fervent caress, she melted against him, returning his kiss, swept away in sweet surrender. Her arms went around him, and his embrace tightened as his kiss intensified. The world went away, and her problems dissolved. There were only the two of them, the night breeze, and the nickering horse.

Aaron pulled away slowly. Leaning against the seat, he closed his eyes.

She supposed she should say something, but her senses had been ravaged, and words evaded her. Within his arms, she'd found more than solace. Her lips were warm from his kisses, and her heart throbbed. Studying his profile, guilt smote her. How could she have permitted the impassioned kisses? How could the two of them hurt sweet Sarah?

Determined to harness his run-away emotions, Aaron took a deep breath. Even with his mind in a state of flux, the information he'd gleaned that afternoon played havoc with his senses, whipping his suspicion into full gallop. He craved answers, but didn't want to press this lovely girl too far. "I appreciate the way you helped my family today."

She smiled. "I was glad to."

He reached out, reconsidered touching her, and withdrew his hand. Watching for her reaction, he said, "Today, at Zimmerman's, people were discussing David Wenger's daughter."

She drew a quick little breath. "*Wass* did they say?"

He shook his head, wondering if a negative statement would bring more of a reaction. "She ran away from home and deserted her teaching."

Even in the moonlight, her face seemed to grow pale. "Did they . . . say why?" Her voice sounded choked.

"No one seems to know."

"Well . . . she'll probably go home soon."

"*Ja.* Probably, Amber." Her woe-be-gone expression lured him. Reaching out, he pulled her into his arms and his mouth found her warm, sweet lips.

Minutes later, he forced himself to release her. He doubted this young woman was from Mercer County. If she wasn't who she said she was, who was she? Suspicious, yet lured, he had to grab the reins to keep from embracing her again. Ransom needed no urging to start off in a trot.

Martha clasped her hands in her lap, apparently to keep them still. "Maybe David Wenger's daughter had a reason for leaving home."

"*Ja*? Like what?" Was it possible that this sweet young woman could be the missing daughter of David Wenger? He was convinced of her integrity, even though she seemed to be evasive. But, if she were innocent, why would she withhold the truth? Gazing into her lovely face and reading her apprehension, he was encompassed by warmth that stirred his innermost being, and a desire to protect her flooded him.

She looked away, and apprehension seemed to impede her speech. "Did you meet David Wenger's daughter?"

"No." He watched for her reaction. "I learned her name's Rebecca."

"Is she Amish?"

"Mennonite." Aaron frowned. If Martha were Rebecca, would she be asking such questions? He pictured Margie and the flashy red car she drove. "Rebecca has an *Englischer* cousin who may have wrongly influenced her. Although being raised Mennonite, I'm surprised that she went astray." He turned to look directly at her. "Are you sure you don't know her?"

"How . . . could I know . . . a girl from around here?" Her apprehension stuck out like porcupine quills in a dog's nose.

"I'll take you to meet David Wenger."

Her smile appeared forced. "That would be nice."

He'd decided not to press her, yet he continued to probe, praying her answers would dissolve his concern. "When can you go?"

Grappling for an excuse, Rebecca focused on the horse's rump. "I've . . . met so many new people lately, I'd like to wait awhile." Her excuse sounded feeble—even to her, but Aaron seemed to accept it.

He stopped his buggy by Beilers' gate. Sarah stood on the porch. In the moonlight, she looked like a doll with a sweet china face. No wonder Aaron loved her. Reliving his kisses, Rebecca tingled with excitement; then guilt over betraying Sarah's trust seared away her ecstasy. She must try to forget the intimate moments.

Sarah moved down the porch steps to the yard. Moonlight gleamed on her white apron; the soft halo of light from the window shimmered on her white cap and made her appear angelic. Expecting Aaron to be transfixed in awe as he beheld the girl, Rebecca glanced at him, gasping when she discovered he was watching her. Their eyes met, and she blinked. "Are you . . . coming in?"

"Not tonight." He gently grasped her hand. "I'll see you in the morning."

"*Ja*," she whispered, reminded that this was Saturday. Church services were held every other week. She wished tomorrow were an off Sunday. Why did meeting have to be at the Beilers'? What if one of the Amish attending worship had seen her in Lancaster?

"*Is alles recht* (are you all right), Amber?" Aaron asked in a voice low enough that Sarah would be unable to hear.

"*Ja. Gute Nacht* (Good night)." She quickly left his buggy.

Sarah smiled as she approached the gate. "Did everything go well?"

"*Ja*," Aaron answered. "My family adores Martha." He chuckled. "Even Nancy has completely accepted her."

Instead of jealous sparks, Sarah's smile broadened. "We think Martha's an angel. *Der gut Man* was gracious to send her to us. *Gel?*"

"*Ja*." He sounded a little cautious. "I'll see you ladies in the morning." Turning his horse, he headed down the lane.

Rebecca watched the vanishing buggy, warmth spreading through her in caressing waves. Praying her expression didn't betray her emotional chaos, she slowly faced Sarah. "I asked Aaron to come in, but he seemed to be in a hurry."

"*Ja.*" Sarah frowned. "This is Saturday night, so he's probably anxious to leave for town. Eli left earlier."

"Does Eli have the car Ruth keeps talking about?"

"*Ja,* I think." A shadow crossed her lovely face. "I suspect Aaron has one as well."

Keeping the knowledge of Aaron's vehicle from Sarah increased Rebecca's sense of betrayal. Then, envisioning Aaron's kiss, her heart raced. Turning away, she battled to smother the smoldering embers before they could explode into flames.

Sarah sighed. "Aaron won't discuss joining the church. I suppose, like Eli, he needs more time." Linking her arm in Rebecca's, they headed toward the porch. "I should've explained about Nancy, but I didn't think about it until after you left with Aaron. Did he tell you about her before you got to his place?"

"No. He assumed you had."

"*Es speit mic*h that I didn't." Sara paused with her foot on the bottom step. "Did you have trouble?"

Rebecca climbed to the porch, then turned. "Nancy acted negatively at first, but everything worked out all right—possibly better than if I'd known. Has she been that way from birth?"

"*Ja.* Intermarriage in some of our families sometimes causes misfortune with their children."

"Nancy's a sweet child."

Sarah laughed softly. "Most of the time."

Sarah's trust made Rebecca feel ill, and she vowed to harness her emotion with Aaron.

Sarah headed for the door. "*Kom ann*, Martha. Elizabeth is here, and we have a visitor."

Rebecca's stomach cramped. *Now what?* She hoped she would be able to improvise without being dishonest.

Sarah moved to the screen door. "Elizabeth and Elam went to school together, before his family moved away, so they're enjoying discussing old times."

Hoping to disguise her trepidation, Rebecca entered the kitchen. The Beilers were present, except for Eli.

Elizabeth came forward, a sweet smile brightening her face. "Martha, I'd like you to meet Elam Miller." She turned to the man. "This is Martha Kauffman. She's from Mercer county, too. Maybe you know her family."

Mercer County! seared through Rebecca's reeling brain.

Elam smiled. "*Un wie gehts?*"

"Doing *vell*," she said, struggling not to cringe as she greeted him.

Elam's warm-brown eyes assessed her from over a wavy light-brown beard. "*Wass* part of Mercer county are you from?"

"Near . . . New Willmington."

He smiled. "Then, you must know several Millers."

"*Vell* . . . I . . ." Her temples throbbed as she fought an impulse to run.

"*Wass's* your father's name?"

"David." At least that wasn't a lie. She felt cornered and corrupt. Hot tears burned the back of her eyes and blurred her vision.

Elizabeth touched her arm. "Is something wrong?"

"Talking about . . . my family or home . . . makes me miss them so much."

Elam looked pensive. "*Es speit mich* that I upset you."

She took a deep breath, hoping to quell the tremor in her voice. "Did your wife come to Lancaster County with you, Mr. Miller?"

He hesitated, then said, "My wife died two years ago."

"Oh!" Would she invariably say the wrong thing to this man? Crossing the room, she chose the farthest chair.

"How old are your boys, Elam?" Esther asked.

"Daniel's six. Jesse Mark's three." He sighed. "I depend a lot on my younger sister to watch them."

"Leah was cooperative, even as a young girl," Sarah said, sighing. "We were such good friends."

Elizabeth glanced out a window. "I hope Eli isn't too late."

Elam smiled. "I'll be going back to Zooks' soon. I have Jacob John's buggy, and I'll be glad to drive you home."

Elizabeth looked pleased. "*Herzlich Dank.*"

Rebecca caught the flicker of interest in Elam's eyes, and Elizabeth's cheeks were slightly flushed. With his wife gone and Elizabeth's husband dead, well—

Rebecca was grateful when she could excuse herself and go to bed. Hiding could be foolish, she supposed, but still apprehensive and frightened, she closed her eyes and shivered.

"Oh, God," she prayed, "I was so foolish to try to find a garden of Eden on my own. Lord, please give me courage to do what you would have me do." In the darkness, tears wet her pillow case.

When Sarah came in, Rebecca feigned sleep.

As the night wore on, anguish, doubt, and fear held sleep at bay. *I want to be honest, God. Please help me.*

She stared at the dark ceiling, listened to a tenacious fly tick against the plaster, and massaged her temples in a futile effort to ease her thunderous headache.

Hours passed. Guilt continued to plague Rebecca and she felt lost in a sea of loneliness. The worst part is, *I've created this abyss*.

"Dear God, I—" Her prayer faded into nothingness as nausea waved over her. Jumping out of bed, she raced downstairs to the bathroom to vomit, thankful that some of the Amish in Lancaster County had the facilities. Bishops in a lot of Amish communities forbid indoor bathrooms, for they consider them a luxury. Because the water had to be supplied by gravity, the bathroom was on the first floor. Rebecca thanked God the rest of the family had gone to bed.

Sarah appeared. "Oh, Martha." Wetting a cloth, she knelt beside Rebecca to wipe her forehead, waited patiently, then offered her a glass of water.

Weak and trembling, Rebecca climbed the stairs and stumbled back to her room. "*Dank an hunnert mohl (thanks a hundred times)*," she murmured to God and to Sarah as she collapsed across her bed.

"Try to get some sleep, Martha," Sarah said softly, pulling a quilt over her.

Exhaustion coiled around Rebecca like a huge serpent, dragging her tormented mind into one nightmare after another.

At dawn, Sarah got up and dressed. Blinking, Rebecca struggled to sit up.

Sarah hurried to the bed and placed her hand on Rebecca's forehead. "You're not running a fever, Martha, but you look pale."

"I . . . don't feel good." She slumped back to the mattress.

"I'll call Mama."

"No, Sarah. This is a busy day for her. Please, just let me sleep."

"You must've eaten something that upset you. I'll bring you a cup of peppermint tea."

"Don't bother. You have too much to do."

Smiling, Sarah bent to kiss her cheek. "It's no bother, Martha."

Rebecca closed her eyes. Sarah's sweetness was unbearable, for it intensified Rebecca's guilt. When Sarah left, Rebecca propped herself on a shaky elbow, glanced out the window at the trees shrouded in the first pinkish rays of light, and wondered what would transpire before the day's end.

She sighed. "I just wanted to earn enough money to be on my own so I could get away from *Mammi's* pressure and enter nurse's training." Margie's speeches about freedom had tempted her, but the girl's promises had been delusions. Was her cousin aware that her way of life had nothing to offer?

"I'll help you discover the true meaning of being a Christian,

Margie," she vowed, not attempting to bribe God, yet wondering if her pledge bore any weight with Him. *First, I have to get my own life straightened out.*

She closed her eyes. An image of a huge black vulture hovered over her, seemingly intent on battering her with its evil wings. Its vicious talons flexed, and it gnashed its serrated beak as though it longed to rip off her flesh and expose her deceitful heart. Gasping, she blinked the horrid vision out of existence.

Sarah entered the room with a tray. "I brought you a cup of tea, some toast, and a poached egg." Using her foot, she dragged a chair to the bedside, then placed the tray on it.

"*Gross Dank*, Sarah." Rebecca eyed a dime-sized hole in the black sweater that draped the back of the chair.

"I hope something to eat helps you to feel better." Smiling, Sarah left.

The refreshing peppermint tea settled Rebecca's stomach. She nibbled on the toast, but could hardly look at the egg. The yolk was like an eye, watching her every move. She covered it with her napkin. Tortured by conflicting thoughts, she stared at the beige walls.

"I'll watch as the Amish families approach, studying each face to see how many of them I've seen at one of the markets," she whispered. A frown creased her brow as she remembered the numerous occasions she'd accompanied her father to the frozen-food locker in Zimmerman's as well as the feed store. Recalling everyone she'd seen was impossible. Faking an illness was unnecessary, for she really felt sick. Her anxiety rose with the sun, until her nerves were a jumbled mass of vibrating cords.

Sarah appeared with a basin. "I brought you water to wash." Smiling, she set the basin on a stand and placed a folded lavender wash cloth beside it. "With the confusion downstairs near the bathroom, I assumed you'd prefer to remain up here." She grinned. "There's a container under the bed I use at night."

Rebecca smiled. "*Viel Dank*."

Laughing softly, Sarah retreated and closed the door.

Getting up, Rebecca shoved the sweater-draped chair back in

front of the window and went to the stand to splash cool water on her heated face. She wondered if her complexion was livid, but there are no mirrors in Amish homes. Going to the dresser, she picked up the brush Sarah had loaned her and stroked her hair. Too fatigued from the ordeal to roll it and put on her cap, she sprawled on the bed with her tresses waving down her back and drifted into fretful slumber.

Oblique shadows of indistinct shapes chased her. Claws seized the folds of her dress and ripped away fragments of the material. She fled through the mist, praying her bright-red underwear did not show. A huge hand snatched her cap, allowing her long hair to tumble down her back. She ran on through the thickening fog, searching in vain for a place to hide.

Waking, she gasped for breath. Beads of sweat moistened her forehead. She licked her dry lips, finding it difficult to swallow. Afraid of nightmares, she fought sleep, but fatigue won the final round, sucking her into a deepening state of unconsciousness.

Light-blue mist swirled around her. As the fog lifted, she discovered herself in a swamp. A snake hissed at her. Leaping away, she stumbled, but seized a tree limb to prevent sprawling in the muck that covered her ankles. The more she struggled to get out of the deepening ooze, the more futile it seemed.

The water began to bubble and froth. She backed away until her back scraped against a gnarled tree. The snarling branches coiled to ensnare her. The water continued to churn and swirl.

Breathless, she glanced around. To her right, she saw an island with grass, shade trees, and vivid arrays of flowers. A butterfly fluttered peacefully near the blossoms, the sky was azure-blue, and birds were singing. She wished she could get to the island paradise. It was only two hundred feet away, but she slowly sank to her knees in the tar-like substance under the tree, and the gnarled limbs held her captive.

The riling water humped in a huge wave. Breaking the surface, a grotesque figure rose from the depths of the murky pool. Staring at the lumps on the huge creature's gray, watery bulk, Rebecca tried to scream, but her constricted throat prohibited any sound.

"Why are you frightened, Becky?" The creature gurgled—tingling her spine. "I'm what you wanted."

"No!"

"You left home to find me."

"I was searching for my garden of Eden."

The thing laughed raspingly. "When you chose your own way of freedom, then told lies, you turned your back on anything resembling Eden."

"*Wer bisht Du* (Who are you)?"

"My name is Worldly. You're part of me, now." His wicked laugh curdled her blood.

"Go away!"

"Never." His huge eyes glowed as he reached for her with seaweed hands. "You belong to me."

"No!"

9

"Oh God, please have mercy and help me!" A brilliant shaft of light seared through the tree limbs near her and penetrated the water beside the grotesque creature.

Bellowing, the monster shriveled, then sank into the ooze.

Peace emanated from the radiance; Rebecca's terror diminished. The illumination collected into a sphere, then took the form of an angelic being. "Come with me," the vision said, reaching for her hand.

Rebecca gripped the proffered fingers and drifted with the being to the peaceful island. Relieved, she began to cry.

"Why do you weep, Rebecca?"

"I'm so lost and alone."

"I'll guide you to joy and peace if you'll trust me."

Rebecca gazed at the vision's lovely face. "Who are you?"

"I'm a messenger of Truth. Jesus said, 'I am the way, and the truth, and the life.'"

Remembering that she wore a torn dress that partly exposed her red-lace underwear, she lowered her head to toy absently with a daisy. "I feel . . . wicked."

"Jesus loves you, Rebecca."

"I know, and I want to be honest, but . . ."

"If you confess your wrongdoings, Jesus is faithful and just and will forgive you and cleanse you from all unrighteousness."

Rebecca leaped to her feet. "It's easy for you to spout Scripture. What do you have to fear?"

"Nothing—for I am pure. If you trust God, He will give you strength and courage to be honest."

Tears rilled down Rebecca's face. "I just wanted to be free to fulfill my calling."

"I realize that, but don't your guilt and shame have you incarcerated?"

"The Beilers don't ask questions anymore, and neither does Aaron, so I don't have to tell them more stories."

"Does that really make you free?"

Rebecca stared at the ground. "I guess so."

"Then I can't help you."

Glancing up, she discovered she was alone. "Wait! Please, come back!"

"When you decide to be honest, I will return," a fading voice said.

Rebecca searched for the light. It was gone, and she was back in the swamp. The ground under her was dry, but moss draped over her face, and gnarled vines held her captive. Horses' hooves drummed the earth. They were coming closer, and she lay in their path. Would their metal shoes grind her into the ground?

Gasping, she discovered she was in her bed. The quilt was tightly twisted around her body; her pillow half-covered her face, the case draping across one cheek. Wiggling free, she wiped the sweat from her face. The messenger of Truth was right! Deceit had imprisoned her and made her ill.

She massaged her temples. *My dreams are becoming more real! I still hear horses*! There were also buggies and the sound of many voices.

"Oh, *ja*. Worship service." Flipping the quilt, she sat up. Struggling out of bed, she gripped a bedpost. Her nightgown tickled her bare feet, her cap was gone, and her hair tumbled over one shoulder in disarray. Shakily, she went to a window, grasped the sweater-draped chair and peered down into the yard.

Two buggies approached the house. The first stopped at the gate to let a woman and four children out, then the driver drove toward the barn where Eli and a friend waited to lead the horses to pasture. Caring for them was quite a chore on meeting day. Rebecca wondered how many people would be coming. Three more horses trotted up the lane with carriages filled with strangers. Rebecca studied faces, afraid that each new one would be someone who might identify her.

Elam Miller stopped the next buggy in front of the house. Elizabeth got out carrying Priscilla and headed toward the porch. Pausing at the gate, she turned to look at Elam. They smiled at each other and something warm seemed to pass between them.

Rebecca looked away, not wishing to intrude on their tender moment. Elam was leaving for Mercer County in the evening, and it was apparent that Elizabeth would greatly miss him.

Slumping onto the chair, she thought about her father. He'd be going to worship this morning with *Mammi*. She yearned to be comforted by her father's reassuring smile, to be solaced in his strong arms, and even be reprimanded by *Mammi*.

Peering through the hole in the sweater, she thought she saw several people who might have noticed her in town. Could they identify her—now that she was dressed Amish? Aaron had seen her. It was enough to make him suspicious, yet his assumptions were inconclusive, weren't they?

The boys who secretly had cars worried her the most. Margie had visited on Saturdays. They frequently shopped, but often cruised downtown in the flashy red sports car. Confusion and worry scrambled Rebecca's brain. Her eyes fell on Sarah's Bible. "You shall know the truth, and the truth shall set you free," she whispered, sighing.

Amish homes had movable partitions on the first floor, so they could be set aside to make room for the worshipers on meeting Sundays. They clattered as men moved them against the outside walls; benches clacked as they were put in place. The hum of many voices drifted up the stairway, but through Rebecca's closed door, words were indistinct.

Cautious not to be seen, Rebecca peered between the sweater-draped chair and the single drape at the side of the window. Groups of young people formed here and there. A half dozen girls whispered and giggled near the gate as they stole quick glances at the fellows who congregated under a maple tree. The boys pretended not to notice, but their roving eyes frequently found the objects of their interest.

Eli came out of the barn and strode toward a gathering of men who congregated under the spreading branches of the apple tree. They wore their Sunday black frock coats and black hats. Elam Miller stood relaxed and smiling, his gestures cordial.

Aaron leaned against the tree trunk. Every hook-and-eye in his Sunday frock coat was perfectly placed, making the front of the garment plain and smooth. Frowning, he shoved his black hat back. His expression remained somber as he listened intently to an older man.

The Bishop, identified by the higher crown and broader brim of his hat, stepped closer to Aaron, opened his Bible, and pointed to it. Maintaining a stern expression, he spoke. All the men looked serious, and some furrowed their foreheads in thought — or disapproval. Which was it? Exasperation flickered in Aaron's dark eyes.

Rebecca studied his handsome face. Warmth encompassed her, and her heartbeat quickened. A spark she wished she could deny came to life. Curling her fingers into fists, she drew her lips taut, determined to squelch any attraction she had for the man.

"He's Old Order Amish," she reminded herself. Disregarding her mind's pleas, her eyes moved to his mouth. Reliving his gentle but fervent kisses, her lips tingled and her heart raced until she could feel her pulse throbbing in her temples.

Straightening, Aaron worked his shoulders. She could almost feel his strong embrace. Raising her hand, she covered her trembling lips as she fought to deny her feelings. How could she have permitted her heart to stray so far?

"He's from another world," she whispered. At least, he might as well be. A vision of Sarah's lovely face haunted her. "How could I have failed such a wonderful friend?" Cringing, she rebuked herself for even thinking about the man Sarah had chosen.

"I don't really know him," she whispered. What did he want out of life? What were his plans for his future? Was he intending to join the church and marry Sarah--or did he plan to keep his car? Was his vehicle just a way of tasting part of the world? He was getting too old to be involved in *Rumspringa*. Would he be tempted farther, like Grandfather Simon? If he left the Amish community, would Sarah go with him?

She paced. She'd prayed to be able to help Ruth. Would she succeed or would she only corrupt the girl? She scowled, remembering that she'd used Eli to get to a phone. Was she a bad influence on him? Aaron King had kissed her, and he was practically engaged to Sarah. She pressed her fists against her temples. *Am I a wicked influence on him, too?*

She moved back to the window where she could openly stare through the sweater's hole, yet remain concealed. Retrieving a pillow, she tossed it to the floor, knelt on it and propped her elbows on the chair's seat. The Bishop was still speaking. An older man, apparently a deacon, joined the conversation. They seemed to be confronting Aaron. The Bishop's face creased. Frowning, the deacon scratched his beard. Seemingly distressed, Aaron crossed his arms, slowly shaking his head.

Mouthing a silent prayer, Rebecca wondered if one of the deacons had discovered Aaron had a car. Was he being condemned and pressed to conform? She shook her head. It was not the Amish way to pressure a young person to comply. She tried to convince herself that they were only encouraging him.

Anger flickered in Aaron's eyes. Then the color drained from his face. His jaw set at a stubborn angle; his lips drew taut. His arms dropped to his sides; his fingers curled and uncurled. Again, he shook his head, seeming dismayed. He glanced up at her window.

Gasping, she jerked away. Had he seen her? That was impossible! Her eyes widened as a new thought seared through her mind. Were the men asking Aaron questions concerning Rebecca Wenger? Had someone discovered her identity?

"Oh, Aaron." Was it too late? Could even Truth save her, now? She thought about worms and how they crawl through dark self-made tunnels under the sod. "I should've been a worm," she murmured. Frowning, she wondered if even a worm hurt the ones it loved.

Forming a line, the older men headed for the house. The older women followed. Aaron's mother was absent. Had her condition worsened? The younger men filed toward the porch. Aaron was among them. He glanced at her window, but she was sure she was out of sight. She didn't flinch as she peeped through the hole, boldly watching him until he vanished from view beneath the porch roof.

Grasping Nancy's hand, Sarah led the procession of younger women. If Sarah watched Aaron's sister today, would he kiss her tonight? A band seemed to tighten around Rebecca's heart. Closing her eyes, she gripped the edge of the chair. A strange feeling stomped across her chest. Was it jealousy? She loved Sarah like a sister, but the thought of Aaron kissing the girl made her nauseous. It seemed as though a giant hand was squeezing her insides, and her throat constricted.

"He belongs to Sarah," she whispered, blinking away the excess moisture that pooled in her eyes. *What can I do to obliterate my feelings for him?*

Footsteps resounded on the stairs. Gasping, Rebecca rushed to the door. It sounded as though three or four men were coming. With trembling fingers, she slid the tiny bolt, hoping they wouldn't demand she open the door.

When the men entered the room next to hers, she wiped the moisture from her forehead. She'd forgotten that the ministers met in an upper room before services. She listened to their shuffling commotion. A man coughed, and chair legs scraped on the floor. Picturing the tall, skinny Bishop, Rebecca quietly moved to the wall to flatten her ear against the plaster.

"I don't know what to think about Aaron King, Bishop John," one of the men said.

"He's a good man. But there's something bothering him. I wish he'd confide in me."

"Aaron isn't used to confiding. He accepts his responsibilities and quietly helps anyone he can."

"I know," the Bishop continued, "but he should've joined the church years ago."

"Do you think he's wrongly influencing Eli Beiler?"

"No. That young man's strong-minded, too."

One of the men chuckled. "Liz told me last night that she thinks he's on the verge of settling down. She's been hoping and praying for it long enough."

"He's been seeing your daughter for months. *Gel*? (Isn't that right)?" asked another voice.

"*Ja*, and Liz cares deeply for him."

"*Vell* . . ." the Bishop coughed. "If Liz thinks Eli's coming around, we must be patient."

"Love overlooks faults. *Gel*?" the third voice said.

The Bishop cleared his throat again. "We can be thankful for that—at least when it comes to the Lord forgiving our sins. Chris, you take the first sermon this morning. Benjamin, you take the second."

"Wait a minute," Chris said. "Aaron King may know something that he isn't willing to share."

"*Ja*?" It sounded as though a book crashed to the floor, and again the Bishop's voice rose. "*Wass* do you mean?"

"He's been asking a lot of questions about a Mennonite named David Wenger."

Benjamin gasped. "That poor man's daughter left home and got into some sort of trouble. I hear the police want to question her."

"Concerning what?"

"I'm not sure. There's been some speculation concerning the problem of illegal drugs in Lancaster."

"Hum... Gossip." The Bishop sounded corrective. "We must pray for David Wenger and his family--as well as for our Aaron King. He may be aware of something illegal, but I don't believe he'd get involved."

"Probably not," Chris said, "but he's been trying to find Rebecca Wenger."

"*Fer wass*?"

"That's what puzzles me."

Rebecca gasped and felt dizzy.

"We must be cautious not to listen to hearsay or be drawn into spreading gossip," the Bishop said. "Aaron denies knowing the Wenger girl, but I feel he's withholding information." He paused. "We'll discuss this matter further after service, and I intend to question Aaron, again, about the girl called Rebecca. Now, we must pray and prepare ourselves."

Moving across the room in a daze, Rebecca slumped to the chair by the window and stared down at the now-empty yard. How long would it be until someone discovered who she was? The July sun beat on the porch roof and glanced into her face. Heat rose from the shingles in quivering waves. Rebecca wiped the moisture from her forehead, then crossed the room to ease open the opposite window. Even the breeze felt too warm to breathe. Was it only the rising temperature in the room that made her feel as though she were suffocating?

She sat statuesque on the straight-backed chair until she heard the Bishop and deacons go downstairs; then curiosity lured her to the door. Opening it a crack, she peered out, discovering she could see down the stairway into the meeting room. A number of men sat in her line of vision. Aaron was among them, making it possible for her to study his face during the sermons, yet remain obscure.

At a given moment, every man took off his hat and placed it under his bench. Everyone stood, and the singing began. Noah, Aaron's father, leafed through his *Ausbund*, the hymnal used in Amish meetings. Holding the book close to his eyes, he mouthed the words. It was not difficult for Rebecca to follow the high German, and she knew she would easily understand the sermons.

Deacon Benjamin Zook took his place. "I'm reading from John eight."

Rebecca comprehended the familiar passage, even though the man's words were slightly muffled. When he read the part about Satan being the father of lies, she flinched, and the stories she'd told thundered back to ravage her.

"Being sorry isn't enough," she whispered. She felt she should tell all and trust God to protect her. *That's easier to say than it is to do.*

"Lord God," she whispered. "Increase my faith. Give me strength and courage to do what's right." She swiped at a persistent tear, wondering if it would help to talk with someone. "Oh, God, who can I talk to?"

Informing Aaron would not only be risky, it would be humiliating to admit to having lied. Telling Eli would put an unfair burden on him. She didn't want to ask him to keep secrets about her questionable past from Liz, especially if the girl was in love with him. What about telling Sarah?

The more she considered confessing the truth, the more her head ached. Closing her eyes, she pictured her radiant vision; then the monster of the swamp played on the back of her eyelids, causing her to gasp and blink.

Slumping to a braided rug at the door, she leaned against the wall to listen to the sermons. Becoming drowsy, she shook herself and peered through the crack. The men she could see looked sleepy, too. Noah's eyes closed, his head bobbed, and he blinked, straightening his shoulders. A fly buzzed at one of the windows. Another circled a man's bald head. His dark eyes rolled to watch the creature as it dipped and soared. When it lit on the end of his large nose and he turned his eyes inward to look at it, Rebecca had to stifle a giggle.

During the Bishop's message, Esther and Ruth passed moon pies and a glass of water to the children. Since they became restless during the three-hour service, the treats were given to them halfway through the meeting.

The Beilers were serving schnitz pie and cheese for lunch. According to the number of buggies lined up near the barn, there must be over a hundred people present. Rebecca wondered how many seatings it would take to feed them all.

"I should help," she murmured, but the thought of going downstairs made her ill. Frowning, she closed the door softly and leaned against it. Silence was necessary, for if anyone heard her, there probably would be questions.

Her mind rampaged. Aaron knew she was here. What must he be thinking? Did her absence make him more suspicious? He would probably interrogate her the first chance he got, so it was essential to avoid him.

"Is it possible?" she murmured, nearly choking on the anxiety that bubbled into her throat. "What will I do if he demands to see me?"

10

When the worship service ended, Rebecca sighed. With the commotion downstairs, she could pace without being detected. She circled the room several times, her nightgown whispering against her legs; then curiosity drew her back to the door. Opening it a crack, she saw Sarah at the bottom of the stairs.

"I don't think that would be wise," Sarah said, nervously brushing her hand across her light-blue skirt.

"*Fer wass?*" Aaron asked.

"It wouldn't look right."

He stepped into view. "*Wass* harm could it do, if you accompanied me?"

Sarah sighed. "I've tried to explain how I feel."

"*Ja, vell . . .*" He looked perplexed.

"Please, Aaron, don't pressure me."

Wondering why Sarah would give him a difficult time, Rebecca noiselessly closed the door, sauntered across the room and sat on her bed. "He wouldn't have to beg me," she murmured. Jealousy coiled within her, then struck with wicked fangs. She battled to destroy it.

Retrieving Sarah's Bible, she flipped it open at random and read, "Fear God, and keep his commandments: for this is the whole duty of man. For God shall bring every work into judgement, with every secret thing, whether it be good, or whether it be evil."

She groaned. "Why does everything have to point out my faults?"

Closing the Bible, she struggled to conjure excuses that would appease her conscience. Flipping her long hair across her pillow, she stretched out on the bed, yanked a sheet over herself, and closed her eyes. Exhausted, but afraid dreams would invade her rest, she fought sleep. In spite of her effort, she drifted into slumber.

Aaron sat at the bottom of the stairs, frowning. He admired Sarah's virtue, but this time he felt she was acting more than a little prudish. Determination seizing him, he stood. "Sarah."

Tossing her dish towel over the back of a kitchen chair, she came to him. Her smile was cooperative, but the set of her delicate shoulders belied it. "*Ja*, Aaron?"

He kept his voice low, but spoke firmly. "I'm going upstairs to see Martha, with or without your company—or approval."

"Isn't your father anxious to start home?"

His jaw tightened. "He'll wait." Turning, he placed his foot firmly on the bottom step.

"I'll go with you." She brushed by him, then her footsteps slowed as though she were reconsidering.

He vowed not to be deterred as he followed her. Opening a bedroom door, she looked in, then stepped aside to permit him access. Striding to the center of the room, he paused. Martha lay on her back under a rumpled quilt, her hair waving in a tawny-gold mass across the pillow and over her shoulder.

"She's asleep, Aaron," Sarah whispered, pausing at his side. "She had a bad night, so we shouldn't disturb her."

He moved to the bed. "Martha," he called softly. She didn't rouse. *Would she respond if I called her Amber—or Rebecca?* Sarah's standing watchdog not only discouraged his brash impulse, it made guilt simmer in the back of his conscious thought.

Sarah touched his arm. "Noah and Jesse are probably ready to leave."

Pulling away, he bent over the girl in the bed. "Martha." Wondering if she had a fever, he placed a hand on her forehead, then at the side of her smooth face. Golden-tipped lashes lay motionless on her pale cheeks. Unable to resist, he picked up a handful of her hair, then let the silken strands stream through his fingers.

"Aaron!" Sarah's tone was hushed, but corrective.

Ignoring her, he looked at Martha's slightly parted lips, and the memory of their kisses seared through his restless mind. Was she who she claimed? If not, who?

"Aaron!" Jesse's voice echoed up the stairwell.

Aaron straightened. "Tell Jesse I'm coming."

Sarah looked pensive, hesitated, then hurried from the room.

Aaron turned back to Martha. Lured, he bent to touch her warm lips with his. Tasting her sweetness created a desire to embrace her, but Sarah's returning tread encouraged him to head for the door. He glanced over his shoulder. Martha lay peacefully, her hair forming a seductive tawny-golden cloud around her sweet face. Envisioning her within his embrace, he missed a step and nearly tripped over a braided rug.

On his way to the buggy, he pondered Martha's reservation, and doubts frolicked in his mind like inebriated frogs. His jaw tensed as he vowed to unearth the truth surrounding her before someone else did.

"Martha," Sarah's sweet voice summoned.

Rolling to her side, Rebecca propped an elbow on the mattress. "*Ja?*"

Sarah set a tray on the bedside chair. "I brought you something to eat."

"The peppermint tea smells good."

"*Mammi* Hazel made it for you. She says it's good for a riled stomach." Picking up the steaming cup, she proffered it.

"*Gross Dank.*" Sitting straight, Rebecca sipped the refreshing brew.

Sarah glanced out a window. "You tossed a lot last night."

"I was plagued by dreams."

"*Ja.* Sickness sometimes makes for weird imaginings, *gel?*"

She thought about seeing Sarah at the bottom of the steps with Aaron and longed to ask her what he'd wanted, but that would be confessing to eavesdropping. "Has Aaron left?"

"*Ja.* Nearly everyone has."

"Was Anna King well enough to attend meeting?"

Sarah frowned. "No. They're taking her to the doctor tomorrow."

"That's good." Setting her cup on the saucer, Rebecca nibbled on a piece of toast. "Did he know I was up here?"

"*Ja.*" Sarah sighed. "He insisted on coming up to see you. I tried to explain that it would be improper, but he argued there'd be no harm, if I accompanied him."

Strangling a gasp, Rebecca blinked. So, that was what Aaron had been pressing Sarah to do. "I'm glad you talked him out of it."

"*Vell...*" Sarah looked perplexed. Avoiding Rebecca's eyes, she straightened the bedcovers.

Rebecca pictured the young people's Sunday night sing. "Does Aaron still attend *Younga*?"

"Sometimes."

"Will he be there tonight?"

"I hope so. He asked if you would be going."

"What'd you tell him?"

"I said you probably would, if you were feeling well." Sarah went to the door. "I'd better get downstairs. There are still dishes to do."

Figuring no one had discovered her presence, Rebecca began to improve. Even the schnitz pie tasted good. As she ate, she thought about *Younga*. Could she risk being identified? Aaron would probably bring Sarah home. The image of the two of them together on a buggy seat awakened something that wriggled painfully within her.

Eli would have to bring me home, she thought. *What if he wants to take Liz home?*

When the neighbors were gone, Rebecca dressed and ventured to the living room. Hazel sat in a rocker, her aging hands clasped in her lap. Her sagacious brown eyes studied Rebecca, making her wonder if the old lady saw through her facade.

Esther moved forward to touch Rebecca's forehead. "How are you feeling, Martha?"

"Some better." She sat on a chair, hoping she didn't appear too healthy.

Eli swept into the room, stopped with a jolt, and smiled at Rebecca. "You going to *Younga*?"

"I don't believe."

"We always have fun. I'll introduce you to my friends."

"I'd be a drag," Rebecca argued sweetly.

Isaac looked up from his Bible. "The fresh air might do you good."

Rebecca pressed her fingers against her temples. "I think it would be wise for me to stay home and rest."

Sarah came in, wearing lilac and looking radiant. "Oh, Martha, you're going with us."

"Not this time."

The girl looked disappointed, then turned to Eli. "I'm ready."

Eli glanced at Rebecca, then went to the shed for the buggy. After they'd gone, she excused herself and went back to her room. Time passed slowly. She continued to glance at the battery clock on Sarah's dresser. Sitting on the edge of her bed, she listened to her radio, intending to hide it quickly if Esther unexpectedly came to her room.

The night wore on. Finally, she heard a buggy and glanced at the clock. It was two a. m. Where had Aaron taken Sarah before he brought her home? Had he stopped under the oak to kiss her? Taking a deep breath, she tightened her jaw. She must control her effusive heart.

Getting up, she went to the window. The shade was drawn to the sill, so she pulled it away from the frame to peer out into the night. When the buggy stopped at the gate, Rebecca tried to see into the darkened interior, but moonlight shimmered on the windshield, obscuring the occupants.

After a few minutes, Sarah got out. As the buggy turned, Rebecca strained her vision to see Aaron, but the driver remained hidden in a shadow.

When the buggy rumbled down the lane, Sarah came into the house, quietly ascended the stairs, and slipped into the bedroom.

"Did you have a good time, Sarah?"

"*Ja*."

"I thought maybe Aaron would come in for awhile."

Sarah snapped on her battery lamp before she spoke. "Aaron was only at *Younga* a short time. When he approached me, I thought he was going to offer to bring me home. Instead, he inquired about your health." She sighed. "He said he'd take you to the doctor when he takes Anna."

"That won't be necessary."

"I told him I thought you'd be well, soon." Taking off her cap, she removed the pins from her hair. "He asked me to come over to sit with Nancy tomorrow."

Rebecca experienced a twinge of dismay.

As Sarah stroked her waist-length hair, the straight blond strands shimmered in the lamplight. She clattered the brush to her dresser. "Eli vanished about the same time as Aaron. I figured he'd taken Liz Lapp somewhere, so I wasn't concerned. Then, I noticed Liz sitting in a corner, looking miserable." She sighed. "Eli used to drive her home after every sing, but lately he's been driving her crazy!"

"Do Eli and Liz have a special relationship?"

"I used to think so." A smile softened her tense features. "You'd like Liz, Martha."

"I'm sure I would, since she's a friend of yours." Rebecca pictured the buggy, realizing the horse had not been Ransom. "Who brought you home?"

"Andrew Lapp, Liz's oldest brother. She was with us."

"Tell me about her."

"She's sweet and quiet like you, Martha. Her hair is black, and her eyes are green. They sparkle like emeralds when she's happy." Sarah laughed. "They snap if she becomes angry. Tonight, they sparked. I think Eli's in trouble."

"Does Liz have a temper?"

"Not usually. She could have any fellow she wanted." Catching her lower lip between her teeth, she frowned. "Except Aaron," she added softly.

"Sarah, I have no right to ask, and you can refuse to answer, but I'd like to know what's between you and Aaron."

"I care a lot, Martha, but lately he's. . . been acting strangely."

Unpinning her apron, she folded it.

Rebecca pictured the car she'd seen him driving. "Do you think Aaron and Eli are together?"

"*Ja.* I know my brother has a car. Aaron admitted a long time ago that he wanted a vehicle." She sighed. "Oh, Martha, what's gotten into him?"

"Maybe the same thing that's lured Eli."

Sarah's eyes widened. "You think Aaron has a car?"

"*Vell* . . . he never mentioned owning one."

"I pray he doesn't go the same direction as his brother." A tear sparkled at the corner of her eye, and she swiped it away.

Witnessing her torment, Rebecca winced. How could Aaron hurt a girl who was so genuinely sweet?

Sarah undressed, slipped into her nightgown, and collapsed across her bed. "I'm exhausted, and tomorrow's wash day." She bolted upright. "*Ach! Es speit mich* that I didn't ask you how you feel."

"I'm fine, and don't worry about the wash. I'll help, so you can sleep in."

Sarah laughed softly. "If I slept in, my family would think I'd died."

Rebecca tossed and turned. Aaron King was spoken for. When he settled down, it would be with Sarah. *I have to get out of this situation before it's too late.* In spite of her turbulent mind, she drifted into fitful sleep where confusing dreams tormented her.

"Martha," Sarah called, shaking her.

Blinking in the darkened room, Rebecca gasped.

"You were moaning."

"I was dreaming." She wiped the sweat from her forehead. "*Es speit mich* that I woke you."

"Don't worry about that. Go back to sleep." Padding barefoot across the room, Sarah fluffed her pillow and slumped onto her bed. "*Gute Nacht.*"

Exhaustion pulled Rebecca into unconsciousness, where she found herself in a courtroom. She wriggled on her chair beside her elderly defense attorney, wondering why her accident with Vance's station wagon required a court trial. Looking at her lawyer's withered face, she was dismayed, then assumed his many years of experience could be in her favor. Scanning the whispering spectators, she tried to avoid their accusing eyes. Then, she looked into the jeering faces of Joe Dinger, Doug, and Gene. Shivering, she turned away.

"This is exhibit number one," the prosecutor said, lifting a small tray that contained a milk glass vase. "This was turned over to the police by Greg Mattis."

In icy silence, Rebecca stared at the vase.

"This vase has a false bottom that contains a packet of cocaine. It is believed that Rebecca Wenger used this means to sell narcotics."

"No!" Rebecca cried.

The judge's gavel banged and his penetrating eyes accosted her.

Joe was called to testify. Taking his seat, he smiled at the prosecutor.

"Since Rebecca Wenger is the one who placed the cocaine in this vase —"

Rebecca's lawyer pulled himself to his feet, then wobbled on feeble, arthritic knees. "Objection!" his voice cracked. "That fact has not been established."

"I'll restate my question, your honor," the prosecuting attorney said, then turned back to Joe. "Mr. Dinger, is this the type of vase used in the Flowers by Vance florist shop?"

"Yes."

"Did Rebecca Wenger work for Vance Troy?"

"Yes."

"Did she make the flower vase deliveries?"

"Most of them."

"Did she have access to this vase?"

"Sure." Glancing at Rebecca, he grinned.

"Did you ever see her putting the packets into the vase bottoms?"

"Lots of times. She told me they were flower freshener."

"That's a lie!" Rebecca cried.

Murmurs traveled through the courtroom.

The judge's gavel cracked. "Silence, please." He peered at the prosecuting attorney from under straggly gray brows. "Proceed."

The prosecutor smiled. "Mr. Dinger, were you with Rebecca Wenger when she delivered vases like these?"

"No way! I just found out that she and Vance were in business together."

"That's not true!" Rebecca leaped to her feet. "It's not true."

Her lawyer rested his gnarled hand on her arm. "Please sit and refrain from your outbursts."

Her knees weak, she slumped to her chair. "You aren't doing anything to prove my innocence!"

"Innocence?" He peered at her with opaque eyes, his gray brows knit.

Rebecca suddenly realized that even her lawyer was convinced of her guilt. Her horror exploded.

The case continued, each witness making matters worse. When the jury was dismissed to confer, Rebecca's lawyer accompanied her to a small room to wait. She pleaded with him to explain why he hadn't tried to win her case, but he only rubbed his aching joints as though he were oblivious to her pleas.

"Why won't you try to uncover the truth?" she asked, jerking on his shirt sleeve.

"Truth?" the old man wheezed. "You don't know Truth, do you?"

"Yes!"

He shook his shaggy gray head. "No you don't."

Tears coursed down her face. "I want to be honest!"

The old lawyer grappled for a bottle of pain pills, took one, and groaned. "If it's Truth you want, you'll have to be honest."

"I will. I promise!"

"Now?"

Sarah's alarm jangled, shocking Rebecca awake. Her hair was wet with perspiration and her hands trembled. *This is ridiculous!* she thought. *I don't even know what was in those stupid packets!* She moaned.

Stretching, Sarah glanced across the room. "Are you still not feeling well, Martha?"

"I'll be . . . fine." She tried to keep her voice from quavering.

Sarah sat on the edge of her bed. "You'd better sleep in this morning."

Rebecca flipped back the quilt. "Today, I intend to do my share of the work." Picturing her scarlet-lace underwear, she closed her eyes. She'd washed it and hung it behind the bed to dry, hoping no one would discover it. Instead of getting up, she waited for Sarah to dress.

Snatching the disgraceful undergarments, she shoved them under her pillow.

"I'll see you at breakfast." Smiling, Sarah left the room.

Leaping out of bed, Rebecca jerked the nightgown off, donned the scarlet bikinis and lace bra, then reached for the lavender dress Sarah had loaned her. The door swung inward. Squealing, she seized the garment and held it in front of her.

"Oh, Martha!" Stepping into the room, Sarah closed the door and leaned against it.

"The underwear isn't mine. I mean, I don't want it to be mine." She grimaced. "I only bought it to prove I could."

Sarah laughed. "Martha, you're wicked."

"I don't mean to be. Are you going to tell Esther?"

Sarah grinned. "I won't tell, if you let me wear them sometime."

Rebecca joined the girl's mirth. "Sarah, you're wicked, too!"

Grabbing the sheet, Sarah began to strip her bed. "Mama's ready for the white things."

Rebecca dressed quickly, intending to help gather the rest of the sheets.

"Oh!" Sarah cried as she flipped Rebecca's pillow onto the floor. A ray of sunlight streamed through the window and played on the bright chrome trim on the tiny radio. Picking it up, Sarah turned it over in her hand; then her eyes slowly moved to meet Rebecca's.

11

Sarah giggled. "You really *are* wicked, Martha!" She ran her fingers over the radio case. "How do you turn this on?"

"The top knob. The second knob is the tuner."

Sarah snapped the radio on, and music flooded the room.

Gasping, Rebecca seized the instrument to bring the music to a safer level. "You'll have Ruth in here!"

"We can't have that." A spontaneous giggle bubbled from her.

"Sarah!" Esther called from the foot of the stairs.

Sarah's eyes widened. "Do something with that thing." She moved to the door, opened it, and called, "*Ja*, Mama?"

"Are you coming with those sheets?"

"*Ja!*" Rushing across the room, she seized Rebecca's sheet and jerked it from the bed.

Ramming the radio into her paper bag, Rebecca helped Sarah. When they got downstairs, Esther had the first basket of clothes ready to hang on the line. Sarah grabbed the basket. Rebecca took the clothespin bag, along with a damp rag to wipe off the line, and headed across the lawn.

Setting the basket on the grass, Sarah grabbed a pillow case, gave it a flip, and pinned it to the line. "Aaron said he'd come for me about one o'clock." She hummed as she worked, evidently dreaming about being with him.

The laundry was finished, dinner over, and the dishes washed, when Rebecca heard a buggy coming. Glancing out the window, she watched Ransom prance up the lane. The horse stomped and blew as he halted near the gate. Aaron jumped from the buggy and hurried up the path. He was early.

Opening the door, Rebecca stepped aside to let him enter.

He smiled. "You're feeling better, Martha. *Gel?*"

"*Ja. Gross Dank.*"

Esther pulled out a kitchen chair. "Have a seat, Aaron. Sarah will be up from the cellar shortly."

"How's Anna?" Rebecca asked.

Sighing, Aaron slumped to the chair. "She seems worse, and Dad's worried."

Esther set a cup of coffee and a plate of cookies in front of him. "Who did her wash?"

"No one — yet. Aunt Nan was supposed to come over, but she's unable to."

Rebecca stepped toward him. "I'd be glad to help."

"*Ja,*" Esther said. "If you bring the laundry over, Martha and I'll do it this afternoon."

He paused ponderingly. "I don't have time to make a return trip and get Mother to the doctor in time."

Rebecca glanced at her borrowed lavender dress to make sure it was presentable. "I'll accompany Sarah," Rebecca said. "We can do the laundry while you're gone."

Aaron peered at her with questioning eyes. "If you mean that, I accept."

Sarah closed the cellar door and smiled at Rebecca. "You're always thinking of ways to help."

Rebecca searched the girl's face for a hint of jealousy, but only kindness and understanding emanated from her.

Eli swept into the kitchen like a swarm of bees, then stopped abruptly to appraise Rebecca. "You're looking better."

Esther rested her hand on Aaron's forehead. "You don't seem too perky. Are you coming down with something, too?"

A weary smile crossed his face. "I'm just tired."

Eli laughed. "That's because you've been out late the past several nights."

Aaron's glare wiped the grin from Eli's face.

Turning to Rebecca, Eli said, "I'm going to Bird-In-Hand this afternoon. Would you like to accompany me?"

"*Viel Dank*, Eli, but I'm going to Kings' to help with Anna's washing."

It was Eli's turn to glare, but Aaron turned from his accusing eyes and studied the too-familiar calendar by the stove.

Sarah tied the strings to her bonnet, picked up a small basket of treats, and headed for the door.

Looking at Rebecca, Aaron grinned. "Get your bonnet, girl."

She realized he'd been watching her and apparently missed Sarah's sweetness. How many times had the man overlooked the girl's virtue?

At the buggy, Sarah paused. "You can sit in front, Martha."

"I prefer the back." She figured by tagging along, she'd already infringed too much on Sarah's time with Aaron.

For several minutes, they traveled in silence, then Sarah looked at Aaron and sighed. "Don't be so glum. I'm sure Anna's going to be fine."

"*Ja*." He stared straight ahead.

"*Wass's* wrong?"

"*Vell* . . . I uncovered some disturbing news last night."

"About what?" she gently pried.

"I don't wish to talk about it right now."

Some of the color left Sarah's face. "Is . . . a member of your family in trouble?"

"No one except my prodigal brother, but that's a worn refrain."

Sarah looked dismayed. "Has something new developed concerning him?"

"We haven't heard from him for several weeks."

Rebecca cringed. Had Aaron uncovered information concerning her? Sarah turned her head to watch a child playing with a litter of puppies. Twisting in his seat, Aaron's eyes found Rebecca's. Blinking, she pretended to be amused by the puppies, but Aaron's stare had revealed his intention to confront her the first chance he got. How could she avoid his interrogation?

When Aaron stopped Ransom at Kings' front gate, Sarah

climbed from the carriage. "I'll see if Anna needs help getting ready to go."

Rebecca climbed from the carriage on the passenger's side and followed Sarah through the gate. Aware that Aaron was close on her heels, she increased her pace and swept through the door into the kitchen.

Catching up, he gripped her shoulder.

"I must start heating wash water, Aaron." She flashed him an innocent smile, but his expression remained somber.

Nancy skipped into the kitchen. Spotting Rebecca, her face lit up. "Martha!" Racing across the room, she flung herself into Rebecca's arms. "Let's play dollies."

"Martha came to help Mama," Aaron said.

She frowned. "Mama's sick."

"You be a good girl for Martha and Sarah," Aaron said softly.

Nancy's large dark eyes surveyed his face. "I'm good. *Gel*?"

Aaron hugged her. "*Ja*, you are."

Breaking free, she ran to the corner to retrieve the doll. Holding it up, she pointed to the apron Rebecca had made. "Dolly likes it."

Anna appeared in the doorway from the *Dawdy Haus*, her features drawn and her complexion pallid. "I wish Noah hadn't gone to town."

"He had business, Mama," Aaron said.

Sarah held Anna's arm as the woman crossed the kitchen. Staggering, Anna gripped the back of a chair.

Rushing forward, Aaron supported her. "I'll help you to my buggy." He glanced at Martha. "The washer's ready, and Jesse and I took the laundry to the summer kitchen."

"We'll manage," Rebecca said, smiling to reassure him as she opened the screen door for them.

He and Sarah supported Anna until they reached the buggy. Aaron helped his mother in and waited for her to get seated. Sarah handed her a small pillow, making sure she was comfortable. Rebecca waited on the porch with Nancy.

Aaron glanced back. "Jesse's at the barn, Martha, if you need anything."

Sarah watched the carriage until it disappeared around a bend, then slowly approached the house. Was it love that shimmered in her blue eyes?

Nancy bounced across the porch. Grabbing Sarah's hand, she yanked. "Read story."

Sarah smiled. "First, we must get the washing under way."

Sweat trickled down Rebecca's face as she hoisted one pair of broadfalls after another to the line. Finally, the wash was flapping in the breeze.

Sarah brought a basin of cool water, and Rebecca washed her face. She was brushing her hair as the sound of an approaching buggy reached her. She straightened her center part, rolled her long hair quickly, pinned it to her head, and donned her prayer cap. She turned to see Aaron entering the house alone.

Nancy ran to him. "Where's Mama?"

Rebecca glanced out the window at the empty buggy; then she studied Aaron's tired face.

"It's pneumonia," he mumbled.

Sarah touched his arm gently. "Where's Anna?"

"The doctor put her in the hospital. He said, with medication and rest, she'd be all right in a few days."

Jesse burst into the house, smelling like manure.

Aaron glared at the boy's boots. "Jesse!"

The boy laughed. "You're getting as fussy as an old woman."

"If you had to keep this floor scrubbed, you'd be more particular."

"Mother hen," Jesse chided.

Aaron looked stern. "The next time this floor needs scrubbed, you can do it instead of Mother."

"Scrubbing isn't a man's work. Get yourself a woman, Aaron."

"Not being the one to clean doesn't give you reason to be heedless."

Jesse sobered. "*Wass's* eating at you?"

"Get your smelly boots out of this house!"

With slouched shoulders, Jesse slunk back outside to scrape his boots on the grass. He glanced back. "I'm going into town with a friend."

Aaron sighed. "You can go when the chores are done."

"*Ja.*"

"Be back early."

"*Ja.*" He headed for the barn, then spun to face the house. "George had her kittens. They're in the fodder room." He looked at Rebecca. "I promised little John one. You can pick it out for him."

Rebecca turned to tell Sarah she should be the one to pick little John's kitten, but when she saw how the girl was looking at Aaron, she decided to give them time alone. As she turned, the monster of jealousy reared its ugly head. Battling it, she fled across the barnyard.

In the fodder room, she paused to listen. Tiny mews issued from behind a small pile of hay. Finding five kittens, Rebecca tried to choose. The yellow tiger was cute, but the black one with a tiny white bib had a sweet personality.

"I'm leaving, now," Jesse said, coming from farther back in the barn. Glancing at the kittens, he grinned, then hurried to a car that pulled to a stop in the barnyard.

Within moments, Rebecca heard footsteps compressing the straw behind her. She turned. "Aaron." Reading the questions in his dark eyes, she leaped to her feet. He stood like a mountain between her and the open doorway, so she turned to flee.

"Wait!" His tone was sharp.

Her heart racing, Rebecca headed for a flight of steps at the back of the barn. If she could make it to the second floor, she could escape through the upper barn door and get to the house. Aaron wouldn't bombard her with inquiries in front of Sarah.

"Wait!" He quickened his footsteps.

With thudding heart, she climbed the steps—Aaron rapidly closing the distance between them.

"Martha, stop!"

Gaining the upper floor, she whirled and raced toward the open door. Before she reached the exit, Aaron's fingers gripped her upper arm. Intent on freedom, she wrenched loose, stumbled, and nearly fell in a pile of hay. His fingers tangled in the bow of her prayer cap, yanking the strings loose. Regaining her footing, she sprang for the partly open barn door.

Aaron leaped forward, grasped her arm, and swung her to face him. Her prayer cap fell, and her hair tumbled down her back. As she tried to jerk free, her foot slipped on chaff. Losing her balance, she toppled to the hay. Not relinquishing his grip, Aaron plummeted with her. She wrestled, but he seized her other arm.

"Stop it," he said, his face close to hers.

Feeling pinned like a butterfly to a board, she met his stare. "*Wass* do you want?"

"Answers!"

"Did you need to attack me?"

"Apparently."

The sweet-smelling hay gave her a heady feeling, and his nearness did strange things to her senses. "Let me go."

"If I do you'll run." His gaze softened, and a muscle jerked in his cheek.

"You . . . lost your hat," she said, peering at the dark locks that dangled on his forehead.

"*Wer bisht Du* (who are you)?" he demanded, but his tone was softening.

"Martha Kauffman." The lie strangled her, and she fought tears. In a moment of silence, a lone bee hummed over a dried clover blossom by her head.

Aaron's grasp tightened. "The fear in your eyes tells me you're not being honest. I've been wondering if your name is really Martha."

"You have a powerful imagination."

"It's an extra sense I have."

She wrestled in a futile effort to escape. "You don't act like you have any sense at all."

"I want you to confide in me."

"*Fer wass?*"

He looked exasperated. "*Wass's* frightening you?"

"Your insanity." Again, she tried to wrench away, but he held her securely.

"I can read fright in your eyes."

"That's because you're attacking me!"

"Amber."

"Stop calling me that!"

"Martha, please." As he perused her face, his expression softened. "I want to help you."

"Then let me go." The tears that had threatened suddenly materialized and streamed down her face.

"Martha. Oh, Martha . . . I . . . I . . ." He watched a tear creep from the corner of her eye, cruise along the side of her face, then lose itself in her hair. "Oh Martha," he whispered. His face lowered and his mouth covered hers.

Picturing Sarah, Rebecca felt she should stop his foolishness, but as his kiss deepened, her senses reeled, and she weakened within his grasp. Her heart raced in wild abandon as his warm lips caressed hers. Her arms went around him as she returned his kiss.

Pulling away slightly, he peered at her. His fingers entwined in her hair, then trailed its length, and his lustrous eyes caressed her face. "Martha . . . I . . . I . . ." Releasing her, he sat up.

"Aaron . . ." Her heart raced, and her vow to control her emotions became confused by desire.

"You . . . better go," he choked. "We'll . . . talk later."

She sat up. Her insides were gyrating, and she tried to hide her trembling hands in her lilac skirt. A thick lock of hair fell over one shoulder and the rest tumbled in carefree abandon down her back. Bits of hay that had caught in her waves protruded from odd angles.

Compassion shimmered in Aaron's eyes, but something deeper seemed to be smoldering as well. Reaching, he picked a dried grass stem from her hair. "Martha . . . you . . ." As though lured, he pulled her into his arms, and his lips sought hers.

She rested back against the sweet scented hay. Though enchanted, she tried to fight his allure, knowing she would suffer guilt when she faced Sarah. However, as the pressure of his mouth increased, all trace of Sarah vanished from her consciousness.

A man cleared his throat.

Aaron jerked upright with a gasp. Propping herself on an elbow, Rebecca peered into a dark corner.

A man laughed. "So, Aaron, you're not above a romp in the hay, eh?"

Aaron leaped to his feet. "Joseph!"

"*Ja.*"

She could not see the man, but his voice sounded familiar. So did his chuckle. She shivered.

Aaron's hat rested at the top of the stairs where he had first grabbed her. Sauntering across the barn floor, he retrieved it, slapped it against his leg to knock off the chaff, then shoved it onto his head. "Does Dad or Jesse know you're here?" he asked the man who remained obscure in a deep shadow.

"No. I didn't know if I'd be welcome."

"The community prays for you, but no longer considers you part of it."

"Shunning is practiced by the church, Aaron, but I haven't joined. Besides, we're family. *Gel*? Have a heart."

"You're one to talk, after the way you broke our mother's." Aaron sighed. "*Wass* do you want this time?"

"I want to stay."

"Stay?" Aaron's eyelids half closed. "Or hide out for awhile? Are you in trouble?"

Getting to his feet, the man stretched and yawned. "I've just discovered that I have information you'd love to hear, brother."

"*Wass* is it?" Crossing his arms, Aaron set his jaw.

"You going to cooperate with me?"

"I'm not promising anything, Joseph. State your purpose."

"*Ja, vell* . . ." As the man strode forward, a beam of light that seared through the crack between two boards in the side of the barn struck his face.

Joe Dinger! Rebecca's mind shrieked. Realizing he was Aaron's brother, Joseph, did nothing to calm her frenzy. Now, Aaron would discover she was a deceitful fraud who had disobeyed God and hurt everyone she loved. Her heart pounded as Joe moved closer.

Maybe he doesn't recognize me, she thought, wanting to hide her face, run, or burrow into the hay. But, as though paralyzed, she sat staring at him.

Joseph strode methodically to her, hunkered, and looked directly into her eyes.

Rebecca's stomach knotted. Joe had been her friend. Or had he? Panic bubbled into her throat. The threat of shame and humiliation made her blood feel cold. Mesmerized, she could not turn from his sagacious gaze.

Joe's grin broadened.

"*Wass* . . . do you want?" she whispered.

"Martha . . . is it?"

"I . . . *Ja.*"

"Martha what?"

". . . Kauffman."

"*Vell, wie gehts* . . . Martha Kauffman. You look good with your mane flying free." Chuckling, he reached to touch her hair.

"Leave her alone," Aaron said.

Joe stood. "My, my, you're touchy." Propping a hand on his hip, he glanced at Rebecca, then stared at his brother. "My information will shock your shirt buttons and unweave your straw hat."

"Let's hear it."

Gasping, Rebecca leaped to her feet.

Aaron's brows lifted as he jerked his head to look at her. Then, turning to his brother, he narrowed his eyes. "Start talking."

12

Joseph laughed. "You're too anxious, Aaron. I don't think coherently on an empty stomach." He scratched the two-day's stubble on his cheeks. "I can hardly wait for some of Mama's cooking."

"You'll have to. She's in the hospital."

Joseph sobered. "What happened?"

"Pneumonia. Probably over the heartache you've caused her."

Joseph looked dismayed. "I always get blamed."

"Only when you're at fault."

Rubbing the back of his neck, he studied Aaron. "I want to come home."

"For good?"

"*Ja.*"

Aaron eyed his brother's white jeans; then, his focus lingering on the man's yellow flowered shirt, he looked dubious. "You'll have to do considerable changing, *gel*?"

"*Ja.*" He massaged the sides of his face. "But I'm not sure where to begin."

"You can start by giving me the information you were speaking of."

Joseph looked at Rebecca's beseeching face, cleared his throat, then eyed his brother. "I want something to eat, first."

"I'll get you a sandwich."

Rebecca picked the bits of hay from her hair, rolled it into a bun, secured it with the few remaining pins, and replaced her cap.

Aaron frowned. "Sarah's in the house."

"*Ja*! You have a woman in the house and one out here as *vell*?" Joseph's taunting laughter echoed through the barn as he pointed a finger at his brother. "And you accused me of wanting a harem, *gel*?"

"Cut it out!" Aaron scowled, then turned to Rebecca. "Get back to the house." Tension made his tone brusque.

She raced from the barn, but slowed her footsteps as she neared the gate. Nancy rocked erratically in the porch rocker. Sarah stood near her, distress dimming the sparkle in her blue eyes.

Still tingling from Aaron's kisses, it was difficult for Rebecca to meet Sarah's gaze. She tried to smile. "The kittens are cute."

"Did you . . . choose one . . . for little John?"

"The black one with a white bib is my choice." Following the girl's line of vision, she noticed a piece of hay that had stubbornly clung to her lavender skirt.

Sarah's eyes misted. "Where's Aaron?"

"In . . . the barn." Rebecca bent to pull weeds in the flower bed, assuming guilt would show on her face.

Sarah slowly descended the three stairs, then sat on the bottom step. "What . . . detained you?"

Taking a deep breath, Rebecca straightened. "Aaron's wayward brother is out there."

"Joseph?" Sarah whispered.

Nancy leaped from her rocker. "I told you, Sarah! I said I saw Joseph! Can we see him some more?"

"Later, Nancy . . . I hope."

A small twig from a maple tree drifted to the porch. Nancy scampered across the floorboards, snatched the stick and tapped the railing in a sporadic beat. "Joseph's home. Joseph's home," she sang off key.

Sarah frowned. "Anna's been through so much with Joseph. Maybe it's good she isn't here."

"He's hungry, and Aaron promised him a sandwich."

Sarah stood. "I'll fix it."

"Wait! It might be wise if you let Aaron tell you about his brother's return."

Stomping to Sarah's side, Nancy pouted. "I saw him first!"

Sarah hugged the child. "You're a good girl, Nancy." Appearing perplexed, Sarah faced Rebecca. "Aaron doesn't talk much about Joseph. None of us do, but we pray he'll change and come home."

The man's plea echoed in Rebecca's mind. "Maybe he will, if we show him understanding and help him to readjust."

"*Ja.* He's a good man, Martha. He just got mixed up with the wrong crowd." Sighing, she gazed wistfully at the outbuildings.

Aaron stepped from the barn and walked briskly toward the house. He wore an enigmatic expression, but his stride and the stiffness in his body betrayed his agitation. When he glanced at Rebecca, something undefinable flashed across his face. Saying nothing, he entered the house.

"He didn't see Joseph," Nancy whimpered.

Sarah patted the girl's shoulder. "You rock your dolly. We'll talk about Joseph after while."

Obediently, Nancy went to the porch rocker, scooped up her doll, and rocked vigorously.

Moments later, Aaron reappeared carrying something in a small paper bag. "I have to go into Lancaster." Checking his pocket watch, he frowned." John Zook is picking me up, and I don't have time to drive you ladies home."

"Someone will have to watch Nancy. We'll stay until you return." Sarah's eyes flicked to the barn, but quickly returned to Aaron.

His frown deepened. "I'd rather you went home.." He hesitated, then looked dubiously at Sarah. "Do you think you could handle Ransom?"

"*Ja.* We'll take Nancy with us, and you can stop on your way back." She eyed his parcel. "What's that?"

"A paper bag," he said, apparently deciding not to tell Sarah about Joseph's presence. His eyes shifted to Rebecca. "I want to discuss something with you, Martha, and tonight will be as good a time as any."

She smiled, but her stomach cramped. His fingers tightened on the top of the bag; then he strode quickly away. Rebecca stared at his broad back until he vanished into the barn, wondering what all Joseph had told him, and apprehension wrapped her in an icy cocoon. A car came up the lane. The driver slowed the vehicle and rolled down his window, but apparently seeing Aaron step into view, he waved, passed the house, and stopped at the barn.

Aaron got in the passenger side. Instead of speeding out the lane, John stopped the car at the gate. Aaron looked worried. "Be careful, Sarah." He frowned. "Don't dawdle. I want you to leave right away."

She nodded. Rebecca bit her lower lip. Why was he avoiding talking to Sarah about Joseph's possible return? She noticed his frown deepen as the car pulled away. Her apprehension mounted. Was Aaron's disquiet over Sarah's driving Ransom—or over what Joseph had revealed?

When the car engine faded in the distance, Sarah sighed. "Aaron probably doesn't want us here because of Joseph. I'll get our bonnets."

Rebecca looked at Ransom. He stomped restlessly. The beast still had a heart for the race track.

Sarah helped Nancy tie her bonnet and don her shawl. Then she smiled confidently at Rebecca. "Let's go."

They climbed into the buggy, but before Sarah turned Ransom to head out the lane, she looked toward the barn. "*Der gut Man* (God) bless you, Joseph," she whispered, then flipped the reins. Ransom started instantly, jerking the carriage.

When they passed the phone shack, Rebecca thought about her father. "Can we stop to make a phone call?"

"We've been gone all afternoon. Mama will need help with supper." She smiled. "You can drive Ransom back."

Rebecca agreed, not wanting to admit her lack of experience. A great uncle, *Mammi* Mary's brother, was Amish, and she'd driven his buggy. She pondered the few times she'd driven it, and shrugged. She'd had no trouble, so what was her concern? Ransom was just more spirited than her uncle's animal. She studied the way

Sarah controlled this beast. *No problem*, she thought.

In front of the Beiler house, Sarah turned Ransom, handed Rebecca the reins, and got out. "*Kom ann*, Nancy. You can help Esther, too." Taking the girl's hand, she hurried to the porch.

Prancing, Ransom snorted.

I'd be crazy to try this. Her uncle's nag was a stuffed puppy compared to this snorting beast. Reversing her decision, she opened her mouth to call Sarah, but Ransom decided it was time to go and trotted down the lane toward the road.

Gripping the reins, Rebecca drew in her breath. What if this animal decided to run?

By the time the phone shack came into view, beads of perspiration dotted her forehead, and her hands cramped from gripping the reins. Anxious to speak with her father, she guided Ransom to the side of the road and pulled on the reins. "Whoa." She was amazed as well as relieved when the horse obeyed.

Leaving the buggy, she raced across the meadow to the phone shanty. Seizing the receiver, she suddenly realized she had no money with her. She stared at the instrument, feeling as though her heart had dropped six inches and now rested at her waist. Slowly replacing the receiver, she battled tears.

A car horn blasted. Whirling, Rebecca looked out the window. A bright-red sports car careened around the bend. Its engine roared, and the wheels spun, flinging loose gravel at Ransom.

The horse whinnied and reared. The vehicle slid sideways on the gravel, barely missing Ransom's flailing hooves.

The horse's terrified whinny rent the air. Flinging open the shanty door, Rebecca ran toward the animal. Before she reached him, he leaped forward and took off at a run.

"Whoa! Whoa!" Rebecca screamed. Horror-stricken, she watched the horse and buggy vanish around a bend.

The man driving the red car stopped and rolled down his window. A lock of mousy hair flopped onto his forehead, and his pudgy round face twisted into a snarl. "You people should park your carriages off the road."

"I did!"

"Buggies shouldn't be allowed on the road. You nearly caused me to wreck."

Ignoring his ignorance, Rebecca stared down the road. Ransom was gone. How far would he run? Her heart throbbing, she raced after him.

As they neared Lancaster, Aaron looked out the passenger window, wishing he could keep his vehicle at his farm. He glanced at John, thankful for his Beachy Amish friend. The man had a round face, sparkling eyes, and a nose with a bulb that one almost expected to light up when he laughed.

He thought about Sarah's driving Ransom and fought anxiety. Should he have encouraged her to drive? What else could he have done? He hadn't wanted to leave her and Martha at the farm with Joseph in the barn. Was his brother serious about changing?

"Is something bothering you, Aaron?"

"I'm concerned about Sarah Beiler driving Ransom."

"You needn't worry about the Beiler girl. *Gel?*"

"*Ja*, but . . ." He frowned. "It's just this feeling I have."

"Should we go back?"

"Would you mind?"

John grinned. "Where shall we head?"

"Isaac Beiler's place."

Anxiety churned within him, but he fought his gut feeling that something was wrong. When John headed down Beilers' lane, matters became worse.

"I don't see my buggy," Aaron said as the car pulled up in front of the house. Leaping out, he raced to the door.

Esther opened it. "What's happened, Aaron?"

"That's what I'd like to know." He saw Sarah and relaxed. "I guess my anxiety was over nothing. Where's my buggy?"

"Martha took it to the phone shack."

"*Wass!*" Aaron's stomach felt as though he'd swallowed a horseshoe.

Sarah looked worried. "I didn't think you'd mind."

"The buggy wasn't at the phone shack." In spite of his effort to halt his galloping imagination, his anxiety mounted. Racing back to the car, he jumped in.

"Where to?" John asked.

"Martha took my buggy and went to the phone shanty, but she wasn't there when we drove by."

"We'll find her."

Before Rebecca reached the main highway, she heard a car's tires screech, a horse's scream, and the sickening sound of scraping metal and splintering wood. Her heart thudding, she raced on.

Rounding a bend, she halted abruptly and stared. Aaron's buggy was wrecked beyond repair. She stared in horror at the blue car that had careened off the road and crashed against a tree. A woman clutched a crying child, and a man stood beside the vehicle. Seemingly dazed, he stared at the scattered remains of the buggy. Apparently Ransom hadn't stopped at the intersection.

Breathless, Rebecca ran toward them. "Is anyone hurt?"

The woman looked at her. "Is that your buggy?"

"It belongs to a friend."

"There was no one driving!" the man said. "Thank the Lord no one was injured."

A tongue-lashing would have made her feel better than this couple's kind words. Her recompense would come, though, when Aaron caught up with her.

Cars lined both sides of the highway, and people had begun to gather. They curiously looked at the car and examined the wreckage of the buggy.

"Where's Ransom?" Rebecca asked, but no one listened. Was the horse lying somewhere in pain? Was he dead?

A police siren wailed, and a new terror smote her. Now she was responsible for two accidents. *I won't run from this one*, she vowed, fighting the temptation to race across the field. How could she answer the trooper's questions? What if a reporter photographed her? Mattis and his friends would discover where she was hiding. She felt faint.

"Miss, are you all right?" a man asked.

Unable to answer, Rebecca dropped her face into her hands.

"Come and sit by my wife," the man said soothingly." She'll help you."

Sitting on the grass, she looked again at Aaron's ruined buggy. A police siren came closer, then the trooper's car jerked to a stop near the wreckage. Realization washed over Rebecca in huge waves that threatened to capsize her. She blinked as she felt herself sway; then she was sucked downward into darkness.

Aaron gripped the edge of the car seat as he saw the snarled traffic on the highway ahead. Horrified over what might have happened, he prayed earnestly for Martha's safety.

John rolled down his window to speak to another motorist. "What's the problem?"

"An accident. An Amish buggy was demolished."

Leaping from the car, Aaron raced toward the scene. His heart drummed with new anxiety as he wondered how badly Martha had been hurt.

Approaching the scene, he glanced feverishly around, trying to locate her. His eyes flicked over his splintered buggy, but Martha was his concern. Spotting her facedown on the grass, his heart sank. She lay so still.

He pushed his way through the crowd to kneel beside her. "Martha. Martha!"

Slowly propping herself on one elbow, she blinked and peered up.

Finding out she was alive, relief flooded him. "Are you hurt?"

"No."

"*Dank der gut Man.*" Gathering her into his arms, he held her close. "Oh, *Dank der gut Man.*"

"Your . . . buggy," she said into his shirt. "Oh, Aaron."

Releasing her, he stared into her upturned face. "What happened?"

After explaining, she glanced at the approaching trooper, then quickly turned away.

Aaron watched the color ebb from her lovely face. "I'll handle this." He stood to intercept the officer.

"That your carriage?"

"*Ja*. A runaway horse."

"Your name, please."

"Aaron King."

"You have insurance?"

"*Ja*. I just caught up. Was anyone hurt?"

"Not seriously. Where's your horse?"

John hurried toward them. "Aaron, Ransom is grazing about a half-mile down the road. He's fine, but so skittish no one can get near him."

"I'll get him, later, John, *gross Dank*."

The officer kept glancing at Martha. Was he going to blame her for the accident? She kept her head down, her face hidden by her black bonnet. People were taking pictures. Aaron usually didn't mind tourists taking snapshots, but this afternoon, it irked him.

"Hey, girl," a man called, aiming his camera. "Look up."

Facing the officer, Aaron frowned. "Let me get her out of here, sir. I'll be back to answer any more questions."

"I understand your concern for your young lady, Mr. King, but you can't leave the scene, yet."

Aaron sighed.

"I'll take her to Beilers'," John offered.

"*Herzlich Dank*." Aaron helped Martha to her feet.

"Oh, Aaron." She continued to avert her face.

He hugged her. "John's here, and he'll take you home."

"*Viel Dank*," she murmured into his shirt, returning his embrace. Then, her head bowed and her face turned away, she accompanied John. Aaron watched until they got to the car. Opening the door, John urged her inside. Assuming she would be all right, Aaron turned back to the officer.

Questions tumbled through Rebecca's chaotic mind. Had anyone gotten a picture of her before she'd covered her face? Would Aaron tell them she was responsible for the accident? Would the troopers come to Beilers' to question her? What about Aaron? She didn't relish facing him after his shock wore off.

John started the engine, crossed the corner of a hayfield, turned up a dirt road to avoid the snarl of vehicles, and headed for Beilers'. Rebecca knew this was only a temporary reprieve.

I'll call Margie, she thought. "John," she said cautiously, "instead of taking me to Beilers', would you mind driving me into Lancaster?"

He gave her a suspicious side-glance. "I'd like to oblige, but Aaron told me to take you to the Beiler place."

"Aaron King doesn't make decisions for me, *gel*?"

"*Ja*, but this time I feel I must abide by his wishes."

Trying to decide what to do, she slumped against the seat.

John stopped the car at Beilers' gate. "If you need help, let me know."

"*Fer wass*?" Rebecca smiled to soften her sarcasm. "So you can ask Aaron if it's all right? *Gel*?"

He laughed. "Aaron has your best interest at heart."

"*Gross Dank* for bringing me home."

"Glad to."

Holding a fixed smile, she closed the car door and went into the house. The aroma of fried chicken wafted to her. Instead of whipping her appetite, it made her stomach churn.

Sarah glanced up from the pot of potatoes she was mashing. "*Dank der gut Man* you're back. I was worried." She grinned. "I guess Aaron was worried, too."

"*Ja*." Rebecca gripped the back of a kitchen chair.

Sarah's attention returned to her potatoes. "Did I hear a car?"

"John Zook brought me home. Where are Esther and Ruth?"

"Ruth's gathering the eggs, and Mama's visiting Nancy Stoltzfus, Elizabeth's mother-in-law."

Ruth bounded into the kitchen, yanked open the cupboard door, and began counting plates. "Mama's coming," she said breathlessly. "She'll expect the table to be set."

Nancy skipped in on Ruth's tail. Giggling, she clapped her hands. "Hurry, Ruth!"

Sarah studied Rebecca's face. "You look pale."

"I . . . I . . ."

"You're trembling. *Wass's* wrong?"

"Ransom ran away with the buggy while I was at the phone."

"*Ach!*" Sarah's eyes widened. "Did Aaron catch up with him?"

"Not until . . . after an accident."

Sarah's hands flew to her face. "Ransom?"

"He's fine, but the buggy is demolished." Tears spilled over and ran down her face. "Aaron will be furious, when the shock wears off."

Sarah took a deep breath, but her face was pale. "He'll be thankful to *der gut Man* that you're all right."

"I'm not going to be here when he arrives."

"Where will you go?"

"Anywhere is better than having to face him."

Ruth laughed. "I think it'd be fun to watch."

"Ruth Beiler!" Sarah gave her a stern look, then quietly finished mashing the potatoes. She frequently glanced out the window, her eyes misty, apparently watching for Aaron.

The Beiler buggy came up the lane and rumbled toward the carriage shed. Moments later, Esther came in with *Mammi* Hazel and the little boys. "Isaac's coming, girls, and Eli's back."

When everyone was seated around the supper table, Eli looked at Rebecca. "That was some wreck!"

Too upset to eat, Rebecca rolled a small whole beet around her plate with a fork.

Isaac spread butter on a slab of bread. "You helped Aaron gather up the debris, Eli. *Gel?*"

"*Ja.* It was a mess. The *Englischer* who hit the buggy could've been mad."

"He had a right to be," Rebecca said quietly.

Isaac nodded. "They're usually furious, even when the accident is their fault. *Gel?*"

"Now, Isaac," Hazel said. "They just don't understand our ways."

Eli swallowed a mouthful of chicken. "Aaron's the one who's mad! His buggy's done for."

"We're grateful that Martha wasn't injured," Esther said. "Aaron can replace his buggy."

"*Ja*, Mama, but with the waiting list, it could be two years before he gets a new one."

Rebecca felt nauseated. She'd forgotten how long Amish could wait for a new buggy. Aaron had a right to be furious. "Excuse me, please," she said softly, left the table, and hurried upstairs.

Taking off her borrowed lavender dress, she draped it across the bed, put on her own blue one, and seized her paper bag.

"How can I slip away without the family seeing me?" she whispered. Her bonnet and cape were in the kitchen. Glaring at her paper bag, she wondered how to camouflage it, then grinned victoriously.

Opening the window, she shoved the bag through and released her grip. It landed on the grass with a plop. She'd slip outside, collect her bag, hurry to the phone, call Margie, and make arrangements for her *Englischer* cousin to pick her up. Confident, she went downstairs.

"I'm going for a walk," she said, not forgetting to put on her bonnet this time. Her fingers trembled as she gripped the doorknob. Smiling to deploy her deception, she opened the door. Gasping, she leaped back.

"*Un wie Machts*, Martha?" Aaron stood on the threshold, proffering her paper bag. "This just fell from your bedroom window. Is it yours?"

13

"Aaron!" Rebecca blinked in disbelief.

He dropped her paper bag onto the bench beside the door without taking his eyes from hers.

Hoping to appear innocent, she smiled.

"I want to talk with you in private, Martha."

She reached for her bag. "I'll take this upstairs."

He caught her wrist. "Sarah will take care of it."

Rebecca's eyes spanned the Beiler family as she sent out a silent plea for assistance. Isaac and Esther looked at Aaron, Eli stared at his plate, Ruth grinned, and the boys slipped tidbits to Jed.

Pink hue crept across Sarah's cheeks. "I'll take your bag to your room, Martha." She smiled slightly and understanding shimmered in her light-blue eyes.

Pressured to comply, Rebecca stepped onto the porch. Jedidiah scrambled through the open door before it closed.

At the gate, Aaron's dark eyes met Rebecca's, and she considered running. His fingers tightened around her wrist as though he'd perceived her intention.

"Amish don't believe in violence. *Gel*?" she said softly.

"*Ja*, but we're human." Not releasing his grip, he headed toward the barn.

Shackled, she glanced over her shoulder. No one followed. Jedidiah yipped and frolicked around them; but neither paid heed to the canine's invitation to play. As they passed an open shed door, the scent of fresh manure hung heavy in the still moist air. A cow lowed, and a cat watched them expectantly. Under the overhang of the barn, Aaron sat on a wooden bench and tugged on Rebecca's wrist.

"Do you have to handcuff me?"

"Sit." He removed his straw hat, slapped it on the bench near him, and peered at her.

She lowered her gaze to the scattered bits of straw by her feet. Aaron's irritation worried her, but a different emotion took precedence. Denying the feeling became futile. The words, *I love him!* ricocheted through her tormented mind.

"This has been a long day," he said quietly. Hurt as well as vexation shimmered in his dark eyes.

Her thoughts chaotic, she sat beside him. Had Joseph betrayed her? Did Aaron know the truth? His fingers on her arm created havoc with her senses. "Please release me, Aaron."

"You'll run, and I don't feel like chasing you."

"I won't."

His steady gaze held hers. "Promise?"

"*Ja.*"

His fingers relaxed, and he withdrew his hand. Sighing, he leaned forward to prop his elbows on his knees. "I talked to David Wenger this afternoon."

She strangled a gasp. Forcing control, she asked, "Where'd you see him?"

"Zimmerman's store."

The term *charlatan* exploded in her brain as she asked, "Was his daughter with him?"

"No."

"Did you ask about her?"

"*Ja.*"

"Did he explain the situation?"

"No."

Who was interrogating whom? His vague answers made her want to scream, but she forced nonchalance. "Did he say his daughter would be with him the next time?"

"No."

"She's with him often. *Gel*?"

"*Ja* . . . in the past."

Tightening her lips, she looked away. "I hope you had a more interesting conversation with him than you're having with me."

"I did."

Anxiety frothed within her, until she thought she would choke on the bubbles. The setting sun turned the trees on the horizon to a dark uneven line. The deep-crimson color of the sky made it appear as though they were aflame. The young corn stalks in a nearby field took on a reddish hue. Jedidiah stretched out by Rebecca's feet. Thumping his tail, he licked her shoe.

Aaron sighed. "David Wenger's daughter isn't home, yet."

"Maybe she'll go home soon."

His sagacious eyes perused her face. "In private, David calls his daughter Amber."

"You knew that." Removing her black bonnet, she put it on the bench, untied the strings of her prayer cap, and wiped a hand across her moist forehead.

"The police want to question Rebecca." He sounded as though he had a mouthful of mashed potatoes.

She assumed it was because she'd worked in the flower shop, but she had no more information than she'd already given them.

"Tell me the story of your life . . . Martha."

She laughed, but it sounded hollow. "There isn't much to tell."

"I'm listening."

She shrugged. "My mother's name was Anna, the same as your mother's." That much was true, but what else could she tell him that was, without revealing too much?

"Where's your brother?"

"I . . . My father knows I'm with kind Amish folks, but I probably won't be here much longer." In one way or another, she figured that was also true.

"Where will you go?"

"Back to my family, or . . ." She had nearly said, "with my brother," but bit back the untruth.

"Have you written to your parents lately, Amber?"

"I've... talked by phone." She squared her slender shoulders. "Didn't you bring me out here to discuss the buggy accident?"

"*Ja* ... among other things."

"How's Ransom?"

"Skittish, but otherwise all right." Leaning against the side of the barn, he stretched his long legs. "I shouldn't have permitted Sarah to drive Ransom."

"Sarah did fine! What happened was my fault."

"I know."

"I knew Ransom was frisky. I shouldn't have been so anxious to make a phone call."

He eyed her expectantly. "Did you contact the person you wanted to talk to?"

"No." A gray feather from a barn swallow fluttered from a nest and lit in her lap. Picking it up, she studied it, glad to have something to look at besides Aaron's sagacious eyes. "I forgot to take money with me."

He sighed. "All that for nothing."

Squirming, she perched on the edge of the bench. "Having no buggy, how'd you get here?"

"I rode my horse."

"I didn't see him."

"I figured I'd be here for awhile, so I turned him loose in the pasture."

"I'll get a job and pay for your buggy."

"That isn't necessary. Not having one for months is going to be an inconvenience, though."

"You have a right to be furious with me." She met his eyes with bravado, but inside she was tremulous.

"I've uncovered some interesting facts, Amber, and I'm beginning to put a picture together. It'll be easier for the both of us, if you tell me what's going on."

She shrugged. "Concerning what?"

He set his jaw. "Did you recognize Joseph?"

"Is that what he said?"

"Don't hedge." There was an unusual sharpness to his words.

His dark eyes narrowed. "Do you know my brother?"

Rebecca's heart galloped. "You told me about your wild brother, so I assumed Joseph was he."

Aaron's determination mounted. "There's more to it." Instead of answering him, she studied a nearby corn stock. This was getting him nowhere. He felt as though he were putting this lovely young woman in a vice, then slowly tightening the squeeze. What did he hope to gain? *I want to prove she's Martha—not Rebecca*, he thought, his doubt surfacing. Pronouncing his words slowly and distinctly, he asked, "Do you know Joseph?"

"I've . . . seen him."

"Where?"

She waved her hand casually. "Maybe in Lancaster--or Strasburg."

"When?"

"Before I came to the Beilers."

David had protected his daughter, refusing to answer Aaron's questions. Since Mary did not believe in images and prohibited photographs, David could avoid being pressured by the police or the Press to produce one. No picture of Rebecca had appeared in the papers. Aaron felt perplexed. "I want desperately to disprove my assumptions, Martha, but . . ."

"Assumptions are usually incorrect, so it's better to forget them."

"I can't." This girl was frightened of something, and enigma surrounded her story. Feeling protective, he covered her hand with his, and his fingers tightened.

Eli rounded the corner of the barn, prompting Aaron to release Martha's hand quickly. She smiled at Eli and a relieved expression captured her delicate features.

Eli glanced from Aaron to Martha, then his gaze lingered on the straw hat on the bench. He side-stepped and cleared his throat. "I figured you'd had time to discuss what was on your mind."

Snatching his hat from the bench, Aaron rammed it onto his head. "I've had enough time to generate more questions." When would he get the next chance to corner Martha? He wished he could decide whether or not his imagination had run amuck.

Rebecca fought a frown. Aaron's interrogation had probably just begun. She pictured how Joseph had grinned at her in the barn after he'd witnessed Aaron kissing her. Could God be using Joseph to pressure her to confess her identity? *No! God doesn't play games.*

A shadow moved at the corner of the barn. She looked up. "Sarah!" Grasping her black bonnet, Rebecca got up and joined her.

"Has Aaron been difficult, Martha?"

"I feel like I've been fed through a meat grinder."

Sarah laughed. "You don't look like hamburger." Her eyes moved to Aaron, and she sobered. "He does, though."

As they strolled out of earshot, Rebecca said, "He's worried about Joseph." Aaron wasn't the only one who was worried. She must solve this crisis. *Or run*, she thought. Aaron was on the verge of discovery. Loving him made the threat of exposure more alarming.

She strolled to the house with Sarah, but Eli remained at the barn. Aaron was probably comparing notes with him, hoping to uncover more facts concerning her. Her heartbeat quickened. Had Joseph returned home because he'd discovered the mysterious powder that had been hidden in the vases? She shuddered. What if he were the guilty party? Could the police be after him? She bit her lip.

Sarah touched her arm. "Are you all right?"

"I'm ... tired." She smiled to cover her anxiety. The Beiler farm had turned from a sanctuary into a trap. *I must leave before it's too late.*

For the next two days, Rebecca watched for a chance to leave, but it seemed as though someone was monitoring her movements. Were the Beilers becoming suspicious? What had Aaron told Eli? Even Sarah seemed to look at her with questions in her blue eyes.

While they prepared dinner, Rebecca studied Sarah. The girl had not been laughing much the past two days.

Has she discovered Aaron kissed me? An image of Joseph formed in Rebecca's mind. She shivered. If he had revealed her secret, wouldn't Aaron be here to further torment her with questions? *Or condemnation!*

Isaac and Eli came in and took their places at the table.

"After dinner, Eli and I are going to Kings' to help Aaron build a new chicken coop," Isaac said.

Esther looked pensive. "I should go to help in the kitchen, *gel*?"

"Anna's sister came with her three daughters, so they can handle the kitchen work. We'll not stay for supper."

Esther nodded. "I'll make sandwiches and send them with you."

Sarah looked at her father with beseeching eyes. "I'll make lemonade. I'd love to go with you. I haven't seen Aunt Nan or the girls for ages. Besides, extra help is always appreciated."

Eli laughed. "I don't suppose Aaron King has anything to do with your generosity."

Sarah tried to look indignant. "I'll be in the house with the ladies."

"*Ja*." He held his grin. "Until time to serve your lemonade. *Gel*?"

"Behave, Brother." She turned away as her cheeks colored.

Not wishing to be in Aaron's presence, or to be confronted by Joseph, Rebecca wrestled to conjure an excuse not to accompany Sarah. However, when an invitation wasn't forthcoming, disappointment tangled her emotions like wild grapevines.

The men headed for the barn to harness the horse, while Esther and Sarah bustled around the kitchen, making sandwiches. The little boys romped in the yard with Jed, and Rebecca helped Ruth with the dishes.

When Esther left the room, Ruth stepped close to Sarah and gave her a playful poke. "Don't forget to sneak your lipstick."

"Ruth." Sarah appeared abashed, but her cheeks colored.

The younger girl's eyes twinkled. "I saw you with it, just yesterday."

Sarah tightened her lips. "I wouldn't sneak."

"*Ja* you would." Ruth giggled. "I found the lipstick in your top dresser drawer."

Sarah gasped, then lowered her lashes. "It's only a light pink shade."

"*Ja.* I tried it."

Sarah's eyes widened. "Ruth!"

"I found your tiny mirror, too." The younger girl laughed. "Don't let *Mammi* catch you. She'll accuse you of being a hussy. *Gel?*"

"Ruth Beiler!" The pink hue on Sarah's cheeks deepened and cruised across her lovely face. "You shouldn't root through my dresser."

"I won't tell on you, Sarah." Gold specks danced in Ruth's eyes. "If you blot it, *Mammi* might not notice."

"You're a naughty girl, Ruth."

"*Ja?*" Her rosy cheeks dimpled. "You, too, *gel?*"

Isaac halted the carriage by the gate. Eli jumped to the ground, rushed into the kitchen, and seized the jug of lemonade with his good hand.

Ruth stared at him. "*Wass* help can you be with your right arm still in a cast?"

He grinned. "I can do as much with one arm as some men do with two. *Gel?*"

"*Ja!*" She giggled. "You do a lot with your tongue, too."

Picking up the basket of sandwiches, Sarah headed for the door. "I'll be home in time to help with supper, Mama."

"Don't worry about that. I have Martha and Ruth."

Sarah looked at Rebecca and smiled. There was a sparkle in her blue eyes that had been absent of late. The tinge of deeper pink on her lips revealed a trip to her dresser. Her cheeks were flushed as she followed her brother outside.

Rebecca stood on the porch watching the buggy until it vanished around the bend. She felt deserted. The thought of Sarah's being alone with Aaron was disturbing. "Sarah will make him a good wife," she whispered. "They belong together."

A cold hand of isolation smote her. She didn't belong here. "Where's my Eden, now?" she murmured, realizing it was farther away then ever. Would she ever find it?

Lifting her head, she gazed at the blue sky. Esther, Ruth, and the little boys were the only ones here. This presented an opportunity to leave. Intending to collect her belongings, she turned toward the door.

Esther pushed open the screen and smiled. "I left a hammer hooked over the last manger toward the back of the barn. Will you get it for me, please?"

"*Ja.*" *Detained*, Rebecca thought, *not thwarted.*

As she crossed the barnyard, she planned her departure. Margie was probably frantic to learn what had happened. "When I phone her, she'll be after me in a flash," Rebecca said.

Entering the barn, she made her way toward the back. She glanced at a fresh pile of hay beside her, thought about her tumble with Aaron, and her hand went to her mouth. Pausing, she relived his kisses. Chaotic emotion rampaged through her, and her lips felt warm beneath her fingertips. She quickly made her way to the back of the barn. Aaron would never kiss her again. He wouldn't know where she'd gone.

Retrieving the hammer, she turned to go, but a man descended the shadowy back stairs and blocked her path. She froze, and her skin prickled. "Joseph!"

"I want to talk with you, Rebecca."

"Don't call me that!" Her heart continued to race. "Have you revealed my identity to Aaron?"

"No."

"*Wass* are you waiting for?" Remembering his love for flashy outfits, she perused his broadfalls, single suspender, and dark-blue shirt. "What happened to your pretty clothes, Mr. Joe Dinger?"

He flinched. "Becky, I mean Martha, I used a different name."

"*Fer wass?*"

"To get a job, I had to apply for a social security number. Since Amish don't believe in it, I didn't want to use my own name."

"Using a fake name on a document is illegal. *Gel?*"

"*Ja*, but . . ." He looked pensive. "I was serious when I told Aaron I wanted to come home." He smiled. "I was surprised to find you."

She ran her hand along a manger, smoothed from an animal's teeth. "I shouldn't have fled from the scene of an accident."

"The scrape wasn't much, and I figured you were scared."

"I was. . . . but there was more to it." She studied his sober face and wondered if he knew about the vases. She decided to find out. "How deeply were you involved in the illegal operation?"

"Operation?"

"*Ja*. I can't believe it was only packets of flower freshener that were hidden in the false-bottomed vases."

Looking blank, he scratched his head. "*Wass* vases?"

"The milk glass ones we used for some of the arrangements."

"False . . . bottoms," Joseph mumbled, rubbing his chin in thought. "Right after you vanished, so did the shelf of milk glass vases. They were replaced the next day with crystal ones."

She shivered. "Do you think those packets could have held an illegal drug?"

"It's possible—I guess."

"Who do you think might be responsible?"

"I have no idea." He hesitated. "Vance seemed like a great guy."

"Gene and Doug were friendly, too. Did either of them look like a crook to you?"

Joseph laughed.

"This isn't funny!"

"*Ja*. I know, Rebec--Martha, but a crook doesn't often look like one."

"How can we find out who's responsible?"

He leaned against a manger. "I don't want any part of it."

"I sent one of the packets to the police station."

Joseph's eyes widened.

"Were you hunting me the day I ran?"

"*Ja*. After I made my deliveries, I decided to meet you in Strasburg and ask you to join me for pizza."

Rebecca studied his worried expression. "I've listened to news reports, but I haven't heard anything." She explained the broken vase and Greg Mattis's phone call.

He listened intently, then shrugged. "Mattis could've been

talking about something that had nothing to do with you."

"Maybe, but I'm scared."

"*Ja, vell*, if there was something illegal going on, the evidence was removed before the police could investigate."

She suffocated a groan. "Will you help me get away from here?"

"*Fer wass*?"

"If I stay, Aaron is bound to discover my deceit. I couldn't bear it."

He pursed his lips as he thought. "If you want to remain hidden from Mattis awhile, and I can understand why you'd want to, your pretending to be Amish is perfect." He grinned. "When I saw you in the hay with Aaron, I could tell you were in love with him."

"Aaron deserves someone better than me. Besides, I can't hurt Sarah, and she's in love with him."

Joseph sobered.

Rebecca watched him. "What'd you tell Aaron about me?"

"Nothing."

"But, that day in the barn, you said you had interesting information for him, then you looked at me."

"I said that to frighten you, so you'd be quiet until I could speak with you. I'd hoped we could strike a bargain."

"Bargain?"

"I don't want my family to know what all I did when I was living like an *Englischer*."

"You didn't do much that they would disapprove of."

"*Ja, vell*." He shrugged. "If you don't tell Aaron you know me, I won't squeal on you."

"He suspects we know each other. He asked me about it."

Joe paled. "When?"

"The night Ransom ran away and wrecked the buggy."

"What'd you tell him?"

"That I'd seen you somewhere, probably in Lancaster. Joe, please help me get away." She pictured Margie. "Drive me to Terre Hill."

"I can't. When I decided to come home to stay, Bec—Martha, I sold my car. In order to prove my sincerity, I showed Aaron my driver's license; then I destroyed it in front of him." He grinned. "Maybe Aaron'll help you. He's strict--in most cases, but he secretly owns a car."

"I know, although I haven't told anyone."

He chuckled. "It surprises me how you fooled the Beilers—as well as Aaron. You being an *Englischer*, how'd you do it?"

"I was Mennonite; now I'm . . . ashamed. I've been deceitful."

"I'm guilty of that, too." He sighed. "From now on, it's going to be different for me."

She fumbled with the hammer. "How are you going to explain your disobedience?"

"Most of it isn't necessary. They just consider it my *Rumspringa*. The Bishop understands. I've been forgiven, and I'll be joining the church in a few months."

"*Dank der gut Man.*"

Reaching out, he grasped her hand. "Please stay. If I don't tell Aaron about you, he probably won't find out."

"I should go to talk with the police."

"*Ja, vell*, there's time for that—later." He rubbed his chin. He seemed to be remembering something and a deep furrow ridged his brow. Slowly, worry captured his features.

Alarm wriggled within Rebecca, and she gripped his sleeve. "What is it, Joe?"

14

"I wonder. . ." Joseph ran his fingers through his dark hair which was still too short for Amish custom.

Rebecca yanked on his arm. "Wonder what?"

"Right after you took off, Vance offered to set me up in a candy and gift shop. I was tempted, but I'd already decided to come home."

"Then, Vance must be all right." She turned to pet the velvety neck of the horse in the nearest stall.

"*Ja, vell . . .*"

She jerked her head to face him. "You think otherwise?"

"Martha!" Esther called.

She gasped. "I have to go." Whirling, she ran to the house.

Esther waited on the porch. "Did you have trouble finding the hammer?"

Trying to appear collected, Rebecca smiled. "I got sidetracked. *Ich hab es net tue welle* (I didn't mean to do that)."

"*Gross Dank*, dear." Taking the tool, Esther vanished into the house.

Turning, Rebecca watched Joseph jog across the field toward Kings' farm and disappear behind a row of bushes. Her mind whirled. Should she run? Would it be wiser to stay, maintain her disguise, and pray to escape detection? Until she could decide, she must keep busy. Getting a hoe, she went to the garden and began chopping weeds around the cabbage plants.

When Sarah came home, her cheeks were rosy, and her eyes sparkled. She almost floated around the kitchen. "You should see

Aaron's new chicken coop, Mama!"

Ruth peered curiously at her. "There's nothing about a stupid chicken house to excite anyone, even when it's full of cackling hens. *Gel?*"

"Don't be silly, Ruth." Sarah set an extra place at the table, then put the knives at the wrong side of the plates.

Rebecca watched silently. Ruth giggled.

Esther glanced at her youngest daughter. "Ruth, you can fetch *Mammi.*"

"*Ja*, Mama." She skipped across the room and vanished through the doorway into the *Dawdy Haus.*

Esther sawed slices from a huge loaf of bread. "You can fill the water glasses, Sarah."

Going to the refrigerator, Sarah retrieved a pitcher of milk and began to pour it into the glasses.

Mammi Hazel entered the room, stared at Sarah, and her gray brows rose sharply. "Sarah! *Wass's* got you so befuddled?"

"*Ach!*" Sarah glanced at the milk pitcher in her hand, then stared in disbelief at the table.

Ruth laughed. "You'd better get your mind off of Aaron King."

A pink hue crept across Sarah's face as she emptied the glasses back into the pitcher.

"My, my," Hazel clucked. She accepted Rebecca's help until she was seated at the table.

Picking up a masher, Esther plunged it into the pot of potatoes. "There's a lot of hoeing to do. Tomorrow morning, we'll get an early start."

The men washed and came in for supper. After silent grace, Eli grabbed for the plate of bread.

Isaac looked at Esther. "Joseph's home."

"*Ach.* It's a good thing Anna's still in the hospital." Esther looked abashed. "I shouldn't have said such a thing."

"You'd be right, Mama," Eli said, swallowing a bite of pork chop, "but Joseph's changed. He's sorry he left, and he's going to join the church."

"*Dank der gut Man.*"

Hazel eyed her oldest grandson and her thin lips twitched. "Maybe you can join at the same time. *Gel?*"

He shrugged.

"Joseph worked hard this afternoon, Mama," Sarah said. "He wasn't there when we arrived. While I was serving the lemonade, I noticed Aaron staring across the hay field. I glanced up to see Joseph jogging toward us." Gripping her fork, she pushed a sliver of pork fat to the back of her plate. "He's wearing Amish clothes. He says he's sorry for leaving."

"You spoke with him?" Esther asked.

"*Ja*, but . . . he was so busy." Pushing her plate away, she got up. "I'll serve the pie, Mama."

Ruth dimpled. "You still remember what a pie is?"

"Ruth," Esther reprimanded softly.

The younger girl refrained from further comment, but mischief danced in her dark eyes.

"The sooner Sarah marries Aaron and settles in her own house, the better," Eli muttered, reaching for another slice of bread. His eyes met Rebecca's. "It would be better for everyone. *Gel?*"

"*Ja.*" She lowered her gaze. The thought was painful.

Somehow, Rebecca managed to get through another Sunday, but she continued to thank God it was an off week. By next meeting Sunday, she planned to be elsewhere.

Monday morning was taken up with doing the wash. The rest of the day, Rebecca had helped with the hoeing. She moaned as she lowered herself into a tub of warm water. Her back pained, her arms ached, and every muscle in her body wailed in sympathetic misery. Tomorrow, they would hoe tobacco.

Finishing her bath, she climbed the stairs, staggered to her room, and crumpled onto her bed.

"Martha," Sarah said. "May I listen to your radio for awhile?"

"*Ja.* You spent all morning helping with laundry and hoeing, then watched Nancy all afternoon. Where do you get your energy?"

Sarah laughed softly. "Lately, happiness has given me wings."

Rebecca figured the girl must have spent considerable time with Aaron. She proffered the radio. "Did you talk much with Aaron's brother today?"

"Jesse?"

"Joseph."

"*Ja.*" Sarah clicked the radio on and tuned it in.

"What was he like before he . . . went away?"

"He was one of the nicest boys in our *Younga*. He was handsome." She chuckled. "He still is, but his hair is too short." She thought a moment. "He smiled more before he left, though."

"Why'd he take off?"

Sarah sighed. "The Bishop discovered Joseph had a car, and some of the older men pressured him to join the church, although they called it encouragement. Joseph was restless, and before I knew it, he was gone."

"*Vell*, he's back, now."

"*Ja*, but he seems worried about something." She turned our her stomach and propped herself on an elbow. "He used to talk to me about what bothered him."

"Were you close?"

"I . . . suppose so."

"*Wass* about Aaron?" Rebecca cringed as she waited for Sarah's answer. "Were you seeing him, before Joseph left?"

"No. I'm six years younger than Aaron. That used to seem like a lot. Joseph's two years older than I am."

Rebecca couldn't help prying. "Then, there was something between you and Joseph?"

Sarah paused, then said, "I haven't talked about him to anyone, since he went away. But, telling you my secret seems easy and right. Joseph used to come to call on me. It hurt when he left." She flopped onto her back. "Aaron has been wonderful. He helped me get my thinking straight."

"Are you saying six years doesn't seem like such a difference, now that you're older?"

"*Ja*. Aaron's a good man. He has a lot of responsibility, and he handles it well." Lifting her head, she looked at Rebecca. "A woman can be sure of a man like Aaron. *Gel?*"

"*Ja.*" Rebecca withdrew into silence. Sarah trusted her. Her emotions threatened to run amuck as she relived Aaron's kisses. They had betrayed Sarah, and it made her feel rotten.

As faint notes of a melancholy tune drifted across the room, remorse spread through her. She hadn't only betrayed Sarah, she'd lied to Aaron. Love for him made her miserable.

I'm not worth a man like Aaron, she mused. Overwhelmed, she began to cry.

Sarah turned the radio off. "Martha?"

Rebecca choked back a sob, unable to speak.

Getting up, Sarah crossed the room and knelt on the braided rug beside Rebecca's bed. Moonlight streamed into the room, bathing the girl in its soft glow. Her blond hair fell around her face, forming a halo.

Rebecca stared, recalling her dream. Sarah looked like the dream's messenger of Truth. It was too much, and her body jerked with a new flood of sobs.

"*Wass's* wrong, Martha?"

"I'm not worth your friendship. I don't deserve the kindness your family gives me."

"Don't be silly. We love you. We're so happy to have you staying with us."

"I'm not just staying." She gasped, hesitated, then blurted, "I'm hiding."

"Hiding from what, Martha?"

"My name isn't Martha. I've been deceitful, and I can't stand it any longer."

Sarah handed her a handkerchief. "We'll work this out."

Rebecca blew her nose and sat up. The night wore on as she unburdened her heavy heart, confessing everything — except her love for Aaron. Sarah was so sweet and sympathetic, it made Rebecca feel worse about betraying her with Aaron. "Oh, Sarah, I'm so lost and alone."

"You're not alone. I'm here, and your secret is safe with me. Besides, what you did isn't really that bad." She smiled. "I'll continue to call you Martha."

"What am I going to do? There's no way to excuse my action, unless Joseph—" She clamped a hand over her mouth.

"Joseph?" The color drained from Sarah's face until her complexion resembled mother-of-pearl in the moonlight.

"*Es speit mich* that I said that." Dropping her face into her hands, she moaned. "I promised him I wouldn't tell anyone that we knew each other."

"Please, tell me everything."

Rebecca took a deep breath and told her sordid tale, except for the mysterious packets.

Sarah listened intently. "Sunday night at the sing, some of the young people were talking about Rebecca Wenger."

"I wish I'd never left home."

Sarah smiled. "Then, we never would've met you."

"I have to leave."

"*Ach*, haven't you learned by now that you can't continue to run away from trouble?"

"Once your family discovers I'm a fraud, I won't be able to face them."

Sarah patted Rebecca's hand. "They don't need to know. You've confessed to me, and I know *der gut Man* has forgiven you for your mistakes. Let's just go on from here." She studied Rebecca. "You seem a bit different, but—you are Amish, aren't you?"

"Mennonite." She gripped Sarah's hand. "I don't deserve your understanding or the love your family shows me."

Sarah smiled. "None of us deserves the love that's showered on us, not only by our families, but by *der gut Man*." She looked pleadingly at Rebecca. "Please promise you won't leave."

"*Ja*," Rebecca whispered, confused over what she should do.

Sarah hugged her. "You relax and get some sleep. Tomorrow, we have to attack the tobacco field." Handing over the radio, she went to bed. "*Gute Nacht*."

Rebecca sighed. "*Schlof gut* (Sleep good)."

Rebecca woke as the first rays of dawn cast a soft glow in the room. *I really should leave*, she thought.

The clock-alarm sounded. Both girls got up. Sarah chose a worn blue dress for working in the garden. Rebecca donned a faded light-green one that had belonged to Elizabeth and followed Sarah downstairs.

After breakfast she looked at Esther. "I'll do the dishes. You and the girls can go on to the tobacco field."

Esther smiled. "You're an angel, Martha."

Rebecca lowered her eyes.

When the kitchen was sparkling, instead of going to hoe tobacco, Rebecca went upstairs. Donning the medium-blue Amish dress she'd made, she packed her belongings into the paper bag, tucked it under her arm, and went downstairs. After making sure Hazel was napping, she left the house.

Part way out the lane, she stopped to look back. No one was in sight. With a heavy heart, she turned away.

When she was nearly to the highway, she heard a buggy. If she had left only a couple of minutes earlier, she could have been inside the phone shack, out of sight. She turned her head to hide her face from the occupants of the carriage, but alarm wriggled on her insides.

Aaron whistled softly as the buggy he was driving rumbled along the highway. Noticing Martha walking out a side road with a paper bag under her arm, he sighed. Had Sarah been right about her possibly leaving? Turning right, he slowed, then stopped near her. "Where are you going?"

Her head jerked toward him. Surprise flashed across her lovely face, then she masked her expression. "For a walk."

"With your bag?"

"*Ja.*"

He frowned. "You've walked far enough. Get in."

"*Viel Dank*, but I prefer to walk." Maintaining a plastic smile, she headed on down the road.

"*Kom* back here."

She increased her pace.

"Martha?"

She refused to look back.

He felt exasperated. "Martha! Wait!"

She paused, but kept her back to him.

"Please, get in the buggy."

She shook her head.

He sighed. "If you don't get into this buggy, I'm coming after you." He kept his tone soft, but commanding.

As though having no other choice, she retraced her steps and climbed to the seat beside him. She met his gaze, then turned away.

"Yesterday, Sarah told me you were upset about something. She was afraid you'd leave unexpectedly. That's what you were doing. *Gel*?"

"*Ja*," she said softly.

He grasped her hand. "Are you meeting someone?"

"No."

Her sweetness, as well as the mystery surrounding her, lured him, and he battled the desire to take her in his arms. "You can't just take off with no place to go."

"You assume I have no destination?"

"Tell me where you want to go, and I'll drive you." Her silence and the set of her soft lips spoke louder than her words. Renewing his determination to make sure she stayed, he released her fingers, and clicked to his horse. "I'll take you back to Beilers'."

"Wait."

"For *wass*?"

"I've put the Beilers' out enough."

"Nonsense. You've been doing your share of the work." He eyed her. "Is there another reason why you'd leave?"

She looked cornered, then erased the concern from her features. "You're fortunate to have another buggy so soon."

"This was ordered a long time ago. It's supposed to be Jesse's."

"Now that Joseph's back, won't he need one, too?"

"Jesse's gracious. He's offered the use of this buggy to both Joseph and me." He frowned. "What do you plan to do, Martha?"

Remaining silent, she blinked innocently.

"*Wass* you're planning to do is unfair to Sarah and her family."

"It's because of them that I should go!"

"That's ridiculous. They trust you." He sighed. "I did, too." He took her hand. The warmth of her fingers played havoc with his senses, and he fought his yearning to embrace her. "Please promise you won't leave without talking it over with me."

"All right," she murmured. "Were you coming to Beilers' to see Sarah?"

"No. I was on my way to Bird-in-Hand." He stopped the buggy by the gate. "I'll be back later this afternoon to help Isaac."

"Will you stay for supper?"

"*Ja*." He gently squeezed her fingers. "I'll see you then."

Rebecca got out of the carriage and went to the porch. At the kitchen door, she looked back. Aaron smiled, waved, and headed out the lane. With slow steps, she went to her room and shoved the paper bag under her bed. Gradually, peace encompassed her, and she felt the closeness of God. Had Aaron's foiling her plan to leave been God's way of blessing her?

Stripping off her clean dress, she re-donned the faded light-green one she'd borrowed to hoe in yesterday. Retrieving the dark-blue man's work handkerchief Esther had lent her, she put it on her head and knotted it at her nape a'la pirate style, the way Amish women did when they worked outdoors.

Taking a deep breath, she went to the tool shed to select a hoe. As she headed for the tobacco field, apprehension crept over her until the hair on her neck prickled. Feeling eyes on her back, she paused and turned to look down the lane. The sun struck her face, but she made out the form of a man who stepped into the shade of a maple tree fifty yards away.

She gasped. *Vance*!

15

Whirling, Rebecca ran to the tobacco field, disregarding the stones that bruised her bare feet. "Sarah!"

"*Ja?*" Sarah glanced quizzically at her.

Rebecca motioned over her shoulder. "I think that man's my ex-employer!"

Sarah squinted to look in the direction of Rebecca's nod. "I'll see what he wants." Dropping her hoe between the plants, she hurried to intercept the man.

Hoeing furiously, Rebecca kept her back to him, but she couldn't help peering over her shoulder. Sarah stood where the man would have to turn his back to Rebecca. Since his mannerisms were different from Vance's, her anxiety diminished.

When he strode quickly down the lane, Sarah returned to the row of tobacco she'd been hoeing. "That was an *Englischer*. His car stopped out on Harvest Drive. He was hoping we had a phone. I gave him directions to the nearest *Englischer*'s house." Retrieving her hoe, she bent to work.

Drawing a deep breath, Rebecca released it slowly. As the morning progressed, she began to enjoy cultivating the tobacco. Then, questions surrounding the strange packets invaded her mind. Gritting her teeth, she hacked off a weed.

"Tomorrow's meeting Sunday," Esther said as she shoved an apple pie into the oven.

Rebecca's dread mounted. How could time pass so quickly?

Sarah crimped the edge of another pie. "Meeting is at the

Jonah Stoltzfus farm."

Ruth pinched a dead leaf from a vine in the window box. "Anna King is home from the hospital, but is she well enough to attend service?"

"No," Sarah said. "I told Aaron I'd stay with her."

Rebecca brightened. "I'd be glad to stay with Anna."

"*Viel Dank*, Martha." Sarah smiled at Rebecca, and understanding passed between them. "Joseph said he'd come for me early, but he won't mind if you go in my place."

Sunday dawned bright. Rebecca's heart sang as joyously as the birds. Alone, she slid open the dresser drawer Sarah had given her and grappled for a hidden sheet of paper. She'd written three names, Vance, Gene, and Doug. Under each, she had two columns. She'd listed the reasons why they might be involved in selling drugs and the reasons why they might not be. Intending to show the paper to Joseph, she shoved it inside the small beige purse Sarah had given her.

She moved to the wall where the clothing hung on pegs, touched her new peach dress, and smiled. For a long time, she'd wanted a garment of that color, but *Mammi* Mary had forbidden it. Last week, Sarah had returned from town with a gift for Rebecca. She'd been thrilled to discover it was peach material. Since Amish in this district were permitted to use pastels, she'd begun the dress immediately. Taking the garment from its hanger, she donned it and tediously fastened the straight pins.

"At least as a Mennonite I had buttons," she murmured, wondering why Mary had permitted them. When she got home, she would sew on buttons. *Mammi Mary won't let me wear peach*, she thought. Sighing, she went downstairs to wait for Joseph.

Sarah set a small pitcher of cream on a tray laden with breakfast. "*Mammi* never misses meeting, and her energy is limited. I like to serve her breakfast in bed on meeting Sundays." Smiling, she headed for the *Dawdy Haus*.

A twinge of remorse pinched Rebecca's heart. Why hadn't she ever thought of serving *Mammi* Mary breakfast in bed? *I will*, she vowed.

Shortly after breakfast, a horse snorted near the front gate. Ruth ran to a window. "Kings' buggy," she announced.

Rebecca tied her new navy bonnet. Going outside, she hurried to the carriage and climbed in. Clutching her purse and picturing the notes inside it, she took a deep breath and faced Joseph. Her eyes widened. "Aaron!"

"*Un wie Machts* (And how are things)? Amber." His dark eyes sparkled as they appraised her.

"I came in Sarah's place, so she could attend meeting."

"I appreciate your willingness to sacrifice." He grinned as though he knew she was delighted to escape attending service.

Not amused, she stared at the beige purse in her lap, wondering when she would get a chance to talk with Joseph. She should've known the driver would be Aaron. After all, he'd been expecting to pick up Sarah.

Aaron watched her. "Eli is going to Lapps' for Liz, so I'll come by tonight to pick you and Sarah up for *Younga*."

Her heart lurched, but she camouflaged her alarm with a smile. "Will your brothers be accompanying you?"

"*Ja*."

She glanced sideways, noting how intently he studied her. Not squirming took a monumental effort. He took her hand. His warm fingers curled around hers, creating rivulets of pleasure within her. She'd vowed not to betray Sarah, but after only minutes with Aaron, it was happening, again. Blinking back tears, she gently pulled her fingers free.

"Are you promised, Martha?"

Her eyes flashed to his face. "*Wass*?"

"Do you have a gentleman in Mercer county who's waiting for you?"

"No."

Taking her hand, he held it firmly. "If you had a problem, Amber, would you confide in me?"

She laughed nervously. "Why would I have a problem?"

He shrugged. "Confiding is difficult for some." He looked at her with serious eyes. "Joseph got into trouble."

She gasped. Had Aaron's brother betrayed her? "Has he explained . . . what he did after he left home?"

Aaron frowned. "Some, but Joseph doesn't talk much about what he did."

"Does he have to describe his sins? Can't he just be sorry for them?"

"I don't know."

"When Jesus forgives us, why should we have to broadcast our faults to the world?"

Aaron chuckled. "I guess what matters most is that we're honest."

The word "honest" ricocheted through Rebecca like a savagely walloped racket ball.

Aaron swung the buggy into Kings' lane. "We'll return from service as soon as possible, Amber."

"You don't need to rush your meal. I'll get dinner for Anna."

"Whoa," he said, stopping the buggy in front of his home. "Mother thinks you're an angel." His eyes teased her. "Is she right?"

"Martha!" Nancy bounced on the porch. "*Kom* and see what Joseph got for me!"

Rebecca tugged her hand free from Aaron's fingers, thankful to have an excuse to disregard his question. Stepping from the buggy, she hurried to Nancy and accepted a wiggling brown ball of fur. "He's darling, Nancy."

"His name's Martha."

Rebecca laughed.

"He's a German Shepherd," Aaron said close to her ear.

Unaware that he'd followed her, she jolted, nearly dropping the wiggling canine.

Aaron jumped forward. His arms encircled Rebecca from behind to catch the puppy before it left her hands. His warm fingers cradled hers, making a sanctuary for the animal.

Rebecca tilted her head back, met Aaron's lustrous eyes, became flustered, and tore her gaze from his. "He's a darling kitty, Nancy."

The girl's eyes grew large. "Kitty?"

Aaron laughed.

Handing the puppy to Nancy, Rebecca hurried into the house to see Anna. Aaron's warm chuckle followed her.

Rebecca stood in the center of the bedroom she shared with Sarah, staring at the paper in her hand. The evening sun streamed through the window, reminding her that it was nearly time to leave for young people's Sunday night sing. Her heart fluttered, and her hands began to tremble until the paper in her fingers vibrated.

"*Kom ann*, Martha!" Sarah called up the stairway. Kings are here to drive us to *Younga*."

Quelling a shudder, Rebecca pinned the list to the inside hem of her peach dress and made her way to the buggy.

"You can sit in front, Martha," Sarah said, getting into the back with Joseph and Jesse.

Bewildered, Rebecca complied. As she straightened her skirt, the piece of paper she'd pinned to the inside of her hem crinkled. She watched Aaron from the corner of her eye, wondering if he'd heard it. He sat stiffly holding the reins and staring ahead. She glanced at her hem to make sure the pin hadn't puckered the material, thus giving away the hiding place for her notes. Would she get the chance to pass Joseph the paper?

Aaron glanced at her with questioning eyes.

"Is something wrong?" she asked.

"You tell me."

She shrugged, fighting to calm her rattled nerves. "How far is it to the Jonah Stoltzfus' farm?"

"Another fifteen minutes." He glanced over his shoulder at Sarah and frowned.

The closer they got to their destination, the more jangled Rebecca's nerves became. When Aaron stopped the buggy near the barn, she got out, discovering that her legs would hardly support her. Apprehension spit sparks within her that threatened to ignite panic.

"*Kom ann*, Martha," Sarah said, taking her hand. "I'll introduce you to my friends."

Worried, Rebecca glanced at her.

"Trust me," Sarah whispered.

Rounding the corncrib, they stopped at the large open barn door. Lanterns, placed in various places, created spheres of soft golden light. Benches lined the perimeter, leaving the barn floor clear. Two young men strummed guitars in one corner. Having seen the tallest one in Lancaster on a number of occasions, Rebecca peered at his round, boyish face and stifled a gasp.

"You know one of them?" Sarah whispered.

"I've seen the dark-haired one in town. He's probably seen me, too." She swallowed. "Oh, why'd I come?"

"That's Christopher Lapp's second son, Peter John. The short brown-haired one is Andrew, Peter John's older brother." She squeezed Rebecca's hand. "If Peter John seems to recognize you, I'll handle it."

Struggling with doubt, Rebecca moved to a shadowed area and took a seat on one of the benches. Aaron followed her, but sat on the other end of the bench. Rebecca bit her lip. If any of the boys said anything, he could easily overhear.

Sarah approached with a pretty, dark-haired girl. "Martha, I'd like you to meet Elizabeth Lapp."

Rebecca stood.

Liz's green eyes sparkled. "Sarah's told me so much about you."

"She's spoken well of you, Liz, and so has Eli."

The girl's smile broadened, and the few freckles on the bridge of her small nose seemed to dance.

Peter John Lapp joined them, his round face wearing a quizzical expression as his green eyes assessed Rebecca. "Haven't I seen you somewhere?"

Rebecca forced a smile. "Probably. I've been here for two weeks."

He shook his head, making his straight dark hair sway. "I think I saw you before that."

Aaron moved slightly closer and tipped his head as though he were straining not to miss a word.

"Martha has relatives in the area, Peter John," Sarah said. "You could've seen one of them."

He furrowed his brow. "The girl I saw several times wore *Englischer's* clothes and let her long hair whip in the breeze."

Rebecca laughed, willing her nerves to remain calm. "Then why would you think it had been me?"

Peter John chewed his lower lip. "She sure looks a lot like you."

"I've heard that before, Peter." She laughed softly, then jolted when she saw Aaron's scowl. "I think I'll get some fresh air." Trying not to run, she went outside. Cloaked in moonlight, she glanced over her shoulder. Aaron was speaking with Peter John. Joseph hurried to join them.

"I pray I can count on you, Joe," she said, moving into the shadow created by the corncrib.

Strolling to a fence, she gazed at the stars. A cow ambled toward her and lowed softly. Reaching out, she petted the animal, slightly calmed by the gentleness in its large friendly eyes. A horse whinnied from across the pasture, and a cricket called from a nearby woodpile. The young people were singing a sweet melody, but the music in Rebecca's heart hit sour notes. A hand rested on her shoulder. Gasping, she whirled.

Peter John grinned. "*Vell, Martha, wie gehts?*"

Fright bubbled into her throat. "I'm . . . fine."

"Did I scare you . . . Martha?"

She tightened her lips, hoping to appear disgusted. "Why'd you sneak up on me?"

He shrugged. "I like to make people jump."

Remembering seeing him in Lancaster driving a car, she tilted her chin sweetly. "I hear you secretly have a car."

He sobered. "Where'd you hear that?"

Hoping to hit a vital spot, she said, "I also hear you tip cans that aren't always Pepsi."

His complexion seemed to pale in the moonlight. He bent to pick up a couple of stones, then rolled them in his palm like dice.

Watching him gave her another idea. "You've been known to gamble, too." Seeing her statement had rattled him, she became more confident. "I hear you dress like an *Englischer*, so you won't get caught."

He frowned. "You're just guessing."

"Am I, Peter?"

"What about you? Did I see your cousin in Lancaster, or was it you? Is your name really Martha?"

Rebecca bit her tongue and struggled not to lie. It was her turn to become rattled. She wrestled to hide it.

"What are you two doing out here?" Joseph asked.

Rebecca turned to face him. "You'd better set this guy straight."

He faced Peter John. "You seem uncomfortable. *Wass's* bothering you?"

"Her." Peter flipped his hand toward Rebecca. "She looked scared when she came, and she's acting sort of . . . odd."

Joseph laughed. "You're probably frightening her."

"Maybe she has something to be frightened about."

"*Kom ann*, Peter. You've been reading too many mysteries." Joseph paused. "Maybe I should tell your sister about the worldly novels you have hidden in the hay mow."

"You've read a few of them, too, Joe. *Gel*?"

"*Ja*, and they gave me ideas. Martha's okay."

Peter frowned. "I'd like to ask her more questions."

"If you do, she'll be free to ask you some."

Encouraged by Joseph's support, Rebecca laughed softly, flashing her amber eyes at Peter John. "I might investigate what else you do in town."

Joseph cleared his throat. "Remember what I told you a few minutes ago, Peter?"

He sidestepped apprehensively. "I think I'll go back inside."

Rebecca watched his rapid retreat, and laced her fingers in an effort to still their trembling.

Joseph smiled. "I made some comments that shifted the conversation away from you. Then, I got Peter alone and convinced him to be quiet."

"How?"

"I told him you dressed like an *Englischer*, just as he had, to get a taste of what that kind of life was like, but didn't want anyone to know what you'd done."

"That much was true, but . . ."

His grin broadened. "I know about a few things that he's done that he wants kept quiet, so all I had to do was threaten to talk with Liz."

She laughed. "I think that's called blackmail."

Joseph shrugged. "You would've done the same for me."

Bending, she unpinned the paper from her hem and handed it to him.

Unfolding it, he scowled. "*Wass's* this?"

"A list of reasons Vance or one of his employees might have gotten involved in peddling cocaine. I want you to see if you can recall something I might've forgotten or overlooked."

"I can't see well enough out here to read."

"Take the paper with you, but don't let anyone see it."

He peered at her through half-closed eyes. "What do you have in mind?"

"I thought maybe you could tell the police what you know."

"Not me!" Crumpling the paper into a ball, he hurled it against the trunk of a tree. "I don't know anything."

Retrieving her list, Rebecca blinked back tears. "Joe, if someone found this . . ."

"*Es speit mich* that I was so careless." He snatched the crumpled ball from her. "I'll get rid of it. There's probably nothing illegal going on anyway."

He could be right. She wished she could forget about it.

Joseph glanced toward the barn. "Here comes Aaron."

"Joe, please screen me from any of the guys who might have recognized me."

"You can count on that."

"On what?" Aaron asked, joining them.

Joseph laughed. "Your curiosity."

Aaron's eyes narrowed. "What'd you do to upset Peter John?"

"Would I do that?"

"*Vell*, something was festering in his socks."

Sarah came out of the barn, glanced around, then hurried toward them. "I wondered where you went." She glanced at Rebecca, then at Joseph.

Aaron sighed. "I'm not going to stay much longer."

Joseph chuckled. "You're always in a hurry."

"I have a lot to do tomorrow." He turned to Rebecca. "*Kom ann.* I promised Eli and Liz that the four of us would join them in a game."

"Game!" Joseph laughed. "You?"

Aaron looked exasperated, then motioned to Rebecca.

Fighting trepidations, she joined him and strolled toward the noisy young people. Sarah and Joseph followed.

An hour later, Rebecca glanced around, remembering that she hadn't caught sight of Sarah in several minutes. Aaron was missing, too. Supposing Sarah had gone outside with him, she slipped through the open doorway and into the shadow created by the carriage shed. What Sarah and Aaron did was none of her business; but a feeling of desertion created a canyon of emptiness within her, compelling her to leave the noisy crowd.

Sarah's soft laughter rippled across the night air. Squinting, Rebecca made out two shadows under an old peach tree. The man pulled Sarah into an embrace. Her arms went around his neck as she tilted her face for his kiss. Their shadows melted into one for several moments.

Oh, Aaron. Blinded by tears, Rebecca whirled, intending to lose herself in the darkness, but thudded against a man's chest. He gripped her upper arms. Looking up, she gasped.

16

"Aaron!" Rebecca gasped.

"Why are you always surprised to see me?"

"I...I...thought." She'd assumed he'd been the one kissing Sarah. Mystified, she stared at his somber expression.

Stepping back, he propped a fist on his hip. "Where's Sarah?"

"I... She..." Rebecca refused to divulge Sarah's frivolous escapade.

"Where are Jesse and Joseph?"

"They... were in the barn."

Aaron sighed. "I'm leaving. Wait for me in the buggy."

Hurrying to the conveyance, she found Ransom stomping impatiently. She spoke softly to him, then climbed into the back seat. *Whom had Sarah been kissing? How could the girl be unfaithful to Aaron?*

Sarah stopped beside the buggy. "You can sit in front, Martha."

"The back seat is fine." Sliding to one side, Rebecca made room for Joseph and Jesse.

Sarah seemed befuddled. Joseph eyed her, shrugged, then climbed into the back. Jesse came running and flopped onto the seat beside him. Quietly getting into the front, Sarah folded her hands in her lap.

Joining them, Aaron closed the door with more force than necessary. Grabbing the reins, he headed Ransom out the lane. Rebecca figured he'd discovered Sarah's caper, but was too much of a gentleman to accost her in front of his brothers. The ride was fast, and no one spoke.

At Beilers' gate, Sarah glanced into the back seat at Joseph and smiled. "Having you back made tonight seem like old times."

"It was *wonderbar!*" He grinned. "Better than *wonderbar!*"

"*Gute Nacht* (Good night), Aaron. You, too, Jesse!" she called as she left the buggy.

Rebecca had to get out on Aaron's side.

He bent toward her. "We're going to have a talk—soon."

She read dismay as well as agitation in his expression. Would she be able to wiggle out of another snare gracefully? "*Gute Nacht*, Aaron.*" She hurried after Sarah.

The July sun blazed on Rebecca's back as she picked tomatoes for supper. Eli's arm was out of the cast, so Aaron had not been to the Beiler farm to help. Nevertheless, her love for him grew. He hadn't been able to confront her, for she'd expertly made herself unavailable each time he'd come to call.

Life with the Beilers bred contentment. There were more rules, and she'd worked harder than she ever had, yet she'd found peace. Was this what it would be like to be Aaron's wife? "Stop it, you dunce!" She unconsciously squeezed a tomato until it burst. Juice spurted, dribbled through her fingers onto the hem of her blue dress, then dripped onto her shoe. Dropping it under a plant, she chose another one and headed for the house.

"Is that you, Sarah?" Esther called as Rebecca entered the kitchen.

"It's Martha," Ruth said. "Sarah isn't back from Kings'."

Rebecca stomped on jealousy as it reared its ugly head. "How many tomatoes does Anna usually can?"

Ruth rolled her dark eyes and grinned. "Dozens of quarts, just like we do. Sarah should be back soon, though. She left early this morning."

Rebecca would have gone along, but Sarah had encouraged her to remain behind. "Has she helped Anna before?"

"*Ja*. It's good to impress a future mother-in-law, don't you think?"

"Sarah would've helped Anna regardless. *Gel?*"

"*Ja*, but her interest isn't only tomatoes." She giggled and whispered, "She slipped her lipstick into her purse before she left."

Picking up a knife to peel potatoes, Rebecca pondered. *It's understandable for Sarah to want to keep me away from Aaron.*

Ruth took several plates from the cupboard.

Rebecca counted them as she accepted the pile. "There's an extra plate. Is Aaron staying for supper when he brings Sarah home?"

"Eli is bringing Liz Lapp home for supper."

"*Wonderbar!*"

Ruth turned the flame higher under the potato pot. "Liz didn't like you — at first, because Eli took a shine to you."

"I thought it was his car that gave her competition."

"*Ja*, that, too."

"Did he get rid of it?"

"Not yet, but he probably will." Was it disappointment that shimmered in Ruth's brown eyes?

Rebecca filled the water glasses and wondered if Aaron would get rid of his vehicle as well.

The sound of an approaching buggy drew the younger girl to a window. "Sarah's home."

Rebecca forced herself to remain at the stove until Ransom trotted back down the lane; then she joined Ruth. Sarah came through the gate, the radiance in her smile setting her features aglow.

"How's Aaron?" Ruth teased as Sarah entered the kitchen.

Sarah shrugged. "He was gone most of the day."

Ruth's eyes widened. "Who brought you home?"

"Joseph." She surveyed the table and smiled. "I guess Liz accepted Eli's invitation."

The meal was enjoyable, and the clean-up fun. Afterward, Rebecca followed Eli and Liz to the porch. "Good-bye, Liz."

Pausing, the girl turned to smile and waved before she climbed into Eli's buggy. Her heart-shaped face looked radiant.

Sarah helped *Mammi* Hazel into the porch rocker and adjusted the old lady's shawl. Then, retrieving a torn shirt, she took a seat on a bench. As she worked the needle through the material, she seemed to be deep in thought.

Perched on the railing, Rebecca watched Eli's retreating buggy; then turned her attention to the grazing cows. Her gaze lingered on a calf, then lazily followed the little stream that meandered through the pasture. She looked at the clump of bushes near the fence row, noticed the huge oak, and thought about the first time Aaron had confronted her. So much had happened since, yet she was no closer to a solution.

Yawning, she glanced at the trees at the horizon, then blinked, straightened, and stared. "Is that smoke?"

Sarah glanced up. The rising dark plume caught her attention. Leaping to her feet, she let her mending tumble to the floor. "Papa! Come quick! There's a fire at Kings'!"

Hazel got up quickly, tottered, and sidestepped. Whirling, Rebecca grabbed the old lady, preventing her tumble.

Isaac ran to the porch in his stocking feet to stare at the horizon. Esther hurried outside with his shoes. He rammed his feet into them, then hurried to hitch the buggy.

"I'm going, too," Sarah cried, racing toward the barn.

Esther seized a hand of each of her little boys. Then she and Ruth hurried across the lawn. Rebecca followed, determined not to be left behind. When the buggy was hitched, they piled in, and Isaac slapped the horse into a run. Glancing back, Rebecca noticed the worried look on Hazel's face. The old woman stood gripping a porch post, staring after the buggy.

At the crossroads, they met two carriages coming from the opposite direction. Moses Zimmerman turned his rig down the road to the left. "It's Kings' barn!" he shouted.

The second buggy, bearing Jacob and Emma Zook, turned and raced after Moses' rig.

"Elam Miller's with them," Isaac said, speedily following.

Rebecca figured he'd made another trip from Mercer County to visit Elizabeth. As they neared the King farm, she smelled smoke and heard the crackling and snapping of wood being consumed. Above the racket, a bell clanged, summoning aid.

"Whoa!" Isaac stopped the horse far enough away that the animal would not become alarmed. Leaping from the buggy, he glanced at Sarah and motioned toward the horse. "Take care of Benedict!"

Ruth followed Esther and the little boys toward the house. Sarah guided the carriage horse to a fence and tied him. "*Kom ann*, Martha," she called, heading for the house.

A siren screamed as a fire truck turned in the lane. The wail of the paramedic vehicle followed. Dozens of people were converging from all directions. Rebecca knew she must remain alert not to be identified. *I shouldn't have come*! But with a barn on fire, how could she have done otherwise?

Eli halted his buggy, his horse's nose touching the fence. Liz was still with him. Eli leaped out and raced for the barn, leaving Liz to attend the horse. More buggies arrived, and cars sped in the lane. Rebecca stopped in the barnyard and glanced feverishly around. What could she do to help? Men shouted and futilely carried pails of water to douse the flames.

"There are ten more cows in there!" Joseph bellowed, racing into the smoky interior.

Terrified cattle bawled, and somewhere in the chaos a calf cried for its mother. Moses Zimmerman hurried from the barn, leading one of the work horses.

"I'll get the last one!" Elam Miller raced into the barn.

A mule must be trapped! Its horrified braying penetrated the din. Rebecca's stomach cramped.

Speeding to the barn, the fire truck slid to a stop. Firemen unrolled hoses as the captain shouted orders. Within seconds a stream of water struck the flames.

Men raced in and out of the barn, striving to save the animals. A hand tugged frantically on Rebecca's, and she glanced to her right. "Nancy! Go back to the house."

The girl's brown eyes were wide with fright. "Aaron's horse," she choked.

"Ransom?"

The girl nodded feverishly. "No one knows."

In an effort to calm the child, Rebecca put an arm around her. "Knows what, Nancy?"

"Before Jesse went to town, he put Ransom in the barn."

"Are you sure?"

She nodded until a lock of hair escaped from under her cap and fell across one eye. "I helped."

Rebecca felt nauseous. "Where'd Jesse put him?"

Nancy held up five fingers, designating the fifth stall.

Not wanting to believe it, Rebecca stared at the burning building. "In there?"

"*Ja!*" Nancy clasped her hands and tears filled her eyes. "He's gonna burn up! Oh, Martha, he's gonna die!"

"Go back to the house, Nancy," Rebecca said crossly, knowing the girl would respond if she sounded angry.

"Poor Ransom," Nancy whimpered, tears streaming down her cheeks as she raced for the porch.

Rebecca searched feverishly for someone who could rescue the horse, but the men were concentrating on saving the thirty-one dairy cows. Covering her face with her hands, she groaned. She'd wrecked Aaron's carriage. Now, he would lose his horse. "I can't let Ransom fry!" Seizing an old quilt that had been airing on the clothesline, she sloshed it into the water trough, and raced into the smoky interior.

"Martha!" a man yelled.

Determined, she paid no heed to the man's plea. Smoke swirled around her, but covered by the wet blanket she was able to breathe. Crackling and snapping wood seemed to surround her. A timber support at the back of the barn, weakened by the fire, buckled and slowly fell to rest on another support beam.

In the fifth stall, she found Ransom. He stomped and snorted. As she tried to loosen him, he nearly trampled her foot. The beast screamed as tongues of fire licked through the boards of the adjoining stall. Sparks rained on the hay in his manger. Shying away from them, the horse nearly pinned Rebecca to the other side.

She gritted her teeth. "I'm trying to help you!"

Somehow, she managed to untie him. He screamed, reared,

and almost caught her face with a front hoof.

"Back. Back!" Rebecca commanded, slapping his shoulder, struggling to get him out of the stall. Smoldering straw a few feet behind him made him crazy, and he refused to step backward.

His wild eyes darted frantically as he reared, again. Seizing his mane, Rebecca put one foot against the manger and vaulted to his back. Covering herself with the wet blanket, she jerked off her apron and wrapped it around Ransom's eyes.

He snorted and stomped.

Rebecca knew she'd been foolhardy, and this time her impulsiveness could cost her her life.

Fire seeped through the partition and caught the straw near the horse's legs. Screaming, he pounded the bedding with his front feet. With a poof, the hay in the manger burst into flame. Rebecca opened her mouth to yell a command at the terrified beast, but choked on a mouthful of smoke.

Tugging feverishly on the apron covering his eyes, and yanking on his mane, she managed to back him from the stall. As she did so, a burning board tumbled to the straw where the horse had been seconds before.

Yanking Ransom's head with her apron, she turned him toward the outside door and dug her heel into his flank, but flames now licked tongues across the opening. Turning him to another doorway, she kicked him, forcing him into the smoke-filled cattle shed. The heat was intense. She choked, striving not to gasp for air, knowing it would only suck more smoke into her already searing lungs.

Her need for oxygen increased. She felt dizzy and her thinking was becoming addled. If she were deprived of fresh air much longer, she would pass out. "God, in your mercy, help me!"

Straining to see through stinging, watering eyes, and battling to keep her face partially covered, she guided the beast through the main shed. The smoke was thicker, now. Was the main door to the left? Disorientated, she slumped across the horse's mane.

Apparently sensing an opening, Ransom bolted. Rebecca nearly toppled from his back. He plunged through the doorway just before a beam crashed to the shed floor behind them. Screaming, the horse reared and pawed the air. Rebecca lost her grip and expected to hit the earth with a thud, but strong fingers clamped around her arm, jerked her free of the bucking beast, and prevented her contact with the ground. The sodden quilt flopped over her face and clung to her shoulders. Whinnying wildly, Ransom galloped away.

"Martha!" Aaron yelled, jerking off the quilt. "That was stupid!"

Her cap had loosened and was gone. Her long hair, damp from the sodden blanket, hung limply down her back. Gasping, she coughed. Her throat was parched, her lungs felt seared, and her brain seemed scrambled.

"You could've been killed," Aaron yelled, shaking her.

"Ran-som," she rasped, finding it difficult to focus on his sweaty, soot-streaked face.

"*Fer wass*, Martha?"

"I couldn't . . . let him . . . die."

"He isn't worth your risking your life!"

"You've lost . . . so much . . . because of me."

"I could've lost you, too."

She coughed, weakened, and her knees buckled.

Catching her, he pulled her into his arms. "Martha. Oh, Martha, *Dank der gut Man* you're all right." His embrace tightened. He mumbled hoarsely into her wet hair.

"*Wass*?" Over the roaring flames, screaming animals, shouting men, and general chaos, she'd not heard him clearly. Had his words been a confession of endearment? *No*, she thought, figuring her garbled mind was pulling tricks.

"There's a man trapped in the barn!" Joseph yelled.

Still gripping Rebecca, Aaron whirled to face his brother. "Who?"

"A . . . stranger." Joseph held his burned arms out in front of him, and pain creased his face.

"Where is he?" Aaron yelled above the noise.

"By the granary door."

"Get someone to aid Martha!" Seizing the quilt at Rebecca's

feet, he dipped it into the water trough and raced toward the far door.

An instant replay of what Rebecca had just been through seared through her muddled brain, forming a horrifying kaleidoscope of smoke, flames, and crashing beams. "Aaron!" she cried. "No!"

Flipping the blanket over his head, he raced into the barn.

"Aaron!" Rebecca wailed as he vanished into the billowing smoke. Unable to stand by and witness his death, she raced after him.

"Stop her!" Joseph bellowed.

Liz Lapp seized her arm. "Martha, some of the men have burns and need our aid."

"But, Aaron! Aaron!" Rebecca's lungs seemed choked with smoke, her brain felt like cotton, and sanity seemed evasive. The words *Aaron will die!* echoed through the foggy canyons of her mind, and tears coursed down her soot-streaked cheeks.

Compassion shimmered in Liz's eyes. "Please sit," she coaxed, guiding her to a lawn chair. "The smoke you inhaled is making you dizzy."

Refusing the chair, Rebecca stood statuesque, staring at the doorway through which Aaron had vanished.

"Let's see if we can help Sarah with Joseph's burns," Liz said.

Rebecca permitted the girl to guide her across the barnyard. Seeing Joseph's arms jolted her back to reality. "Are your burns deep?"

He plunged his arms into the pail of cool water Sarah offered. "I'll be all right," he grunted. When Liz rushed away to help someone else, Joseph glanced around, then bent his head toward Rebecca. "That trapped man might've started the fire."

"*Fer wass?*"

"I think I saw the guy a couple months ago with Vance Troy."

Her eyes widened. "Why would he want to burn your barn?"

Joseph's frown was evident, even through his pain. "Vance seemed upset when I refused his offer to set me up in business."

"That doesn't make sense—unless he or one of his other

employees wanted to use you as an outlet for selling drugs."

"I've been wondering about that." Gritting his teeth, he continued to dunk his arms into the pail of water.

She turned to stare at the barn. Groaning, the roof on the bottom of the L-shaped section began to buckle, slowly gave away, and merged into the flames. She covered her face. "Dear God! Oh, Aaron!" A truant strand of wet hair pasted itself to her face and she brushed it back with a sooty hand. Love for Aaron wrapped her in a cocoon of misery. Her knees weakened and she sat on a stump. The section Aaron had entered was not engulfed in flames, but sparks had ignited numerous spots. The heat was unbearable and the black smoke dense. A new surge of tears rilled down her face. "Oh, God, please bring Aaron out safely!"

Sarah brought a fresh pail of water to Joseph. Her eyes filled with tears as she stared at the inferno, her hands clasped in prayer.

Rumbling and groaning, the bottom of the L of the barn began to cave in. Sarah cried out. Joseph sucked in his breath.

Weakened to despair, Rebecca dropped to her knees. "No! Oh, no!" she cried as support timbers snapped.

At that moment, a bulky shadow appeared, and a man stumbled outside carrying a wrapped body over his shoulder.

"Aaron!" Rebecca cried, thanking God in the same breath. Then she noticed the flames that licked the material of his broadfalls from his ankle to his hip. "He's on fire!"

Joseph jerked his burned arms from the pail of water, seized the handle, raced to his brother, and doused the flames.

Jacob Zook and Eli took Aaron's burden and laid the stranger under a tree.

"Don't... know... him," Aaron gasped. Choking, he stumbled.

Elam Miller rushed to him, caught his plummeting body and eased him to the ground. "Bring the oxygen!" Elam's brown hair was singed and blackened by soot. His blue shirt was filthy and his black broadfalls torn. He ignored the blood that trickled into his beard from a scrape near his temple.

A paramedic raced forward to put a mask over Aaron's dirt-streaked face.

Rebecca peered at his leg, thanking God that the fire had caught the material just seconds before he emerged. She hoped his burn was superficial. She glanced at Joseph, then at the stranger's still form. "Is he dead?"

Another paramedic knelt and held the back of his fingers against the man's neck to feel his carotid artery for a pulse. "He's alive... barely," he said, placing an oxygen mask over the stranger's face. "There's a bump on his head, his shoulder's broken, and his leg's badly burned."

The wail of another fire truck seared through the darkness. The first truck continued to spray water on the blaze with no effect. At least the outbuildings had been saved.

Aaron pawed at the mask, pulling it from his face. "Amber," he choked. "Amber."

Elam looked puzzled. "Who do you want?"

Aaron glanced feverishly around until he saw Rebecca. "Go to ... the house."

Noticing his torn sleeve and bloody arm, she gasped. "You've been hurt!"

He glared at her. "Get to... the house!" He tried to prop himself on an elbow, but winced and slumped back to the ground.

"But, Aaron."

"Go!"

Whirling, she fled. Had the stranger been conscious when Aaron reached him? Had someone sent him? Had he told him who she was? Her nightmare had returned.

The women were in the kitchen preparing coffee and lemonade. Sarah looked worried as she rushed another pail of water to Joseph. Rebecca wondered if the girl had been there when she rode Ransom from the flaming barn. Had she seen Aaron's embrace? Had anyone heard his choked murmurings? If so, would Sarah forgive her this time?

Sitting on the porch rail, she stared toward the barn. Night had fallen, and orange tongues of flame lapped hungrily through what remained of the barn's sides. The main section of the roof cracked, snapped, and fell into the inferno. With a mighty groan, the largest side of the L-shaped barn collapsed into the blaze like a dying animal. The sky was black with smoke, and the air was so thick it was difficult to breathe.

Rebecca's lungs felt scalded, her eyes smarted, and her heart ached. The interpretation of Aaron's distorted words, as well as the meaning of his embrace, evaded her, and the haunted look in his dark eyes gripped her tortured mind.

She suddenly realized he would have acted the same toward a sister. What had gotten into her? Had she inhaled enough smoke to make her that daffy?

Joseph came to the house, his face twisted in pain. "Christopher Lapp fell."

Liz's face paled. "Papa!" Jumping off the porch, she raced toward the barn.

Rebecca considered Aaron's command to remain at the house; then thinking about how she would feel if her father had been injured, she leaped from the banister and ran toward the injured man. Eli looked up as she drew closer. His torn shirt gaped open; smears of soot shadowed his face and his straw hat was gone.

"Papa!" Liz cried, dropping to her knees beside her father.

Rebecca stepped to Eli. "Is Christopher injured seriously?"

"He may have a couple cracked ribs, but he'll be all right."

"*Dank der gut Man* it's not worse."

The firemen continued to spray the chicken coop, carriage shed, and tobacco barn, fighting to keep the fire contained.

Struggling to turn his head, the stranger peered in Rebecca's direction.

She turned away quickly, not wanting to risk the man's identifying her. "If there's nothing for me to do here, Eli, I'll go back to help with the sandwiches."

He nodded. "I could use a cold drink."

She intended to flee before the stranger could get a good look at her. She whirled, nearly colliding with a large man. Stopping with a jolt, she stared numbly up at his stern face and gasped.

Narrowing his blue eyes, a state trooper peered down at her. "Where are you going so fast?"

17

Rebecca spun and darted toward the house. The trooper laughed. Shaken, and knowing it would show on her face, she avoided the ladies in the kitchen, rounded the corner of the porch, and leaned against an apple tree, hoping her blue dress blended into its shadow. She flipped her long wet hair over her shoulder, wondering what to do about losing her prayer covering. Boosting herself to a limb of the apple tree, she became shrouded with small leafy branches.

The paramedics took the stranger to the hospital, a Beachy Amishman drove Joseph to the emergency room, and the police continued to ask questions. The tall trooper Rebecca had collided with headed for the house with determined strides. Her pulse throbbed in her throat, and her mouth went dry. What if he'd uncovered her identity?

The trooper stopped near the porch. His blond brows shimmered in the light from the kitchen window. His square chin seemed to give him an added air of authority. "Is Noah King here?"

Aaron's father rose and went down the three steps to the yard. "I'm Noah."

"Do you know the man your son rescued from the blaze?"

"No, Sir."

"What was he doing in your barn?"

Noah rubbed his right elbow as though it hurt. "I don't know."

"Do any members of your family know the man?"

Noah looked old and tired. He scratched his gray beard. "I

don't think so. He could've just been passing through. Sometimes strangers spend the night in a barn."

Do you know Rebecca Wenger?"

"No, Sir."

The trooper propped a large fist on his hip. "Someone must. I'd like to question your sons."

Noah sighed. "Jesse isn't home, and Joseph was taken to the burn unit, but you may speak with Aaron."

"I've already questioned him."

Noah frowned. "What are you hoping to discover?"

"The injured man was only semi-conscious, but according to him, Rebecca Wenger was here during the chaos."

Feeling dizzy, Rebecca clutched the limb.

Noah shrugged. "A number of strangers came to help. A fire draws a lot of spectators, too."

The trooper's eyes spanned the barnyard. "I'm going to question Aaron further."

Rebecca frowned as she watched the officer retreat. Who was the stranger? Had he seen her in the flower shop—or with Vance? "Oh God, please continue to hide me in the shelter of your wings." She intended to go to the police station herself—later, but she prayed to be spared the humiliation of being confronted in the presence of the Beilers or Kings.

When the trooper's car left, Rebecca wiped her forehead with the hem of her blue skirt. Elam Miller approached the house.

Elizabeth hurried down the porch steps. "You're hurt!"

He smiled. "It's just a scratch."

She examined the side of his face. "*Kom* into the house where I can attend to you."

Though fatigued, a luster crept into his eyes. Fire fighters munched sandwiches, drank lemonade and talked boisterously. They frequently discussed the stranger and speculated on how the fire had started.

Aaron walked slowly to the house and sat on the top porch step. One of his cut-off shirt sleeves exposed a bandaged shoulder. The leg of his broadfalls had been split up the seam, apparently to attend to the burn on his leg. Since he refused to go to the burn unit, she assumed his burn wasn't as deep as Joseph's. In the dim glow of lamplight that streamed from a window, she saw lines of concern on his face.

Gripping his battered straw hat, Moses Zimmerman strolled toward the porch. "What about that Wenger girl, Aaron? Did you see her?"

Aaron looked pensive. His dirt-smudged face appeared bronze in the glimmer of defused light from the kitchen window. "I was too busy to notice anyone in particular."

"*Vell* . . ." Moses leaned against a porch post. "That fellow you rescued told the police she was here."

Shrugging his injured shoulder, Aaron winced. His gaze drifted to the pile of burning rubble that had once been the barn. "I have enough on my mind, Moses. The police can take care of arsonists and runaways."

Moses looked at Noah. "It's your business, but if someone burned my barn, I'd want to get to the bottom of it and find out why."

"There's no proof that the injured man set the blaze. It could've been an accident." Noah sighed. "Regardless, we must pray for the man. *Gel* (Is that not so)?"

"*Ja*." Moses scratched his ear, then plopped his singed straw hat on his gray head.

Liz Lapp stepped closer to the rail. "That Wenger girl needs our prayers, too."

"*Ja, vell*." Moses seemed puzzled. "She shouldn't have left home." Yanking out his handkerchief, he blew his nose, the sound trumpeting across the lawn.

Sarah joined Liz at the porch rail.

Scowling, Aaron stood, glanced around the barnyard, then surveyed the porch. "Where's Martha?" His voice sounded controlled, but authoritative.

Sarah smiled. "I'm . . . not sure--right now, Aaron."

He frowned. "Some time ago, I told her to go to the house. Did she?"

"*Vell* . . . I've been too occupied to notice everyone."

Rebecca knew Sarah was being evasive to protect her, and she prayed Aaron wouldn't press her too far.

His irritation seemed to mount. "She lost her prayer covering when she rescued Ransom, but that shouldn't be bothering her too much."

"*Fer wass?* Some of the women might be critical, and Martha's sweet and sensitive. *Gel?*"

"Get her a covering, find her, and tell her I want to talk to her."

Nodding, Sarah vanished into the house.

Jonah Stoltzfus sauntered toward the porch. The brim of his straw hat had been burned off, and the remaining blackened tentacles jutted in various directions. Soot smudged the bridge of his large nose and his dark beard was disheveled. "It looks like we're going to have a barn raising, Noah. *Gel?*"

"*Ja*, but tonight, I'm too tired to think about rebuilding."

Jonah nodded. "You'll have to figure out what lumber you need, and I'll see how soon it can be delivered."

Moses nodded. "When you're ready, let us know and we'll be here to help."

"*Dank an hunnert mohl* for your assistance tonight."

"That's what neighbors are for."

"*Dank der gut Man.*" Noah sighed. "The boys and I couldn't have gotten all the cattle out in time."

Jonah sneezed. "I'm sorry we couldn't save the barn."

Aaron gingerly touched his bandaged shoulder as he gazed at the still flaming ruins. Then turning, he slowly walked to a stump, propped his foot on it, and examined his leg burn in the light that filtered from a kitchen window. He was near enough Rebecca could hear him mumbling, but far enough away she couldn't decipher his words.

Anna came from the house and approached him. "I'm thankful you saved the cows."

Aaron winced. Putting his foot on the ground, he let his pant's leg fall into place. "I know you thought a lot of the mule, Mother, but--"

A shadow crossed her face. "You mean Sally didn't make it?"

"Joseph tried, but she jerked away from him and ran blindly back into the fire."

"*Ach*, poor Sally. The girls are going to miss her," Anna said, referring to the cows.

"We got all of the calves, except two." Sighing, he sat on the stump.

Anna shook her head. "*Dank der gut Man* no one died during the rescue effort. Sometimes men act impulsively."

Aaron snorted. "Not only men!" Clenching his fist, he struck his good knee. "Did anyone tell you about Martha's ridiculous stunt?"

Anna's eyes widened. "Martha?"

Nancy scampered to them. Bouncing, she clapped her hands. "She saved Ransom!"

"She could've been killed," Aaron growled. "She went into the barn after my horse and nearly didn't make it out in time."

Anna's hands flew up. "*Ach!*"

He stared at his mother. "I sent her to the house. Where is she?"

"I haven't seen her."

Gritting his teeth, he scowled.

Anna rested her hand on his arm. "If Martha rescued Ransom, you should be grateful. Did you thank her?"

"No!"

"You should."

"For what? Being foolish?" He curled both hands into fists. "She's the most stubborn female I've ever known!"

Anna laughed. "I think she's delightful."

"Humph."

"You've been through a lot today, Aaron. With the morning sun, things will be brighter."

"I'm going to get to the bottom of what's been disturbing me, Mother—and soon."

She patted his uninjured shoulder. "I'm sure you will." Taking Nancy's hand, she went back into the house.

One by one, families left and Kings' farm quieted. Hot timbers glowed in the dark, and streams of smoke curled listlessly into the night sky. Aaron sat on the stump, his chin in his hands.

Rebecca combed her hair with her fingers. Pondering what Aaron wanted to discuss, she shivered. A noise behind her head made her jump and nearly lose her balance. Strangling a scream, she turned her head and stared into the eyes of a small furry face. "Restless," she whispered. She stroked the cat, figuring he'd been frightened tonight, too.

Sarah stepped from the porch, the ties of an extra prayer cap dangling from her left hand. Hesitating, she looked around the barnyard. Shielding her eyes with her hand, she peered at the carriage shed, then headed in that direction.

Rebecca slipped from the tree limb and hurried through the shadows to the building. "Sarah," she whispered.

The girl jumped and whirled. "Oh, Martha, I've been searching everywhere for you."

"Sarah, that stranger knew me."

"No one knows who he meant when he said Rebecca Wenger was here."

"Sh!" Rebecca glanced feverishly around. "What does Aaron want?"

"I don't know." Sarah held out the prayer cap. "Put this on and go to him."

"Not yet." Twisting her hair, she held it in place. "I promised *der gut Man* not to lie anymore, and I won't know how to answer Aaron's questions." Donning the cap, she tied the strings.

Sarah frowned. "*Wass* can I tell him?"

"Say that I'm not feeling well." She wiped her hand across her forehead. "That would be the truth."

"Where were you?"

"In the apple tree."

Sarah laughed softly. "I wouldn't have thought to look there."

"If you want me, that's where I'll be." As she vanished into the shadows, Sarah went back to the house.

Rebecca sighed. Talking with Sarah had helped calm her nerves, but there was more to come. Thunder rumbled in the distance as though punctuating her thought.

Sarah came out carrying a pitcher and a glass. Stopping beside Aaron, she smiled. "Lemonade?"

"*Herzlich Dank.*" Accepting the refreshment, he drank deeply. When he finished, he handed the glass back. "You're a wonderful girl, Sarah. You'll make a good wife."

She brightened, and even in the dim light, color bathed her cheeks. "I'm going to try."

Rebecca cringed. *Aaron told his mother I'm foolish and stubborn. Now, he tells Sarah she's going to make a good wife.* The truth of it seared through her.

"Did you find Martha?" Aaron asked.

"*Ja,* but she isn't feeling well."

He stood quickly, concern creasing his forehead. "Was she hurt in the fire? Did she inhale too much smoke? Where is she?"

"Resting. She'll be fine."

He gripped her shoulders. "Tell me where she is."

Not feeling up to sparring with Aaron, Rebecca slipped from the limb, hurried around the house, and wandered along the edge of the cornfield. The stalks were now higher than her head. A startled field mouse squeaked as it raced across her toe.

"*Es speit mich* that I disturbed you," she mumbled. Thunder rolled; closer this time. Looking up, she peered at the silhouettes of smaller corn leaves and tassels against the smoke-blackened sky. She'd have to face Aaron sometime, so it might as well be now. After all, he was a reasonable man—well, most of the time.

The haze from the fire hid most of the stars. Lightning streaked across the sky, and another peal of thunder unnerved her. A light drizzle began. Squaring her shoulders, she headed for the house.

"Martha!" Aaron called.

"I'm here," she answered from near the back porch.

He strode swiftly to her. "Are you feeling all right?"

"I'm . . . tired."

He sighed. "So am I, but I want to talk to you."

"Are you still angry about my rescuing Ransom?"

"*Ja.*"

"I wrecked your buggy, Aaron, and I couldn't let your horse die."

"So you foolishly risk your life?"

She tilted her chin. "I didn't see my deed as foolish—in the beginning." The misty rain dampened her clothing, yet she stood unmoving.

Aaron seemed not to notice the storm. "We won't discuss the accident or your rescuing Ransom further, tonight." His eyes narrowed. "Did you recognize the man I rescued?"

Her heart nearly stopped, then it thrashed like a snared hawk. "No." Her voice squeaked.

Aaron's gaze was unwavering. "He was conscious when I found him."

"Did he confess to setting the fire?"

"No, but he said some interesting things."

Thunder rolled overhead, and she tried to swallow the anxiety that bubbled into her throat. His brow furrowed as he scrutinized her face. Determined not to lie to him, she tightened her lips and tilted her chin another degree.

"I want to help you." His fingers tightened on her shoulders. "It isn't only what that man said." He hesitated, then said, "Joseph's been talking in his sleep."

New fright exploded within her, but she held her smile. "Maybe what he did when he was away is bothering him."

"*Ja.*" Sighing, he released her. "He mentioned Rebecca Wenger several times."

She shrugged. "*Wass* do you think that has to do with me?"

"My brother's been talking to you in his sleep as well, and he seems to be confusing you with Miss Wenger."

Rebecca camouflaged a shiver with a shrug. "Dreams are ridiculous sometimes. *Gel*?"

"*Ja*, but there's still what the stranger said."

"Which was?"

"He told me to check out the filly with amber eyes." The rain intensified, pelting them with huge drops, but he stood statuesque with his hands on his hips. "Can you explain what he could've meant?"

Water trickled down her face and wet her clothing, but she

stood unyielding. "I don't need to explain anything! I'm not on trial."

"No? It seems odd that you'd show up the day Miss Wenger dropped from sight."

"Aaron, its raining."

"A little water won't hurt us as much as your keeping a secret might."

She tried to divert him. "Suppose you tell me what I'm supposed to know about Joseph."

"It's what you possibly know about each other that confuses and concerns me."

Rebecca grappled for something to say, but her brain seemed catatonic. "The fire has us all in a tizzy, Aaron."

His dark eyes scrutinized her face. "Tell me where and when you saw Joseph."

"There you are!" Sarah joined them with an umbrella. Shielding Rebecca from the rain, she rested a hand on Aaron's arm and smiled. "We'll be leaving, so I came to say *gute Nacht*."

"*Herzlich Dank* for your help in the kitchen, Sarah."

"I was glad to do my part."

"*Ja*. You always are."

"You look fatigued. Why don't you wash up and get some rest?"

He looked back at Rebecca, his lips taut.

Sarah linked her arm in Rebecca's. "Papa's ready to leave, so we should go to the buggy."

Anger sparked in Aaron's eyes. "I'm not finished discussing something with her!"

"We're all exhausted," Sarah argued sweetly. "You can get your answers tomorrow. *Gel*?"

"I'll get my answers tonight!"

"Aaron." Sarah's eyes widened at his brusqueness, and she stepped backward, gasping as her heel caught on a root.

Leaping, he caught her with his good arm. Scrambling to regain her balance, she dropped the umbrella, clutched the front of his shirt with one hand and his injured arm with the other. He gasped in pain.

She seemed flustered. "*Es speit mich* that I hurt you."

Retrieving the umbrella, Rebecca shielded Sarah.

Aaron faced Rebecca. "It's past time for us to talk."

He crossed his arms, impervious to the storm, his unwavering gaze holding hers.

18

Lightning seared across the sky. A fierce crack rent the air as another bolt struck a tree along the fence row. Thunder shook the earth, vibrating the rock under Rebecca. Larger drops of rain spattered the umbrella, then pelted it with vengeance.

"Good-bye, Aaron," Sarah said, grabbing Rebecca's hand.

Racing through the downpour, they climbed into the back seat of Beilers' buggy. Rebecca laughed nervously. "*Dank an hunnert mohl*! I think you just saved my life."

"Temporarily." Sarah joined her laughter.

"Where are Isaac and Esther? I thought you meant they were in the buggy."

"They will be. Mama said they were leaving, and I figured Aaron would be battering you with questions."

"*Ja*, he was." Lightning flashed, thunder rumbled, and rain drummed on the carriage roof. "Oh, Sarah, I'm so ashamed. I don't want Aaron to uncover my deceit. The longer I withhold the truth, the worse it seems to be." She grappled for a dry handkerchief to catch the raindrops that trickled from her hair.

Sarah peered at the smoldering rubble. "Joseph will do what he can to hide your identity until you're ready to reveal it."

"I've brought so much trouble to Aaron."

"*Ach*, he's all right." She patted Rebecca's hand.

The downpour slackened. Ruth raced to the carriage. Her dark eyes sparkled in the dim light. "Wasn't this exciting!"

Sarah looked perturbed. "Ruth Beiler!"

Isaac and Esther hurried to the buggy, the two little boys in tow. On the way out Kings' lane, Rebecca turned to look out the back window. Aaron stood in the barnyard, staring at the smoldering beams. With his burned hat in his hand, his clothing soaked, and his hair pasted to his head by the rain, he made a forlorn image in the darkness.

When Rebecca looked back at Sarah, she bit her lip. The girl studied the scene with sadness in her expression and tears glistening on her lower lashes. Rebecca thought about Sarah's loving Aaron, and claws of anguish raked her. *I will always cherish him, but for Sarah's sake, I must hide my love for him deep in my heart.*

Staring into the glowing embers of the barn, Aaron gingerly touched his throbbing shoulder. He figured his injuries were a small price to pay for a man's life, whether or not he'd set the blaze. With a laborious sigh, he crossed the barnyard and headed for the house, favoring his right leg. The burn was superficial, but his discomfort was mounting.

After a refreshing shower, he stretched out on his bed. Fatigue gripped his body, yet sleep evaded him. The stranger's statement gyrated through his fitful mind. He flopped to his stomach, but cringed as his weight pressed on his injured shoulder. The phrase, *amber-eyed filly*, continued to spin through his brain. The words tumbled over each other, then whirled faster and faster, making him dizzy and sucking him into the vortex of a whirlpool of tormented thoughts.

When Joseph came home from the emergency room, Aaron got up to intercept him. "I want to talk to you."

His brother looked at him through glazed eyes; then blinking, he headed for the stairs.

"Joseph!"

Jesse appeared at the top of the stairs and watched Joseph ascend. "His arms were burned pretty bad, Aaron. He's had medication for his pain."

"*Ja.*" Aaron considered going back to bed, but followed

Joseph. He waited until his brother stretched out on his bed and got as comfortable as possible. Lighting a lamp, Aaron challenged him. "I must have some answers."

"To . . . what?" Joseph closed his eyes.

"Who is Martha?"

"A . . . lovely girl."

"Who *is* she!"

"She's . . . okay."

"I'm worried about her."

"*Gute Nacht*, . . . Aaron." His words were slurred.

"Joseph!"

"*Ja?*" The syllable dragged.

"I want some answers!"

His brother didn't stir, and his even breathing signified slumber.

Suppressing the desire to shake him, Aaron gritted his teeth. If the stranger's statements were true, Martha could be in trouble. "Joseph!" he called brusquely.

His brother groaned, and looked at him through hooded eyes.

"Martha could need help!"

Joseph's eyes widened as though Aaron's statement had shocked him awake.

"I know you're in pain, but we must talk."

Joseph frowned. "I can't . . . tell you anything."

"Can't—or won't?" Staring at his brother's solemn face, Aaron felt as though he'd treed a coon, but probably wouldn't get answers to his myriad of questions without a struggle.

Joseph's eyelids slid over his eyes as slowly, but as definitely, as a glacier, and the effect sent a cold chill through the room. "We'll . . . talk . . . tomorrow." His words slurred, then faded. The medication had taken effect.

Aaron grumbled, his determination to disclose Martha's secret intensifying.

For two days, Rebecca was careful that Aaron didn't catch her unaware. Sarah remained watchful, too. Aaron had dropped in twice. The first time, Rebecca remained in the carriage shed. The second, she slipped to the basement. Ruth was enchanted, even though she was unaware of the reason for Rebecca's avoiding Aaron.

On the third day, Rebecca was gathering the eggs when she heard a buggy. Peering through the wire across a window of the henhouse, she saw Ransom and caught her breath. Would the cackling hens give away her location? She moved away from the opening, but worried that Aaron might have caught a glimpse of her green dress.

She finished collecting the eggs, set the basket near the door, then leaned against the wall to wait for Aaron's departure. She hoped it would be soon. The hen house certainly wasn't perfumed. The Beilers didn't use cages, and the dust made by the scratching chickens tickled her nose.

When the door swung inward, she pressed herself harder against the rough boards.

"*Hi, wie Machts* (How are things)?" Joseph asked. His one dark suspender made a sharp contrast against his blue shirt. His straw hat shadowed his eyes.

Rebecca let out the breath she'd been holding. "I thought you were Aaron."

"Sarah said I'd find you here." He picked up the basket of eggs. "Let's sit under the apple tree."

When they were settled on the bench, Rebecca studied his perplexed expression. "*Wass's* wrong?"

Sweeping his straw hat from his head, Joseph tossed it to the ground by his feet. "I rode into Lancaster this morning with a Beachy friend. I stopped in the flower shop to see Vance, wondering if I'd notice anything abnormal."

Rebecca's heart jolted. "*Ja?*"

"Vance was his cordial self, and I didn't see anything unusual."

"I'm not surprised." Bending she picked a clover and touched each of its three leaves.

"Vance thought I was there because I'd talked to that fellow who got trapped in the barn fire."

She straightened. "Vance knew?"

"*Ja.*" Plucking a grass stem, he chewed on it. "He'd sent the guy to try to convince me to go into business."

She felt the color draining from her face. "So he set the fire because you refused him?"

"No. He told Vance he'd been smoking and an ash dropped. He tried to put the fire out, but it spread too quickly. In his panic to summon help, he slipped, bumped his head, and knocked himself out."

"Didn't he know better than to smoke in the barn?"

"*Ja*, but he thought he'd be careful."

She sighed. "Did you see Gene or Doug?"

"Doug was in the greenhouse, but Gene's gone."

She blinked at him. "Gone?"

Joseph leaned against the back of the bench and rested his tender arms in his lap. "Vance made Gene the same offer as he did me, and Gene took him up on it."

"You mean help to start a business?"

Joseph nodded. "I visited Gene's Candy and Gifts. Mattis came in while I was there and bought a box of candy. I thought it was a little strange when Gene went to the back room to get a box of assorted chocolates that were exactly like the ones on the display shelf." He sighed. "But when Mattis slipped him extra cash that Gene quickly shoved under the counter, I got suspicious."

She straightened. "Then there *is* something illegal going on!"

"I don't know, Rebecca—but . . ."

"Does Gene know you saw him?"

"I pretended not to notice."

She tossed away the limp clover. "You have to inform the police."

"I don't have proof of anything illegal."

"No, but if the police investigate . . ."

He snatched his hat from the grass, plopped it onto his head, and stood. "I'm not getting involved."

She leaped to her feet and reached to grab his arm, remembered his burns, and withdrew her hand. "You *are* involved!"

He gripped the handle of the egg basket. "I'll take these in to Sarah."

"If you phoned the police—"

Turning, he strode quickly away.

"Joe!"

He waved his hand. "I'll think about it."

Rebecca watched him go, her lips taut.

Isaac took his place at the supper table. "It's only been a week since the fire, and already the cement's been poured and the foundation's ready for Kings' new barn."

"When will the lumber be delivered?" Eli asked.

"Tomorrow morning."

All took their seat as Esther clattered the plate of roast beef onto the table. "We've been baking all day, so we're ready."

Sarah's eyes sparkled. "I can hardly wait."

Ruth bounced on her chair. "Me, either! There's always lots of scrumptious cakes and delicious cookies at a barn raising."

Eli laughed. "And you'll eat your share."

Little John clapped his hands. "Me, too!"

After the dishes were finished and the girls were in their bedroom, Rebecca looked beseechingly at Sarah. "What am I going to do tomorrow?"

Sarah took off her cap to brush her hair. "About *wass*?"

"The barn-raising. I have no excuse to stay away."

"*Fer wass* would you want to? We'll need you to help with preparing the food."

Rebecca lowered herself to her bed with a plop. "Don't you remember why I'm here?"

"Oh! *Es speit mich* that I was so thoughtless." Her hairbrush hovered in the air as she turned to peer at her friend. "I've been so excited."

"Mennonites always come to barn raisings." Tears smarted Rebecca's eyes. "My father will probably be there. I long to see him, but . . ."

Sarah crossed the room to put an arm around Rebecca. "The

mothers will need someone to watch their small children. We keep them at a safe distance from the workers. You can take care of them. I'll set up a spot where no one will notice you."

"Except the mothers of the little ones."

"I'll stay close and cover for you. If you watch who comes, you can identify anyone who would recognize you and let me know."

Rebecca chewed her lower lip. "It'd be risky."

Sarah hesitated, deep in thought, then said, "Liz Lapp is sweet and understanding. We can trust her with your secret. What if I ask her to help?"

"If she knows, she might accidentally call me Rebecca."

"I don't think so, but I'll leave the decision up to you." Bending, she kissed Rebecca's cheek. "Get some sleep. We'll manage fine."

Solaced, though unconvinced, Rebecca slept.

Dozens of buggies lined the fence at Kings'. From a secluded spot behind the house, Rebecca had recognized five people and pointed them out to Sarah.

"Do any of the ladies with small children know you?"

"Not to my knowledge."

"We were right to inform Liz." Sara laughed softly. "It was her idea for all of the young ladies to wear the same shade of blue. With our white caps, it will be difficult to tell us apart—especially from a distance."

A black car came up the lane and pulled to a stop. Rebecca gasped and tears stung her eyes as the driver got out, handed a large food container to one of the ladies, and headed for the barn. "Papa," she whispered, swiping at the excess moisture that dampened her lashes.

Sarah hugged her. "Do you have a message for him, Martha?"

Rebecca's eyes widened. "I wouldn't dare go to him! I'd be seen."

Sarah motioned to the blankets on the line. "I offered to air Anna's quilts." She laughed softly. "They make a super screen, *ja*?"

Joseph rounded the last quilt. "Martha?" He looked as though he were trying to smile, but it was a vain effort.

Hurrying to him, Rebecca eyed him expectantly.

He lowered his voice to a whisper. "I made that call you wanted me to make to the police."

Her eyes widened. "When?"

"About an hour ago."

Her heart did a flip. "What'd they say?"

"Nothing. They just took the information."

Rebecca sighed. "*Gross Dank.* I think you did what was right."

"*Ja, vell* . . . it's in their hands now."

A little boy tugged on her hand. "You promised to tell us a story."

"All right."

The morning proceeded without incident, but when Liz and Sarah hurried forward, alarm exploded within Rebecca.

"I'll watch the children for awhile, Martha," Liz said.

Sarah's eyes twinkled as she approached Rebecca. "Please get me the shawl from the buggy in the carriage shed."

Rebecca hurried to the designated building, careful not to be observed. Slipping through the partly open door, she paused, squinting to see into the shadowed interior.

"Over here," a familiar voice said.

"Papa!" Running, she flung herself into his open arms.

He held her close. "Amber. Oh, Amber."

"I've longed to see you, Papa."

"Honey, please come home." He sighed, then continued as though he would rather not make his statement. "Vance Troy gave the police your name. You received a citation to appear before the district justice concerning your hit-and-run accident."

"What if I put off going to the authorities?"

"If you don't appear at the magistrate's office after a citation, there'll probably be a warrant for your arrest."

"Oh, no." Envisioning her humiliation, she cringed.

"Honey, the accident had minimal damage, and settling it won't be difficult. When you see the magistrate, he'll set a date for your hearing. There'll be a fine and court costs."

"I need to wait another couple of days." Picturing the strange packets, she prayed Joseph's information would aid the police.

"Don't worry. *Der gut Man* will be with you, Rebecca."

She gazed into his weary face. "How'd you know I was here?"

"A girl called Sarah found me alone and told me." He hugged her tighter. "I wish we could visit longer, but if I'm missed, someone might come looking for me."

"*Ja*. I'm staying with the Isaac Beiler family. Tomorrow or the day after I'll phone the police and answer their questions about my accident."

David brushed at the excess moisture in his blue-gray eyes.

Standing on tiptoe, she kissed his cheek. "I love you, Papa. Tell *Mammi* her fried chicken was the best ever. Tell her I love her, and that I'm sorry."

"She's sorry, too. Things will be different when you get home."

Aaron pounded nail after nail, thought about Martha, and his frustration mounted. The past several days he'd been busy, yet he'd taken time to try to talk with her. On each occasion she'd cleverly avoided him. He scowled. Even after trying to convince Joseph of the danger Martha could be facing, his brother refused to tell him anything. *He's hiding something, too.*

Aaron glanced around for David Wenger. After drinking a glass of water that Sarah had offered him, the man had sauntered toward the carriage shed. Several minutes had passed, and he hadn't returned. Why? From high on a beam, his eyes searched among the frolicking children for a glimpse of Martha. If his suspicions were correct, she might try to meet with David. Martha was so difficult to keep track of. Why had so many of the young women dressed in medium-blue today?

Unable to locate Martha, he strode quickly across the barnyard to the carriage shed, slid the door farther open, and stepped inside. Stopping abruptly, he stared.

David chuckled. "*Herzlich Dank* for bringing me the message, Martha."

She appeared startled, but smiled brightly. "*Gross Dank* again for bringing the fried chicken, Sir."

Spinning on his heel, David smiled at Aaron, then left the shed without looking back.

Aaron stared after him, then turned to Martha, his suspicion running amuck. "What was that all about?"

"Like the man said, I delivered a message."

"Concerning what?"

She glanced at the buggy, seemingly flustered. "He brought fried chicken."

"So? Everyone brought something special."

"His wife is dead. It's appropriate to thank him personally. *Gel?*"

"*Vell* . . . it's a bit odd to thank a man in the shed!" He thought about the possibility of David being this girl's father. He narrowed his eyes. "Unless—"

She laughed, cutting off his words. "Sarah sent me to get a shawl from the buggy. The man happened to be here when I came in, so I took the opportunity to speak with him."

Aaron frowned. "Something doesn't add up."

With a nervous giggle, she reached into the buggy and seized a folded cape. Waving it victoriously, she hurried away.

"Martha!"

"Sarah's waiting." She increased her pace.

Setting his jaw, Aaron headed back to the construction site. Tonight, he would insist Martha reveal the truth.

Martha? he thought. *Or Rebecca?* Gripping a hammer, he struck nails with a vengeance.

Rebecca played with the children where she could watch the barn construction. *Aaron knows*, she thought. She was surprised that the knowledge didn't upset her. The gentle witness of the Beilers' trust in God had deepened Rebecca's faith. Now that Joseph had phoned the police about Gene's possible drug-dealing, she felt confident in reporting her suspicion to them.

Tonight, I'll explain everything to Aaron. Somehow, she knew he would understand. *Tomorrow, I'll go to the police.*

Lord God, forgive me for the sins I've committed. Cleanse my heart and make me pure. Peace spread within her. Even though she had made mistakes, God had remained faithful. He had protected her when she'd been afraid, given her an understanding friend in Sarah, and now was filling her with strength, courage, and hope.

"Praise the Lord, for he is good and his steadfast love endureth forever," she whispered, ready to face whatever she had to to clear her name. *Precious Jesus, give me strength and courage to live for You, to keep my faith constant and Your teaching foremost in my heart.* Free at last, in a way the world could not provide or understand, she drew a deep breath and smiled.

She continued to glance at the barn. The foreman separated the men into groups of a dozen, giving them assigned tasks. Beams were soon pulled into place with ropes and fastened. Men scampered up and down ladders and across support beams as joists were nailed securely. Before the noon meal, the skeletal frame of the structure was up.

Long tables stretched across the yard. The women had brought kettles, pans, and bowls of delicious food. The tables almost groaned under the weight of it. There were fried chickens, baked hams, meat balls and gravy. Bowls of candied sweet potatoes rivaled mounds of creamy mashed potatoes and casseroles of scalloped ones. Several containers of fresh garden vegetables seemed to blossom strategically among the meats. Dishes of applesauce, gelatin salads, and puddings competed for space. Various dishes of pickles and relishes sat on a side table. Crowded on a table of their own, dozens of desserts competed for attention.

Peter John Lapp and Eli carried a table to the back of the house.

"Put it here under the hickory trees," Liz said.

Eli looked disturbed. "Why can't the children eat with the adults?"

Liz flipped the tablecloth at him. "Sarah thinks it might be easier this way."

"It doesn't make sense!"

She poked him and laughed. "*Ja, vell*, it's worth a try. *Gel?*"

He grinned. "Whatever you say."

Liz waved her hand. "Go get your dinner."

Watching them go, Rebecca smiled at Liz. "Was this your idea?"

"Sarah and I talked it over and decided the children would be better off away from the confusion."

"*Viel Dank.*" Knowing the real reason, Rebecca laughed.

Liz's green eyes sparkled. "Sarah and I will accompany the children to serve their plates. You stay here and help them get seated when they return."

Rebecca sighed with relief. At least she wouldn't find herself sitting across the table from someone she'd grown up with—or seen on the Lancaster streets.

Snatches of conversation drifted to her from the other side of the quilts. She kept her back to the group, not wanting anyone to accidentally peer through an opening between the hanging blankets and see her face. She was aware of her father's eyes, but knew he would use discretion and not get caught staring.

After the meal, the men hurried back to the barn. Liz finished eating and joined the children. By this time, they were restless, ready to get into mischief.

"After we clear the tables, I'll watch these monkeys," Liz said. "You'll need a break."

Using a row of berry bushes as camouflage, Rebecca sat on the grass and watched dozens of men climb over the frame of the building like giant ants. The steady drumming of hammers mingled into one deafening noise. Gasoline generators roared as they powered electric tools, and saws screamed as they bit their way through planks and siding boards. A diesel engine generated hydraulic pressure for automated tools. The structure seemed to grow in front of her eyes. Every time she became distracted by one of the children, then looked back at the barn, she was amazed at the progress. It was always this way and the thrill never lessened.

Large sections of the barn's sides were constructed on the ground, then attaching ropes, the men heaved them into place and nailed them securely.

By early evening, the building was finished. Some of the

families said good-bye and left for home.

"Smoking time," Moses Zimmerman said, removing his straw hat and patting his head to smooth his tousled gray hair. Grinning, he lit a cigar. Cigarettes are forbidden, but since Amish in the Lancaster area grow tobacco, dry the leaves, and make their own cigars, they are permitted to smoke them.

Joseph joined Moses with a cookie in one bandaged hand and a piece of pie in the other.

Moses laughed. "I'm glad to see you're feeling better. At least you can still eat with both hands. *Gel*?"

Joseph grinned. "I have to keep up my strength. Now that we've lost our milkers, the cows have to be milked by hand."

"*Ja*. I know you hate milking the old-fashioned way, but did you need to burn your hands to get out of it?"

Joseph laughed. "It worked! *Gel*?"

"It's a good thing you have good neighbors or Noah and Aaron would be stuck with milking all thirty-one."

"Jesse does his share."

Rebecca enjoyed listening to the good-natured bantering, but missed joining in on the fun. Cuddling Priscilla, Elizabeth strolled to the peach tree. She gazed west, her expression wistful. Elam had gone back to Mercer County. Was Elizabeth thinking about him?

Sarah took a turn with the children, but was busy cuddling a little girl who had cut her knee, and one of the tiny ones needed her diaper changed.

Sarah looked thoughtful, then smiled at Rebecca. "If you slip in the side door and up the back stairs, no one will see you."

Sweeping the toddler into her arms, Rebecca hurried upstairs to the room designated for the purpose, changed the baby, and picked her up.

A car sped up Kings' lane and stopped. Rebecca peered out the window at the state trooper's emblem on the door of the vehicle and froze. Her heart raced wildly as one of the troopers got out of the car, strolled to the house, and knocked on the door.

Moments later, Liz Lapp ran up the stairs and into the room, her eyes wide. "That officer is asking for Rebecca Wenger!"

19

"*Wass* are you going to do?" Liz asked, her green eyes wide.

Rebecca's heart drummed in her temples. *I'm one day too late*, she thought, wondering why God hadn't protected her until tomorrow. "There must be a lesson in this that the Lord wants me to learn," she said, praying for His strength and guidance.

The words, "I will never leave thee nor forsake thee," drifted into her mind. "Thank you, Lord," she whispered.

"Martha!" Aaron's voice echoed up the back stairway as his tread resounded on the bottom steps.

She crossed the bedroom, paused to take a deep breath, then slowly descended the stairs.

Aaron stopped a third of the way up. "Rebecca?"

She gripped the banister with her right hand; the left one hovered in the space between them. Standing on the next step up brought her eyes nearly parallel to his.

He caught her free hand, his fingers curled around hers, and his face twisted as though he were in pain. "*Wass* do the police want with you?"

"I . . . I damaged . . . a car." She closed her eyes, but picturing the strange packets, she blinked. "I ran, but there were . . . extenuating circumstances. I intended to explain everything to you tonight."

His fingers tightened on hers. "I wish you would've trusted me enough to have told me."

"I explained it to Sarah. She's wonderful. *Gel*?"

"*Ja.*" He released her hand as though mentioning Sarah had made him aware of touching Rebecca.

She took a deep breath. "Where's my father?"

"Waiting in the yard."

Her eyes gazed beseechingly into his. "Please believe in me."

"I do. Oh, Amber." He took her face in his hands.

Aaron stepped away as a trooper stopped at the bottom of the stairs and glanced upward. "Miss Wenger?"

She nodded. Noticing the man's square jaw and handsome face, she realized he was the one she'd bumped into the evening the barn had burned. The amicable way he'd laughed seemed to echo in the canyons of her chaotic recall.

"I'm Corporal Kiefer." His neat blond brows hovered over kind blue eyes, and a smile softened his features, yet his alert stance, his gray uniform, and the holstered gun strapped to his side made him appear imposing. "I have a warrant for your arrest, Miss Wenger," he said softly. "Please come with me."

Lowering her lashes, she continued down the steps and crossed the kitchen with the trooper. He pushed the screen door open. Another officer waited on the porch. He was shorter, but had broad shoulders. His black brows lay over his green eyes in the same fashion as his black mustache rested above his upper lip. He looked friendly, but he didn't smile.

David Wenger hurried across the lawn to meet Rebecca. "*Der gut Man* will help you."

"I know, Papa." She fought humiliation as she glanced at the compassionate faces of her Amish friends.

"Are you David Wenger?" Corporal Kiefer asked.

"Yes." David faced the officer. "What are the charges?"

"Miss Wenger left the scene of an accident, then ignored a citation to appear before a district justice."

"She wasn't home, so she didn't know about the citation."

"She'll have a chance to explain that at her hearing, Mr. Wenger."

Aaron hurried to join the group. Unable to speak because of the lump in her throat, Rebecca met his unwavering gaze.

"If only..." His features were etched with anguish and his arms hung limp by his sides.

Joseph stood by the porch steps. He made a familiar OK sign that encouraged Rebecca.

Corporal Kiefer gently tugged her arm. "We'll take you to the office of the district justice for Strasburg."

Glancing at David, the trooper with the dark brows smiled crookedly, tilting his mustache. "You may follow us."

Corporal Kiefer opened the back door of the police vehicle for Rebecca. As she climbed in and settled on the seat, she glanced out the back window. Sarah hurried to Aaron. He stood staring at the trooper's car.

Kiefer slid into the back seat with Rebecca, and the second officer got behind the wheel and started the engine. As the car turned, Rebecca looked back. Aaron sat on a stump. His shoulders slumped, his head hung, and his hands covered his face. He'd squeezed his hat out of shape, and it lay at his feet like an injured animal. Sarah stood beside him with her hand on his shoulder.

Rebecca sighed. If only she had gone directly to the police, she could have avoided this humiliation. She had permitted her fear concerning possible narcotics to weaken her and undermine her trust in God. She silently thanked Him for His grace and mercy. She knew Christians were not perfect, and that God forgave His children when they erred and repented. She had grown through her ordeal, and vowed that from now on, she would trust God completely. She glanced at the officer beside her. "What happens when I go before the district justice?"

"He'll explain your options."

Options? she thought, praying God would exonerate her. *He already has*, she knew, but the district justice wasn't God. She studied Corporal Kiefer's face. "Will I have to pay a fine?"

"What did your citation say?"

"I haven't seen it."

Kiefer smiled. "I suggest you read it before you agree to anything or sign a statement." The kindness and understanding that emanated from his blue eyes encouraged her.

The trooper who was driving parked the car. Kiefer opened the door, got out, and waited for Rebecca to join him.

She looked around. "Where's my father?"

"He'll have to park his car." Kiefer's warm smile was encouraging, yet her heart raced.

When her father appeared, she took his arm, and together they entered the office of the district justice. The secretary smiled and motioned for them to go into the inner office. Taking a deep breath, Rebecca stepped through the doorway.

"Have a seat, Miss Wenger," the district justice said, motioning to the two chairs facing his desk.

The man appeared pleasant, yet her legs felt wobbly as she took one of the chairs. Her father sat on the one beside her. Corporal Kiefer took a position at the back wall.

The justice looked at Rebecca and smiled. "All we're going to do today is set the date for your hearing." He flipped through his calendar and appointment book, set a date three weeks ahead, then eyed her. "I sometimes waver setting a bond, but you ignored your citation to appear in this office. Since there was an arrest, and there's no guarantee that you won't run again—"

"I won't! Honest!"

The justice thought a moment. "I set bond at five hundred dollars."

Rebecca swallowed. "Plus fines and charges?"

"Those will be levied at the time of your hearing." He toyed with his pen. "The fine for hit-and-run is from fifty to three hundred dollars. In your case, it will probably be fifty. Itemized court charges will be around a hundred. You'll have a chance to plead innocent, in which case, you'll be given a trial."

"I'm guilty," she said quietly.

"I suggest you don't admit guilt or sign anything until you read the charges, Miss Wenger, but we won't get into that today. Now, if your bond is put up, you'll be released on your own recognizance."

David paid the bond, then turned to Rebecca with a smile. "Let's go, honey."

As she opened the door into the outer office, Joseph hurried across the room to meet her. Sarah was with him.

"How'd you get here?" Rebecca asked, hugging Sarah.

"We jumped in your father's car and came with him."

Suddenly, Aaron was there, embracing Rebecca. Overcome with joy and love, she clung to him. Then blasted by the knowledge that, because of Sarah, she had no right to this man, anguish gouged canyons of despair in her heart. The pain of it made her stiffen and turn away, misery overshadowing the euphoria of her newly acquired freedom.

"Is everything all right, now?" Joseph asked.

"It will be."

Sarah gripped Rebecca's hand. "I'm going to miss you dreadfully, but I know your family will be overjoyed to get you home." She blinked, her blue eyes lustrous with happy tears. "You'll visit us soon, *gel*?"

"Oh *ja*." Rebecca watched Aaron from her side-vision. He moved farther away and seemed pensive.

Sarah was effervescent. "When can you come?"

Rebecca's conflicting emotions made her feel dizzy. "I'll try to, next week." She wanted to say good-bye to Aaron, but the lump in her throat cut off her words. Unable to meet his eyes, she pushed open the door and stepped outside.

David turned to face Sarah and Joseph. "I'll drive you folks home."

Joseph smiled. "*Viel Dank*, but I phoned John. He's here to pick us up."

Rebecca looked at the familiar Beachy Amishman with the bulbous nose and friendly eyes. He waved to her as he stopped in front of the building. Aaron got into the front seat without looking back. Waving, Sarah got into the back seat with Joseph.

David took her arm. "Let's go home, honey."

"That sounds like heaven—almost." She accompanied her father and got in his car. Fastening her seat belt, she leaned back and sighed. "*Dank der gut Man* this will soon be over. I'm so happy to put my mistakes and deceit behind me."

David reached to squeeze her hand. "When we confess our

wrongdoings, Jesus washes us clean by His precious shed blood."

She sighed. "I've learned by my mistakes."

"So have I." His smile broadened. "Mary has been rethinking her views, too. I stopped at the phone shack to call her, so she's expecting us."

"How's she going to act when I walk in?"

"She's anxiously waiting."

Soft laughter bubbled into Rebecca's throat. "She'll spend the next three months lecturing me on proper conduct, but I almost look forward to it."

"Mother says you've already suffered because of your sin, so there'll be nothing more said concerning it."

"I didn't appreciate *Mammi*. I suppose it was because I thought about myself instead of trying to understand her. I've learned a lot from the Amish. I can hardly wait to hug *Mammi*."

"Mother feels she has learned a lot as well." He smiled. "We'll just go on from here."

David parked the car in the driveway. Rebecca jumped out. She glanced at the multicolored array of wild flowers along the fence as she rushed through the gate. Pausing, she bent to touch a giant yellow mum at the edge of the round flower bed; then she hurried across the yard and opened the kitchen door. A heart-shaped cake with "Welcome Home" printed on it sat on the table, and the aroma of fried chicken wafted to her. She turned to face the doorway that led from the dining room. Mary stood in the opening, appearing uncertain.

"*Mammi*," Rebecca whispered, moving to her.

There were tears in the old woman's eyes as she held Rebecca tightly. "*Dank der gut Man* you're home." Her voice quavered.

Rebecca kissed Mary's wrinkled cheek. "You're the best *Mammi* anyone could have."

"*Vell* . . . we've all made mistakes, and we'll probably make a few more, but, in the future, I pray we'll handle our disagreements with more understanding."

"Your chicken smells heavenly."

"Now, Rebecca, you shouldn't use the name of heaven so . . .

Ach!" Mary laughed. "I guess old habits are hard to break."

Home really is going to be different! Rebecca thought. Glancing around the familiar kitchen, she gasped. "New curtains!" She whirled to face Mary. "They're yellow!"

"*Vell*," Mary said, looking a bit sheepish. "We'll both have to learn to give a little." A smile deepened the wrinkles around her mouth and eyes. "Yellow isn't so bad. Actually, it's quite pleasant. It makes the room look like sunshine—even on a cloudy day."

"Oh, *Mammi!*" Laughing, Rebecca hugged her again.

Mary had set the dining room table with the best china. Eyeing a new blue tablecloth and blue and pink flowered napkins, Rebecca blinked. Mary had never permitted any except white or a subdued check.

When they were seated and the meal begun, Rebecca faced her father. "Maybe I should look for a job."

Mary's tea cup clattered to her saucer. Her lips moved slightly, but she remained silent.

Rebecca sighed. "I feel I should earn the money to pay my fines and court costs." She shuddered. "And that five hundred dollar bond!"

"I'll get the bond money back after the hearing." David chuckled. "Unless you skip town."

"Never again!" Rebecca noticed Mary's hands trembling. "Are you all right, *Mammi*?"

"*Vell*, the last time you got a job, you--" Closing her lips, she lowered her eyes to her plate.

"This time it'll be different."

Mary dabbed her mouth with her flowered napkin. "Maybe you should consider furthering your education."

Eyeing the old woman, Rebecca held her breath and waited.

Mary sipped her tea and smiled. "Do you still feel *der gut Man* is calling you into nursing?"

"*Ja.*"

"Then, I'll no longer stand in your way."

Was the sun that filtered through the lace curtains the only thing brightening the room? "Do you mean it?"

Although uncertainty shimmered in Mary's eyes, she nodded.

David smiled. "It's not too late to put in your application for the fall semester." He picked up the platter of fried chicken, helped himself, then passed the platter to Mary. "You made a mistake, Amber, but that page of your life is ended."

"*Herzlich Dank der gut Man.* From now on, I'll trust Him."

Tears formed in the old woman's faded eyes, and she dabbed at them with her handkerchief. "Had I agreed to your entering nurse's training, you wouldn't have taken a job in that florist shop, and all this heartache could've been avoided."

Jumping up, Rebecca hugged her. "I love you, *Mammi. Es speit mich* for what I've put you and Papa through."

David helped himself to the mixed vegetables. "The important thing is that we've all learned from this experience. We've grown closer to each other, and have learned to depend more on the Lord."

"*Dank der gut Man* for his grace and mercy," Mary said.

Rebecca's heart felt lighter than it had in months. "Thank you, Jesus," she whispered.

Three days later, Rebecca went to her bedroom shortly after the noon meal. She continued to marvel over the cheery decor. During her absence, *Mammi* Mary had instructed David to redecorate, using colors she'd formerly denied Rebecca, but knew the girl loved. Rebecca's eyes spanned the cotton-candy-pink walls. She smiled. The drab gray-green curtains had been replaced with drapes that had baskets of dainty pink roses on a creamy-white background. The bedspread matched, as did the cushion on the rocker by the window.

Retrieving the catalogue and brochures concerning nurse's training that Margie had given her months ago, she sprawled across her bed and fanned the pamphlets in an arc.

"Rebecca," Mary called up the stairway. "Sarah Beiler wants to speak with you on the phone."

Racing down the stairs, she grappled with the instrument. "Sarah."

"*Hello*, Rebecca. It's so good to hear your voice. I've thought a lot about you. Joseph and I have had long talks."

"I shouldn't have made him keep my secret."

"He's relieved to have it out in the open. Being secretive and evasive was making him sick."

"I have a lot to thank him for."

"I miss you Rebecca."

"I miss you, too." Picturing Aaron, she toyed with the hem of one of the new bright-yellow kitchen curtains, still amazed that Mary had permitted them.

"I hope when you come to visit you'll stay a few days, Rebecca."

"Having the use of Papa's car, I can visit often." Rebecca frowned. There would be nothing to fear, except running into Aaron. Or what was worse, seeing him with Sarah. "Did Eli bring you to the phone shack?"

"Aaron did. I was at his place watching Nancy."

Rebecca entwined the phone cord in her fingers, then shook them free. She yearned to speak with Aaron, but struggled to control her deep feelings for him. She opened her mouth to ask to talk to him, but her throbbing heart halted her request. She reminded herself that he belonged to Sarah, and fought to swallow a persistent lump in her throat. "Tell everyone I said hello."

"I will. And they all wanted to be remembered to you." She laughed softly. "I told Nancy that I was phoning you. She said to tell you she wanted you to come and play."

"Bless her heart."

"Ransom is getting fidgety and Aaron's beginning to pace, so I'd better say good-bye."

"He's probably impatient because you're talking to me."

"He doesn't know. I'll call again before long."

"Tell Aaron . . ."

"*Ja?*"

"Nothing, Sarah. *Der gut Man* bless you both."

"May He bless you, too."

When Rebecca replaced the receiver, she closed her eyes tightly and struggled to bring her effusive heart under submission. Her mind had said its farewell to Aaron, but her tenacious heart continued to yearn for the sweet kisses she'd tasted.

She jumped as the phone rang, jangling her nerves. Taking a deep calming breath and praying to still the tremor she knew would be in her voice, she gripped the receiver. "Hello."

"Hi, Rebecca."

"Margie! I thought you were visiting a friend in Philadelphia."

"I just got back and Dad said you were home. You busy?"

"I was looking through my nurse's training brochures."

"Why? Doesn't that always upset you?"

"Not any more. I've got the green light!"

"You're kidding! Even from the old lady?"

Rebecca's heart reacted against her cousin's frivolous reference to Mary. *"Mammi* has been a peach about it. I'm so excited."

"Me, too!"

"Just don't offer to help me get a job."

Margie laughed. "Hey, because of me, you got acquainted with a lot of kind Amish families. According to what Dick said, I thought you might be marrying Aaron King."

Rebecca laughed, but only felt it in her throat. "Aaron's in love with Sarah Beiler. They'll probably marry this fall."

"Rats! I still think he's a real hunk."

"Margie!" Rebecca sighed, but a grin toyed with the corners of her mouth.

"Hey! Have you been listening to the news? Of course you haven't." Margie hardly stopped for a breath. "Did you hear what happened to Vance Troy?"

"Vance?"

"Yeah! The police received a tip about cocaine about the time you vanished and suspected Vance."

"Oh!" Rebecca gripped the receiver as she recalled mailing the letter to the police station.

"They searched his flower shop, but didn't find anything. An investigator has been watching Vance. Last week, the police received a phone call that cast suspicion on one of Vance's former employees."

Joe's call, Rebecca thought.

"This guy had opened a candy and gift shop a few weeks ago. The cops raided his shop. Apparently he and Vance have been using the store to pass cocaine. The police found enough snow in the bottom of candy boxes to send them up for awhile." Margie giggled. "You quit too soon. You missed all the excitement!"

"Oh, Margie." Rebecca breathed a prayer of thanks, praising God for protecting her.

"I'm going shopping at Park City Mall on Friday, Rebecca. Wanna go?"

"That sounds like where it all began."

Margie laughed. "It all ended well. Besides, now that you're back and Mary's grateful about it, you have permission to enter nurse's training. You've found your Eden, Cousin!"

She thought about her love for Aaron. "Well, not quite."

"Dick's here, so I've gotta run."

Replacing the receiver, Rebecca meandered back to her bedroom. She wished Margie had not brought up Aaron. It made her heart ache. Crossing the buff-colored carpet, she touched one of the sweetheart roses on the drapes, then gazed out the window. A bluebird splashed in the bird bath, then fluffed his plumage. The wild flowers she'd planted along the picket fence bloomed in a multicolored panorama. Pink touch-me-nots quavered in the breeze, and brown-eyed Susans nodded their heads. Leafy branches of the maple tree seemed to wave to her.

The next afternoon, Rebecca sat in the chair by her bedroom window. *Mammi* Mary had finally permitted her to read an inspirational historical novel. Flipping another page, she smiled.

A gray Taurus pulled in the driveway and stopped. An image of Aaron flashed through her mind, and her heart lurched, but there were many cars of that make and color. Her eyes widened as the driver's door swung open and Aaron got out. He wore a light-blue shirt and the usual one dark suspender held up his black broadfalls. She stared as he strolled toward the front porch. Was he no longer keeping his vehicle a secret?

Digging the still-hidden mirror out of her dresser drawer, she quickly applied soft-pink lipstick. Blotting it on a tissue, she checked her reflection, making sure the color looked natural. Smoothing her plain purple dress, she wished she had time to change into the pretty pink flowered one with which *Mammi* had surprised her.

When Aaron rapped on the front door, she jumped. Hurrying to the top of the stairs, she stopped to listen. She longed to race to meet him, but dreaded the possibility of making a fool of herself. Gripping the top newel post, she waited. She forced an outward calm, but her nerves were squealing like startled bats.

"Rebecca," Mary called. "Aaron King wishes to see you."

Taking a deep breath, Rebecca descended the stairs. Mary stood by a brown armchair, studying their visitor. Aaron stood gazing out the picture window at the vivid array of blooms in the flower bed, his straw hat in his hand. As Rebecca's foot touched the last step, he turned.

"*Hello, wie gehts*, Aaron. It's good to see you." Finding it difficult to meet his gaze, she turned and adjusted the perfectly draped pastel striped afghan that covered the back of the cream-colored sofa. "Have a seat."

Excusing herself, Mary quietly left the room.

Aaron sat, his back straight. Clearing his throat, he toyed with the brim of his hat. "Sarah sent me."

Rebecca took a seat on the far end of the sofa and struggled not to let her words falter and betray her. "You should've brought her with you."

"She's very busy these days with canning—and all . . ."

Rebecca fingered the lavender flowered embroidery on a toss pillow that was a shade deeper than the floss. "As long as she's happy."

"*Ja*." He smiled. "She's that, all right." His gaze met Rebecca's. "Sarah would like you to come to help her plan the wedding."

The word "wedding" stung her senses and reverberated her core. Swallowing, she tried to smile.

20

"I'd love to visit Sarah before the wedding, Aaron." Rebecca prayed her smile didn't appear as plastic as it felt. Even though she'd expected a wedding announcement, the words coming from Aaron's mouth had scourged her heart. Squeezing the lavender toss pillow, she shoved it between herself and the arm of the sofa.

"Sarah would like to know when you can *kom*."

"Wednesday afternoon would be good for me."

Sitting stiffly on the other end of the sofa, he studied her with serious eyes. "I can *kom* for you."

"*Gross Dank*, but I'll have the car when Dad gets home from work. When's the big day?"

"The third Thursday in November."

"That's three months away. But I suppose Sarah's excited."

"*Ja*." He laid his hat on the arm of the sofa. "The service will be at Isaac Beiler's and the meal will be served at my farm."

She'd assumed that would be the arrangement. She wanted to appear joyous and shower Aaron with best wishes, but the tenacious lump in her throat restricted her speech, and their conversation lapsed into an uncomfortable silence.

Clutching his hat, Aaron got to his feet.

Rebecca stood. She hated to see him go, for she assumed this would be the last time they would be alone together—until after he was Sarah's husband. "Would you like a cup of coffee?"

"*Herzlich Dank*, Amber, but I'd better be going. I have to deliver a kitchen hutch this afternoon."

She glanced out the window at his car, then back to his face. "You deliver them yourself?"

"Some. I hire a pick-up for larger pieces." His brow furrowed. "There are complications, but . . ." He flipped his hand, evidently not wishing to discuss the problem. "I'll probably see you when you visit Sarah."

She accompanied him to the front door. As she stepped outside, a brisk summer breeze billowed her purple skirt. "It looks like a storm's brewing."

"*Ja*." He studied the gray clouds that charged across the sky, then faced her.

Unable to meet his gaze, she peered unseeingly at the tobacco field near the barn. The plants were nearly ready to harvest. Thunder rumbled in the distance, and a mist dampened the sidewalk and the top of the railing.

"*Vell* . . . I'll see you, Amber."

She nodded, not trusting herself to speak. A leaf from a nearby hydrangea bush, swept by the breeze, skittered across the porch, whispered against her ankle, then tumbled to a stop against the banister. Picking it up, she twirled the stem between her thumb and forefinger. Aaron strode quickly to his car, got in, and shut the door. Starting the engine, he waved, then sped out the driveway.

"Good-bye, Aaron," she whispered smiling vibrantly as she battled the tears that forced their way forward. As his car vanished around a curve, she struggled to swallow what felt like a football and unconsciously crumpled the wet leaf in her hand.

The sound of his motor faded in the distance. Slowly descending the porch steps, Rebecca moved onto the lawn and plucked a wilted blossom from the Mr. Lincoln rosebush. The red petals, shaken by her trembling hands, fluttered to the grass at her feet like tiny lifeless butterflies. Bending, she retrieved one velvety petal. Another gust of wind ripped it from her fingers. Larger drops of rain struck her face and arms, encouraging her to retreat to the porch. She slipped inside, avoided *Mammi's* sagacious eyes, and fled up the stairs.

For the next few days, she struggled with the reality of Aaron's coming marriage. She made herself a cup of tea, propped an elbow on the kitchen table, and sipped the steaming brew.

Mammi came in waving an envelope. "Letter for you."

"*Gross Dank.*" Rebecca glanced at the return address. "It's from Sarah Beiler. I plan to visit her today." Ripping open the envelope, she extracted the letter. Would Sarah expound words of love about her future husband? Afraid *Mammi* would interpret her misery, Rebecca excused herself and ran upstairs. In her room, she unfolded the letter.

"*Dear Rebecca,*

Aaron said you plan to visit on Wednesday. I pray you'll be able to come. Ruth's baking a cake, and Aunt Nancy King will be visiting, too. She's quiet and sweet, much like yourself. I know you'll love her as I do.

Herzlich Dank for agreeing to help me plan my wedding. I'm so excited, although the date seems so far away. See you soon.

Love,
Sarah"

Rebecca changed into the new light-pink dress Mary had given her for her homecoming, but paused to trace around the tiny deeper pink and lavender pansies on the fabric. Smiling, she clutched a creamy-white purse and went downstairs.

Mary sat on the sofa, her sewing basket open by her side. Looking up, she smiled. "Have a good time."

"I will." Rebecca hugged the old lady and kissed her wrinkled cheek. "And *Gross Dank* again for the lovely new dress."

"*Vell*, it was a long time in coming." Her eyes spanned Rebecca's attire. "It might rain. Don't forget to take a wrap, dear." She bit her lower lip as though she wondered if she should have suggested it.

Rebecca marveled over Mary's recent leniency. "I'll take my

new blue cape, *Mammi*." She went to the closet, slipped the garment from its hanger, slung it over her arm, and hurried to the car. Backing out of the driveway, she headed for Route 23.

Pondering her visit with Sarah buoyed Rebecca's spirit, but her exhilaration was dampened by the thought of losing Aaron forever. Her mouth drew taut and her hands tightened on the steering wheel as she vowed she wouldn't let Sarah detect her dismay.

A leaf, its stem caught under the windshield wiper, lay marooned and withered on the hood. *That's what I'll feel like after Aaron marries Sarah.* The rest of the trip, she struggled to bring her emotions into submission.

Rebecca parked the car by Beilers' front gate, got out and headed toward the house. Yipping, Jed romped to greet her. Little John and Reuben stopped their play long enough to grin. *Mammi* Hazel sat in her favorite porch rocker, knitting. Smiling, she nodded.

The screen door burst open. Sarah rushed to hug Rebecca. "It's so good to see you." She beamed. "My wedding's three months away, but I can't help being excited!"

"I'm so happy for you," Rebecca said, hiding her torment.

Esther opened the screen door. "Hello, *wie gehts*."

As Rebecca stepped into the kitchen, the aroma of freshly baked chocolate cake and roasting beef wafted to greet her.

"*Un wie gehts*, Martha, I mean Rebecca," Ruth called, waving her frosting knife and nearly losing a glob of the fluffy white substance. She giggled and her dark eyes sparkled.

Sarah introduced Rebecca to Aunt Nancy King.

"Hello, Rebecca." The plump woman's smile rounded her pink cheeks and her deep-blue eyes twinkled. "Aaron and Joseph have told me so much about you."

Feeling as though she'd acquired an extended family, Rebecca returned smiles and warm greetings. Wearing a print dress and minus an Amish apron, she felt a bit self-conscious, but the genuine hugs and the kisses that brushed her cheeks soon dispelled her apprehension.

Sarah grasped Rebecca's hand. "*Kom ann*. We have so much to talk about. Let's go to our room."

Rebecca pondered the continued use of the words *our room* and held her smile as she followed her friend to the familiar bedroom. Eyeing the chair by the window, she relived the Sunday she'd spied on Aaron.

Sarah clasped her hands. "I can hardly wait until November. Oh, I've waited so long for this."

The words jolted Rebecca back to the present. "Once the ceremony takes place, you'll be married for a long time. *Gel*?"

"*Ja*." Sarah whirled around the room. "Won't it be *wonderbar*!" Her eyes glistened, and her face was aglow.

Rebecca was happy for her friend, but her own heart grieved. She turned away. Were tears going to betray her, regardless of how desperately she battled to hold them back? Wrestling to regain control of her emotions, she fumbled with a pile of partly-finished quilt patches on Sarah's bedside table and hoped the girl was too dreamy to notice her misery. In spite of her supreme effort to appear joyous, her hands trembled.

Sarah sighed. "I know you're happy for me. *Gel?*"

"Oh, *Ja*!" A sob caught in her constricted throat.

"Rebecca?"

Drawing a long breath she closed her eyes hard, battling her tenacious tears.

Approaching quietly, Sarah studied Rebecca's face and gasped.

Forcing a smile, Rebecca swiped at her moistened cheeks. "You'll make a good wife. Aaron's fortunate."

"*Ach!*"

"He's anxious, too, Sarah." Clenching her jaw, she forbade more tears, but one escaped captivity and rolled down her face.

Sarah sobered. "*Es speit mich* that you misunderstood. I thought you knew."

"I've known all along that you and Aaron —" Her voice caught, and she turned away.

"*Ach*! Rebecca, I'm marrying Joseph."

Rebecca whirled. "Joseph!"

"You thought it was Aaron?"

"*Vell* . . ." Weakening, Rebecca sat on the bed. "I discovered you were attracted to him, the first day I came here, and I could tell he cared for you, too."

I adore Aaron—as a brother. But I've loved Joseph for a long time. When he left, I thought I'd die. Aaron helped me a lot." She smiled and pink hue crept across her lovely face. "When I saw Joseph in Amish clothes, again, I was ecstatic!"

Rebecca thought back. "When you returned from Kings', the day they built their chicken house, you were so happy."

"I was flying! Joseph had vowed to remain at home." Laughing, she hugged Rebecca. "I was so befuddled, I poured milk in the water glasses."

"Wait a minute! At *Younga* when I saw you kissing someone, I'd thought it was Aaron, but . . ."

"That was Joseph! I promised him I'd be his sweetheart."

Rebecca's eyes widened. "That's why you tried to get me to sit in the front seat with Aaron. I was so dense, I made you sit with him instead."

"We should've talked about it, but it's fun to fool our families and friends."

"You did a good job of that!"

Sarah smiled. "Aaron wants to start a business."

"*Ja*, but being the eldest, won't he eventually have the responsibility of running the farm?"

"Now that Joseph's back and wants to manage the farm, it frees Aaron."

"Aaron's the most wonderful man I've ever known."

"*Ja*? You don't act like it. He was upset when you snubbed him the day at the justice's office."

"That wasn't because I didn't care!"

"He thought so, especially when you didn't contact him afterwards."

"He would've had to be the one to reach me by phone."

Looking confused, Sarah sat on the edge of her bed. "You could've answered his letter."

"*Wass* letter?"

"You didn't receive one?"

"No!"

"I suggested it might have gotten lost, but Aaron disagreed. He can be stubborn—sometimes." Massaging her temples, she looked reflective. "I longed to call you about Joseph's proposal, but I sent Aaron, assuming once you two were alone together you'd come to an understanding."

"He didn't mention Joseph, so I assumed Aaron was the groom-to-be." She bit her lip. "He seemed . . . distant."

"He came back depressed." Sarah shrugged. "He said you treated him with indifference."

"I hid my feelings because I thought he was going to marry you."

Sarah threw up her hands. "*Ach*, you two!" A vehicle stopped in front, and she glanced out the window. "It's a van." She gasped. "It's Aaron!"

"Van?" Rebecca whispered. "Aaron?"

"*Kom ann!*" Grinning, Sarah led the way.

Battling apprehension, Rebecca followed, but stopped on the porch. Aaron's eyes met hers, and he paused with his hand on the gate.

Sarah laughed softly. "I think you should take her to see your new house."

"House?" Rebecca echoed.

Approaching, Aaron leaned against a porch roof support and appeared dubious. "Would you like to see my place?"

"*Vell . . . ja.*"

Sarah's eyes sparkled mischievously as she looked at Aaron. "By the way, she didn't get your letter."

His brows rose sharply.

Sarah shrugged. "Maybe you forgot to mail it."

"I gave it to Jesse to put in the box."

Stepping forward, Rebecca paused to survey his dark-blue vehicle. "Do you like the van better than your Taurus?"

"It had high mileage. Besides, I need room to haul supplies."

Rebecca accompanied Aaron to his van and got in. "Are you

no longer concealing your vehicle?"

"*Vell* . . ." He looked pensive. "We'll talk about that—later." Starting the engine, he turned the van and headed out Beiler's lane.

Rebecca glanced at the clutter of folded papers on a box between the front seats, then watched as a light sprinkle of rain dappled the windshield. Aaron seemed to have something on his mind. Was he distressed over Sarah's marrying his brother? Or was he involved with someone else?

A cream-colored German shepherd darted onto the highway. Aaron jammed on the brakes. The pile of papers and envelopes sloshed onto the floor. The tires squealed, but the van stopped in time. Aaron whistled.

"That was close." Rebecca bent to scoop up the scattered papers.

Glancing at the haphazard pile as he accelerated, he chuckled. "That's the junk I took out of my glove compartment when I traded vehicles."

One envelope looked sealed. Rebecca flipped it over, read her address, and waved her prize. "Is this the letter you were so sure Jesse mailed?"

He glanced at the handwriting. "*Ja!*"

She slid the letter into her pocket.

"*Wass* are you going to do with that?"

"Just because the stamp isn't canceled doesn't mean it isn't mine."

He laughed, but it sounded strained.

Assuming the letter would explain Aaron's feelings about Sarah marrying Joseph, she was anxious to read it—yet she was apprehensive. Deep in thought, she paid no heed to the direction they were traveling. When he turned into a driveway and parked, she glanced up. A robin fluttered from a maple tree to her left and landed on the grass on the other side of a picket fence. A brick ranch house sat fifty feet back on the lawn. The flower beds were tilled, but nothing had been planted. She looked ahead at a cement block structure. A showcase window displayed a dining room table with six chairs, an exquisite hutch, and a buffet. She read the sign above the door. "King's Furniture," she whispered.

"I'm going into business, Amber."

"You've been busy of late!"

"My friends helped me." He frowned. "I pray my decisions don't devastate my family."

"How could your going into business do that?"

"Look at the house, Rebecca."

She glanced at the blue draw-drapes on the picture window, stared at the ornate lamp by the front door, then noticed the electric and telephone lines connected to the house. She looked back at him. "You need help to remove the drapes and disconnect the power lines?"

He took a deep breath, his hands still gripping the steering wheel. "I'm not . . . disconnecting them."

She blinked and her lips parted. "But . . . you're Amish."

"I am . . . yet." He turned to study her face. "After Joseph returned, I felt free to live my life as I had planned to before he went away."

"Did Sarah know this, previous to Joseph's return?"

"No."

Rebecca struggled with bewilderment.

"In order to protect my parents, I didn't tell anyone." He sighed. "I kept my decision from you, because I believed you were Amish—in the beginning. Then . . . I didn't know how you might react."

She turned away. "I'm still ashamed of the stories I told."

Reaching out, he took her hand. "*Der gut Man* has forgiven you, Amber, and so have I. His grasp tightened. "I hope you know, now, who you can trust."

"I trust you, Aaron. *Es spett mich* that I didn't trust you before."

"Amber . . ." He hesitated as though searching for words, then he blurted, "I'm joining a Mennonite church."

Her eyes widened.

"On off Sundays I've been attending Mennonite services. My decision was after much prayer. I believe in evangelism, and I hope to do some Christian writing." Releasing her hand, he opened his door. "*Kom ann.* I want to give you a tour of the house."

As they approached the gate, the robin hopped farther away, its alert eyes watching them. With her mind and heart in a flux, Rebecca accompanied Aaron to the front porch. He took a key from his pocket, turned it in the lock, and swung the door inward.

She stepped into the vestibule and hesitated. Kicking off her shoes, she stepped onto the plush blue living room carpet. Her toes enjoyed the depth of pile as she crossed the unfurnished living room to examine the stone fireplace along the far wall. The white tile hearth felt cool through her stockings as she paused to caress the highly polished wooden mantel. The light-blue tones of the decor had a warm friendly effect, but empty, the sixteen-by-twenty-foot room seemed huge. "Where's . . . your furniture?"

"I hope to marry soon, and I want my wife to choose it."

"Oh." The anguish that had lessened came crushing back, and the letter in her pocket seemed to grow hot. It must explain his coming marriage. Praying he couldn't detect her surprise and pain—or her facade—she flipped her hand. "I assume the kitchen has King's cabinets."

"*Ja. Kom ann.*"

She followed through the empty but cheery lavender-and-cream dining room and onto the pinkish-beige vinyl in the kitchen. Running her hands over the smooth Formica counters, she studied the intricate parquetry design on the cabinet doors. "They're beautiful, Aaron. Is the wood cherry?"

"*Ja.*"

"She'll love them."

"She?"

"Your . . . future wife."

"Oh."

Rebecca headed down the hallway to the master bedroom, paused inside the doorway, and glanced at Aaron. "Are you going to paint these walls or leave them white?"

"I want to leave the decorating of this room to—my future wife."

Again the word *wife* pummeled her heart, and she quickly entered a small bedroom with light-green walls and beige carpet. "Is this your guest room?"

"*Ja.*"

Stepping onto the cream-colored carpet in the room beside the master bedroom, she stopped to stare. The bottom half of the walls were done in panels of light-blue and soft-pink; the top half had wallpaper with frolicking puppies and kittens, but it was the small white crib containing a baby quilt that caught and held her attention.

Aaron motioned to it. "That was mine when I was an infant, so I thought it fitting for my first child to sleep in it."

His voice echoed in the emptiness, creating vibrations deep within her. She tried to appear exuberant, but her heart ached. Moving to the crib, she placed her hands on the top rail and peered at the mattress. Picturing a baby with Aaron's eyes and smile, she swallowed hard. Who would be the mother of the infant? When Aaron joined her, she forced a smile. Was he envisioning the woman who would rock his children?

She slowly turned away, strode to the living room, and opened the drapes. The sun shimmered through the softly falling rain, and a rainbow spanned the horizon to her left. She pictured bachelor buttons along the walk, vivid multi-colored flowers by the fence, and a rose arbor near the front gate. What woman would live here to enjoy the blossoms? *And Aaron's companionship*? Emptiness yawned within her, making a mockery of the dazzling scene.

"*Vell?*" Aaron said slowly.

She turned to face him.

He held her gaze. "You're disappointed about something. *Wass* is it?"

"Your house is *wonderbar*, Aaron." Lowering herself to the carpet in front of the hearth, she peered at the blue phone on the floor near her elbow.

"If there's something you don't like, I'll change it."

"Once it's finished, it will be lovely, Aaron." She stared into the naked fireplace, feeling as cold and empty as it looked.

Sitting beside her, Aaron sighed. "I sort of got the impression that you cared for me—before . . ."

"I . . . did." *I'm not going to cry*, she vowed, figuring she'd made a big enough fool of herself. The backs of her eyes smarted, but squaring her shoulders, she forced control.

"Is nurse's training all your heart desires?"

"Not . . . exactly." The letter crinkled. She retrieved it, then shoved it back into her pocket.

"The letter explains how I feel."

Afraid her voice would quaver, she sat motionless, saying nothing.

Aaron drew a long breath. "I love you, Rebecca."

Her lips parted. Facing him, she blinked. "Oh . . . Aaron." Her hands fluttered and words evaded her as past situations between herself and this man flashed before her in a vivid panorama. Had her fear of betraying Sarah blinded her to Aaron's feelings?

"I know you feel called to be a nurse. I'd support you in whatever you wish to do." Reaching out, he rested a hand on her shoulder.

It was all the invitation she needed. She melted against him. "I love you, Aaron."

His embrace tightened. "Then, you'll marry me?"

"*Ja.*"

"Soon?"

"*Ja.*"

His mouth covered hers. Warmth of love encompassed them as their kiss bonded the promise of everlasting loyalty and devotion. Rebecca's heart, joined with Aaron's, soared to new and lofty pinnacles of joy and hope. As his warm lips caressed hers, she poised to soar into an unknown macrocosm of ecstasy.

The phone rang.

Aaron pulled away enough to grin at her. "Answer it, darling. You might as well get used to it. *Gel?*"

Gripping the receiver, she swallowed. "Hello. — I mean—King's . . . Furniture."

Aaron's elated chuckle created a song in her heart.

Pressing the mute button, she turned to face him. "Where is your business located?"

"Eden."

She blinked, and her vision blurred with happy tears. "Right under my nose. Oh, Aaron, I've found my Eden!"

His grin broadened. "So have I."

Rebecca gave the man on the phone the information he wanted, then hung up. Sun streamed through the picture window behind Aaron. The shower was over, but the rainbow remained. She pondered God's promises and blessings.

Love shimmered in Aaron's eyes. "Welcome to Eden, darling."

She smiled. "Our own special garden."

"For now and always." He took her in his arms; his embrace tightened, underscoring his vow.

The End

Search For Eden   Barbara Michel

Return To Eden

(The Second Novel in the Eden Series)

by Barbara Michel

In RETURN TO EDEN, Elizabeth, a young Amish widow, rejoices over finding love again. But, can she rip her infant daughter away from her only relatives by marrying Elam and moving over three hundred miles from her family and church district? If she doesn't, will she lose her chance for happiness? Through the many trials that plague Elizabeth, her faith in God remains steadfast. Then, a buggy accident complicates the situation between her and Elam, threatening to dash their hopes for fulfillment. Will the results change her life completely?

About the Author...

Barbara Michel

Previous to losing her sight in her late teens, Barbara was a landscape artist. Although her vision is gone, her artistry still abounds in her descriptions. The imagery she paints in her word pictures in *Return to Eden* proves that even now she is a very capable artist.

Barbara raised three children and is now devoting herself to writing and spending cherished time with her grandchildren.

If you enjoyed **"Search For Eden"** — *you will find the same enchanting character development and fascinating story line about the Amish in her second book in the series. Barbara Michel's latest novel will also thrill your heart!*

Order your copy now from:

Son-Rise Publications
143 Greenfield Road
New Wilmington, PA 16142
1-800-358-0777

$8.95

ISBN - 0-936369-65-5

Other Novels from Son-Rise Publications

DOG JACK, beloved mascot of the 102nd Regiment of the Pennsylvania Volunteers, comes to life again through this historical novel. Written by *Florence Biros*, the story is told through the eyes of Jed, a run away slave boy, who identifies with Dog Jack. Thousands have responded to this unique Civil War drama depicting the life of Pittsburgh's canine hero. Wounded in battle three times — once critically — he was actually held prisoner of war for six months until being exchanged for a Confederate soldier. Illustrated with pictures of the 125th Reenactment at Gettysburg. Four-color portrait cover.
   Trade paper. 0-936369-47-7. **$7.95.**

A visit to her New England roots led *Elizabeth Shaffer* to extensive research and the writing of **DAUGHTER OF THE DAWN.** Descended from Pilgrims Elizabeth Tilley and John Howland, she has created an intriguing romance. Against the background of the storm-lashed voyage of the Mayflower and the privations of the first year of Plymouth Colony, Elizabeth Tilley battles her love for John Howland who is engaged to her best friend. Photos of Mayflower, Plymouth Plantation replicas, and English ports. Four-color portrait cover.
   Trade paper. ISBN - 0-936369-72-8. **$7.95.**

All **LIZA JANE** ever wanted or expected of life she already had: the security and love of her family and a handsome, young suitor. But one summer day, a mysterious veteran from the final days of the Civil War comes into her life with a secret lying heavily on his heart. Now **Liza Jane** must search for truths that never before concerned her, truths about life, love, and God. Until Liza Jane can unlock the mystery of Adam, she might never again know peace.
   For the Love Adam written by *Janis Fedor*.
   ISBN - 0-936369-73-6. **$8.95**